A Theological Aesthetics
of Liberation

A Theological Aesthetics of Liberation

God, Art, and the Social Outcasts

VICENTE CHONG

Foreword by Michael Kirwan

◆PICKWICK *Publications* · Eugene, Oregon

A THEOLOGICAL AESTHETICS OF LIBERATION
God, Art, and the Social Outcasts

Copyright © 2019 Vicente Chong. All rights reserved. Except for brief quotations in critical publications or reviews, no part of this book may be reproduced in any manner without prior written permission from the publisher. Write: Permissions, Wipf and Stock Publishers, 199 W. 8th Ave., Suite 3, Eugene, OR 97401.

Pickwick Publications
An Imprint of Wipf and Stock Publishers
199 W. 8th Ave., Suite 3
Eugene, OR 97401

www.wipfandstock.com

PAPERBACK ISBN: 978-1-5326-4612-6
HARDCOVER ISBN: 978-1-5326-4613-3
EBOOK ISBN: 978-1-5326-4614-0

Cataloguing-in-Publication data:

Names: Chong, Vicente, author. | Kirwan, Michael, foreword.

Title: A theological aesthetics of liberation : God, art, and the social outcasts / Vicente Chong ; foreword by Michael Kirwan.

Description: Eugene, OR : Pickwick Publications, 2019 | Includes bibliographical references.

Identifiers: ISBN 978-1-5326-4612-6 (paperback) | ISBN 978-1-5326-4613-3 (hardcover) | ISBN 978-1-5326-4614-0 (ebook)

Subjects: LCSH: Catholic Church—Doctrines. | Aesthetics—Religious aspects—Christianity. | Liberation theology. | Freedom (Theology).

Classification: BT83.57 .C48 2019 (paperback) | BT83.57 .C48 (ebook)

Manufactured in the U.S.A.   02/06/19

Cover art: La Hora Oscura by Eduardo Kingman

Contents

Foreword by Michael Kirwan | vii
Acknowledgments | xi

Introduction | 1

Chapter 1
A Critical Analysis of Liberation Theology | 9
    The Method of Liberation Theology | 9
    Some Essential Tenets of Liberation Theology | 18
    Liberation Theology and Aesthetics | 51

Chapter 2
Von Balthasar or Rahner? Towards a Theological Aesthetics of Liberation | 55
    Exploring von Balthasar's Theology as a Possible Model for a Theological Aesthetics of Liberation | 57
    Exploring Rahner's Theology as a Possible Model for a Theological Aesthetics of Liberation | 89

Chapter 3
A Theological Aesthetics of Liberation, Part One: A Pneumatology of Liberation through Art | 114
    Art and Transformation | 119
    Art and the Holy Spirit | 153
    God, Art, and Liberation | 159

Chapter 4
A Theological Aesthetics of Liberation, Part Two: A Christology of Contrast in Art | 163
    From the Experience of Contrast in Art to Theology | 164

Schillebeeckx's Theology of Contrast | 180
Correlating Schillebeeckx's Theology and Aesthetics | 215

Conclusion | 222

Bibliography | 227

Foreword

Vicente Chong first proposed to me, in 2012, the notion of doing research in "the aesthetics of liberation theology." The originality of such a project was evident to both of us: up to now, liberation theologians have simply not aligned questions of beauty with the struggle for justice and emancipation. This was virgin territory. And yet it is interesting, and important, to ask why this conjunction should be so surprising and original. Why do we assume that the struggle for justice must preclude appreciation and concern for beauty, and the enjoyment of art something that must be postponed until the struggle is over? Does this not feed into the worst preconceptions of art as a "bourgeois" luxury, a decorative addition to life, which the poor must renounce until "reality" (meaning socio-economic conditions) has been transformed? So, along with so many other valuable human goods, the poor must go without, once again. Put in these terms, the "puritanical" resistance to and neglect of art and aesthetics within liberation theology is a serious omission. Chong's work is intended as a corrective.

A second theme here is Chong's confrontation with the major, one must say dominant presence in "theological aesthetics," namely Hans Urs von Balthasar. The focus in von Balthasar's work upon the "glory of the Lord" (*Herrlichkeit*), and his development of a "theo-drama" as the primary way of describing humanity's relation to God, are a monumental achievement. Von Balthasar's writings are important, but problematic—especially for this project. Von Balthasar acknowledged the importance of liberation theology's concern for the social gospel, but was unsympathetic to its main tenets and methods. The "theo-dramatic" approach engages with themes of human and divine transcendence, but von Balthasar's "canon" is pitilessly Eurocentric, and largely confined to "high" European literature. Also, there is often a feeling with his work that the insights of literature are being "colonized" for theological purposes. If the "voice of the oppressed" in Latin America and elsewhere is to be heard, as aesthetic as well as socio-political yearning, then an alternative foundation for theological aesthetics needs to be found.

It has been commonplace to set up a contrast between Balthasarian approach and an alternative theological trajectory, in terms of the two theological journals set up after the Second Vatican Council. *Concilium* sought to discern God's presence in the world of today; it was and remains the voice of political and liberation, as well as feminist theologians, and represented the voices of the global South. *Communio* was the journal, founded by von Balthasar, in reaction to what he saw as an imbalanced attentiveness to the voices of the "world," as described above: rather, the church's renewal must come primarily from its own rich traditions and inner life.

The *Communio* versus *Concilium* distinction needs careful handling, but if we are to use these labels, then Chong's is, emphatically, a work of *Concilium* theology. He attempts to construct a theological aesthetics from the traces and hints which we find in Karl Rahner and Edward Schillebeeckx, as well as liberationists such as Gustavo Gutiérrez and José Comblin. The inspiration here is David Tracy's notion of an "analogical imagination." Tracy draws our attention to the "classic": an expression of the spirit, which endures over time, and which continues to enrich and nourish long after its original appearance. No culture survives without its classics. This is even more the case with those texts, symbols, stories, and events which a culture labels "religious": and above all the "event" of the life, death, and resurrection of Jesus Christ.

So Chong attempts a dialogue between theological aesthetics and the theology of liberation; between a "northern" and a "southern" theological style. But what, precisely, connects art and liberation? In each case we have a mysterious negotiation of two dimensions of human life: freedom and necessity. There is a "coercive" dimension to great art. It demands and commands our attention; the classic will not allow itself to be ignored. And yet, the experience of great art leaves us deeply free, in a way that other modes of representation (propaganda, pornography) do not. One might say the same for the production of art: the artist is a mysterious compound of liberty and discipline, since artistic creation is impossible without constraints and "rules."

Liberation theology tells the same story, of a people which is emancipated, only to be drawn into the new "enslavement" of a loving, exclusive covenant with God. This lays upon them the responsibility of attending to the widow, orphan, and stranger—precisely because "you yourselves were once slaves and exiles." God is the God who liberates, firstly, his people from enslavement and exile, and secondly, his Son, Jesus, who is "concentrated humanity," from the bonds of death. The single story of these successive liberations continues into the present as a majestic exercise of imaginative sympathy, simply put by Paul when he says: "you are God's work of art."

Chong identifies three ways in which art liberates: as an instrument of protest and hope; as an experience of creative freedom for the artist; and as a total transformation of its recipients. The "transcendental anthropology" of Karl Rahner helps to structure these insights, while the notion of the life and death of Jesus as a "contrast event" is taken from the Dominican Edward Schillebeeckx. On this view, the cross is itself ugly, and we should never aestheticize its cruelty. By contrast, however, the cross refers us to the radiant beauty of Jesus' "pro-existence," his life of solidarity with the poor.

An "ecumenical" project therefore, bringing together a Jesuit and a Dominican theologian (even if both are on the *Concilium* divide of post-Conciliar theology). Nevertheless, I venture to suggest that the spirit of Chong's approach is distinctively Ignatian and Jesuit. In the much-used slogan, the Jesuit seeks to "find God in all things," even in the paradox of beautiful art showing human ugliness. Chong refers to Picasso's painting *Guernica*, a "classic" twentieth-century depiction of wartime suffering. The representation arouses in us, not a serene and detached "beatific vision," but indignation and—hopefully—an incentive to action. Chong finds a similar inspiration in another painting, *La Hora Oscura*, by an Ecuadorian artist, Eduardo Kingman. Here a flogged man is looked on by smiling, clown-like faces. The disjunction is upsetting: how can the same canvas contain such diverse images? And yet the "citation" of Christ, the *ecce homo*, in the figure of the suffering man gives us the clue as to how the smile and the scourging co-exist.

The Jesuit imagination respects the capacity of a person's memory, understanding, will, and senses, when properly organized, to bring us to God. Chong's work chimes with the priorities of the Ignatian pope, Francis, who sees culture, rather than socio-economic analysis, as the most fruitful partner for theology. In Francis we find a similar impulse to correct imbalance, and to connect the joy of the gospel with a real concern for God's poor. Francis certainly has his detractors, but his appeal across a wide spectrum of liberal and traditional believers is striking. It suggests that it is time to move on from the polarizing *Communio* versus *Concilium* debate, and to see how the best of these traditions can be brought together. Chong's theological aesthetics of liberation, in its critical and complementary use of von Balthasar alongside the *Concilium* theologians, reflects and shares this "hermeneutic of generosity." It is, therefore, a work of its time: a work of "Franciscan" Jesuit theology.

Dr. Michael Kirwan, SJ
Heythrop College (University of London) and
Loyola Institute, Trinity College Dublin

Acknowledgments

This book is based on my doctoral thesis submitted to Heythrop College, University of London, in 2016. The completion and publication of my work have been made possible with the help of some kind persons who gave me support in different ways. With gratitude, I want to acknowledge them here. First of all, I thank Dr. Michael Kirwan, SJ, my supervisor, who was always enthusiastic about my theological project, and helped me with his insightful comments. I am indebted to Joseph Munitiz, SJ, for his generous assistance in reading my thesis and suggesting corrections for the English style of the text. I give thanks to Alan Harrison, SJ, for his spiritual support, and to Richard Salmi, SJ, for his companionship. I am grateful to both the British Province and the Ecuadorian Province of the Society of Jesus for giving me the human and financial support to complete my doctoral studies. I express my gratitude to the Pontificia Universidad Católica del Ecuador that granted me a leave of absence in order to go to London and work on my research. I give thanks to Dr. Karen Kilby for introducing me to Wipf and Stock Publishers. Finally, my thanks go to my family and friends for their loving support.

Introduction

This study develops a correlation between theological aesthetics and liberation theology. The result of this correlation might be called a "theological aesthetics of liberation." This work does not presume that this is the only way to connect these two theological disciplines. Indeed, there are other ways to relate theological aesthetics with liberation theology.[1] For this reason, this is not *the* theological aesthetics of liberation, but *a* theological aesthetics of liberation.

In general, there has been a refusal to establish a correlation between liberation theology and theological aesthetics, and this has come from both disciplines. *On the side of liberation theology*, since its emergence in the late sixties of the last century, the main concern of liberation theologians in Latin America has been the socio-political liberation of the poor. Their goal has been to respond theologically to the immediate and urgent reality of material poverty that has existed in Latin America, and to support through their theological reflection the process of liberation that was happening in that continent. Faced with the scandalous reality of social injustice, liberation theologians presumably thought that there was no time and no room for aesthetics, beauty, and art.[2] Probably any theological reflection on aesthetic

---

1. The question about the relationship between theological aesthetics and liberation theology has been explored by authors such as de Gruchy and Goizueta. See Gruchy, *Christianity, Art and Transformation*; Goizueta, *Caminemos con Jesús*; Goizueta, *Christ Our Companion*. It will become apparent in this study that my approach is different from theirs.

2. Some authors have noted that theology in general has paid little attention to aesthetics and the arts. See Begbie, *Voicing Creation's Praise*, xv–xvi; Brown, *Religious Aesthetics*, 1–5; Farley, *Faith and Beauty*, 6–8. Thus, the lack of attention to aesthetics is not a characteristic of liberation theology alone, but of theology in general. However, it is right to say that the situation has changed in the last decades, when studies about the relationship between theology *in general* and aesthetics have increased considerably, while not much literature has appeared on the relationship between liberation theology *in particular* and the arts.

matters seemed irrelevant, secondary, or even selfish. "How can we think about beauty and art when the poor are dying from hunger?" is what some Christians who sympathized with the liberationist movement might have thought. Indeed, "the ethical concern for the poor frequently leads to a criticism of support of the visual arts as an inappropriate expenditure of funds," John Dillenberger writes. Nonetheless, he adds, "Right as their viewpoint may be about the poor, it nevertheless represents a truncated theology."[3]

To some extent, the same attitude towards aesthetics still exists among some people who care for the poor. As Jeremy Begbie says, "Compared to the other pressing issues of our day—the population explosion, the ecological crisis, mass starvation—the arts seem a somewhat trivial concern."[4] Indeed, some people might wonder, "Should not world poverty force us all to become aesthetic 'philistines' in the pursuit of economic justice?" The problem with this "form of philistinism," John de Gruchy observes, is that it seems to be "morally correct."[5] This philistine attitude towards the arts, which still exists among some theologians who are interested in social justice, generally implies a rejection of both the aestheticism and the elitism that may exist in the world of art.[6]

On the side of theological aesthetics, the main focus has been on the relationship between various aspects of the "religious realm"—such as God, theology, faith, spirituality, etc.—and different dimensions of the "aesthetic realm"—such as beauty, art, perception through the senses, imagination, etc. Thus, theological aesthetics has explored questions such as, how can we understand God through the concept of beauty? Or what is the religious dimension of aesthetics? Or in what way can we have a spiritual experience through art? Legitimate and important as all these questions are, they do not have a direct or explicit connection with the reality of the poor and the struggle for justice. Presumably one of the reasons for this lack of social concern in the area of theological aesthetics has been a purist understanding of aesthetics—i.e., the notion that both aesthetics and art are and should be useless and non-instrumental.

The refusal to establish a correlation between theological aesthetics and liberation theology is regrettable. In fact, the assumption in this study is that a mutual and critical correlation between these two disciplines is beneficial for both liberation theology and theological aesthetics, as long as such

3. Dillenberger, *Theology of Artistic Sensibilities*, 255.
4. Begbie, *Voicing Creation's Praise*, xvi.
5. Gruchy, *Christianity, Art and Transformation*, 87.
6. According to Sherry, "The lack of a theology of beauty . . . follows in part from fear and suspicion of the question, expressed in pejorative terms like 'aestheticism' and 'elitism'" (Sherry, *Spirit and Beauty*, 18). I will explain these concepts later in this work.

a relationship helps us to understand God in his relationship with human beings. *On the one hand, liberation theology needs theological aesthetics* for at least three reasons. Firstly, aesthetics can help liberation theology to make attractive the objects of its reflections. Certainly, the emphasis of liberation theology has been on the "good," that is, on issues such as praxis and justice. However, the problem is that these objects of theological reflection have been presented as moral imperatives that do not elicit any attraction. De Gruchy claims that goodness without beauty "degenerates into moralism" and lacks the "power to convince."[7] In this sense, a theology that cares for the good, but that disregards the beautiful, loses its capacity to engage people.[8] Unfortunately, the "denigration of aesthetics in contemporary theology," de Gruchy says, seems to include "various forms of liberation theology."[9] Therefore, liberation theology needs to recover its aesthetic dimension in order to make attractive the objects of its theological reflections.

Secondly, aesthetics can help liberation theology as long as art can be a "source of religious insight," as Alejandro García-Rivera suggests. Art is an "indispensable element" of "theology's vocation to bring insight of the need and way of salvation in its reflections on the social and cultural environment it finds itself in."[10] However, art brings theological insight not through concepts and ideas, but through metaphors and images. This is why Patrick Sherry recommends theological aesthetics, for instead of addressing only people's mind, it would be better also "to approach people through their hearts and imaginations. And an obvious way of doing this is through art and literature."[11] Therefore, art can help liberation theology inasmuch as art can help people understand what liberation is by appealing to their capacities for feeling and imagining.

Finally, as long as liberation theology fails to pay attention to the liberating and transformative power of art, it will keep missing an important dimension of the process of liberation. De Gruchy maintains, "A society that relegates the arts to the periphery of its life . . . is spiritually and culturally poor; it may be committed to transformation, but it has neglected one of the key resources for reaching towards that end."[12] Likewise, a theology that cares for the poor, but disregards aesthetics, is abandoning one of the key elements in the process of liberation of those who are social outcasts. Indeed,

---

7. Gruchy, *Christianity, Art and Transformation*, 107.
8. Cf. Austin, *Explorations in Art*, 83.
9. Gruchy, *Christianity, Art and Transformation*, 105.
10. García-Rivera, *Wounded Innocence*, 34.
11. Sherry, *Images of Redemption*, 3.
12. Gruchy, *Christianity, Art and Transformation*, 254.

Pablo Richard (talking about the future of liberation theology) points out that, in the past, liberation theology engaged almost exclusively in a dialogue with philosophy. "Today we must extend it to other disciplines." For instance, liberation theology should enter into conversation with art and literature because "a liberating movement is taking place" in those areas.[13] According to Frank Burch Brown, "doing aesthetics is not so much a theological option as a theological necessity."[14] Indeed, doing theological aesthetics is a necessary task in the area of liberation theology.

On the other hand, theological aesthetics needs liberation theology. As theological aesthetics helps liberation theology to see the connection of the good with the beautiful, liberation theology allows theological aesthetics to find the relationship of beauty with goodness. Liberation theology can help theological aesthetics to see that God's beauty is essentially related to the liberation of the poor. In other words, the preferential option for social outcasts makes concrete the notion of divine beauty. Furthermore, the question about social justice presented insistently by liberation theology takes the form of a challenge for aesthetics: how can aesthetics be present in the process of social liberation instead of being simply a pursuit of aesthetic pleasure in the contemplation of works of art? Theological aesthetics should answer this question if it intends to be significant in a world marked by social injustice.

Various authors have pointed out the possibility of a relationship between theology and aesthetics. For instance, Sherry says, "Art and literature may help to shape theology, whilst theology may in turn influence art and literature."[15] According to Brown, one can think of many ways in which Christian theology of every kind might "be affected by acknowledging and in some measure incorporating aesthetics. Likewise there are several ways in which Christian theology of nearly every variety might inform aesthetics."[16] George Pattison notes, there are different "paths leading from art to religion and from religion to art." However, "this is not the same as identifying one with the other, or, more negatively, reducing one to the other. The dialogue between art and religion is to be just that: a dialogue, with each partner seeking to appreciate the specific contribution of the other."[17] In this conversation, the relationship between theology and aesthetics can and should be mutually critical. As Sherry says, "the process is two-way: for although art

---

13. Richard, "Liberation Theology," 509.
14. Brown, *Religious Aesthetics*, 37.
15. Sherry, *Images of Redemption*, 161.
16. Brown, *Religious Aesthetics*, 37.
17. Pattison, *Art, Modernity, and Faith*, 8.

and literature may contribute towards religious understanding, and sometimes pass judgement on theology, theology may in turn criticize them as inadequate in some respect."[18] Thus, in a mutual and critical correlation between theology and art, we can make a theological reading of aesthetic reality, and we can make an aesthetic interpretation of Christian faith. However, methodologically speaking, we cannot do both at the same time.[19] In the theological aesthetics of liberation that I will develop here, I will make a theological reading of art first (chapter 3), and then I will make an aesthetic interpretation of a specific aspect of Christian faith (chapter 4).

The area covered by this study is *theological* aesthetics, and not aesthetics in general. Therefore, the focus of this work is neither on philosophical aesthetics nor on the history of art. Those subjects require the knowledge of artists, aestheticians, historians, and art critics. My expertise is not in those fields, but in theological aesthetics, which explores the aesthetic world not in isolation, but in its relationship to the religious realm. Therefore, the authors with whom I will be conversing in this research are mainly theologians and authors who have studied in different ways the relationship between religion and art. This work explores the ideas of different authors as they appear in their books. It does not deal with the issue of what lies behind their thoughts, that is, the influences on their theologies. Therefore, this research does not explore, for instance, the impact of Karl Marx on liberation theology, or the influence of Martin Heidegger on Karl Rahner. That kind of analysis, albeit valid, is not very useful for the aim of this study. Besides, I cannot engage in that kind of investigation for lack of space.

Some authors claim that theologians should pay more attention to what artists say about their artistic work, lest theologians interpret or impose ideas on works of art that were never intended by their creators. Thus, Michael Austin says, "Theologians must be on their guard against commandeering art for religion, must allow artists to speak to them in their own language, and must try to make what they can of what they hear."[20] While I agree with Austin, I have two reservations about his comment. First, to

18. Sherry, *Images of Redemption*, 21; see ibid., 172, 181. See also Austin, *Explorations in Art*, ix.

19. Cf. Brown, *Religious Aesthetics*, 18–19. While recognizing the existence of a correlation between theology and aesthetics, a theologian is not obliged to analyze both sides of the correlation. For instance, Begbie declares that in his book: "due primarily to lack of space, I have had to confine myself to the bearing of theology on the arts. No doubt there will be many who are more interested in the reverse question—what the arts offer to theology? Of course the two are interrelated . . . [However] my major concern is with what theology can bring to the task of understanding and enhancing the arts, not what the arts can bring to theology" (Begbie, *Voicing Creation's Praise*, xviii).

20. Austin, *Explorations in Art*, 33.

some extent, a work of art is independent from its creator as long as it is open to the interpretation of its recipients. I will say more about this later. However, it is important to note here that, although it is important to know what artists say about their own work, the meaning of their work sometimes exceeds what they intend to express through their artistic creations. Indeed, some artists are pleased when viewers find different meanings in their work. Therefore, to some extent, theologians may be allowed to find different meanings in works of art, meanings that sometimes were not intended by their creators.

Second, when authors suggest that theologians should listen to what artists say, generally the assumption is that theologians do not know what aesthetics is because they are not artists themselves. However, what if the theologian is—himself or herself—an artist? Then the theologian can draw on his or her own experience as an artist. Indeed, this is exactly what some authors do in their analyses. Thus, for instance, Brown writes, "I have been aided in part by personal and familial circumstances. Since I have occasionally published poetry and I am active as a composer and musician, my own experience of secular and religious arts, and of music and literature in particular, has naturally proven to be of some value."[21] This is true of my study as well. While I am not a professional artist, I know from my own experience—and the experience of some in my family—about the joys and the toils of creating works of art.

Furthermore, there are different ways to engage in the practice of art. Not only is the artist someone who practices art. The recipient also is someone who engages in the practice of art, namely, the practice of appreciating works of art. Indeed, for the recipient the experience of art implies a personal engagement with artistic works. Other people can tell me about their own experiences of art. However, their information does not stand in place of my own personal experience. In this sense, a theologian, as an active recipient of works of art, can and should turn to his or her own experience to think theologically about such an experience. In this sense, the present study is based on my personal experience, not only as a creator of works of art, but also as a recipient of works of art.

The main focus of this work is on painting. Thus I could speak of the experience I have had when I have seen the works of so many artists that I admire. This is what many authors have done in their books. They analyze specific paintings of different artists, and they infer theological conclusions from such an analysis. I consider that kind of examination valuable and valid. However, in my personal experience, I have often found myself reading fast

---

21. Brown, *Religious Aesthetics*, xiv–xv.

or even skipping those parts of the book in which an author studies specific works of art. Probably this is due to the fact that they refer to works of art for which I do not have any interest, or which I simply do not know. Therefore, instead of analyzing specific works of art—in which potential readers of this work might or might not be interested—I have decided to take an inclusive approach to the phenomenon of art.[22] In other words, although my main focus is painting, hopefully my approach is broad enough to include other artistic expressions. Furthermore, this study is heuristic in the sense that it hopes to enable people to discover for themselves the theological insights that I will explain in this work. My hope is that those who have interest and expertise in other fields of art may find connections, similarities, and differences between their and my own experience of art.

When I say that my study will focus on painting, I am talking about painting in general. Thus my emphasis is not explicitly on religious painting, that is, art that represents explicitly religious themes, such as Jesus, Mary, or the lives of the saints. Besides the fact that art does not have to portray explicit religious objects in order to have a religious significance, the main focus here is on how art can contribute to the process of liberation, and how we can interpret theologically such an event. Since this investigation does not concentrate on explicitly religious painting, it does not study religious icons either. The spiritual, symbolic, and religious aspects involved in Christian iconography require a different kind of analysis.

The structure of the present work is as follows. Given that the goal of the present research is to explore a possible correlation between liberation theology and theological aesthetics, a logical first step is to clarify what are these two theological disciplines. Thus, chapter 1 explicates some essential tenets of liberation theology, including its understanding of God, Jesus Christ, and the Holy Spirit, in their relationships with the liberation of social outcasts. Chapter 2 explains two different types of theological aesthetics, those of Hans Urs von Balthasar and Karl Rahner, in order to investigate which model is more appropriate for the theological aesthetics of liberation that I will develop here. Opting for the model of Karl Rahner, chapters 3 and 4 develop a correlation between theological aesthetics and liberation theology. Chapter 3 gives a theological interpretation of the phenomenon of art, and chapter 4 develops an aesthetic interpretation of a specific aspect of Christian faith, namely, the fundamental event of Jesus Christ. Chapter 3 argues that the Spirit of God works in and through the liberating and transformative experience of art. Chapter 4 suggests that the experience of

---

22. Some works of art will be mentioned in this study. However, I will not make any detailed analysis of those works.

contrast in art helps us understand the life, death, and resurrection of Jesus Christ. This aesthetic interpretation of Jesus Christ in chapter 4 is systematized and expanded with the help of Edward Schillebeeckx's theology.

Not long ago, Pope Francis suggested a correlation between liberation theology and theological aesthetics in his encyclical *Evangelii Gaudium*: "We may not always be able to reflect adequately the beauty of the Gospel, but there is one sign which we should never lack: the option for those who are least, those whom society discards."[23] In those words, the Latin American Pope indicates a fundamental relationship between the Gospel (theology), beauty (aesthetics), and the option for the those whom society excludes (liberation). The present study intends to articulate the connection between these three elements. My hope is that this theological aesthetics of liberation opens possibilities for understanding how *God* works for the *liberation of those who are social outcasts* in and through the experience of *art*.

---

23. Francis, *Evangelii Gaudium*, 195. This encyclical involves a theological aesthetics that has not been fully explored yet. Here I do not intend to analyze the theological aesthetics of Pope Francis because it is beyond the limits of this study and because it is not the main goal of this work. For some texts in which Francis talks about beauty in connection with the gospel, the poor, the good, and the true, see ibid., 7, 9, 36, 42, 116, 167, 199, 230, 257, 264, 276.

Chapter 1

A Critical Analysis of Liberation Theology

In this chapter, we will explore the theology of liberation in Latin America. This chapter explains the methodology of liberation theology and some of its essential tenets. The concepts of liberation theology to be explained here will be correlated with some aspects of theological aesthetics in the following chapters.

THE METHOD OF LIBERATION THEOLOGY

The following explanation is based on the analyses of Gustavo Gutiérrez, Clodovis Boff, and Juan Luis Segundo, who, among the liberation theologians, are the ones who talk more explicitly about their method. Liberation theology is essentially related to its method. Gutiérrez defines liberation theology as a "critical reflection on Christian praxis in the light of the Word."[1] This definition indicates already the method of liberation theology. In its basic structure, the method of liberation theology has three moments: praxis-reflection-praxis. The second moment, i.e., the moment of reflection, involves four mediations, namely, the perspective of the poor, sociological analysis, interpretation in the light of faith, and ideological suspicion. All these steps of the method are interrelated forming a single process.

The first moment of the method of liberation theology is praxis. Gutiérrez calls it the "first stage" of the method,[2] whereas Clodovis Boff calls it the

---

1. Gutiérrez, *Theology of Liberation*, 11.
2. Ibid., xxxiv.

"antecedent moment."³ In any case, both theologians convey the idea of praxis as a stage before the moment of reflection. Therefore, praxis has a priority inasmuch as praxis is *prior* to reflection in the method of liberation theology. This priority does not mean that praxis is more important than reflection, since both praxis and theory are relevant for liberation theology. The priority of praxis is rather methodological.

"Praxis" is one of those terms that some theologies—and other disciplines as well—employ, but it is not always clear what they mean when they use it. In liberation theology, "praxis" refers to the social and political action of those movements that were especially strong during the sixties and the seventies of the last century in Latin America. This movement was fundamentally about the poor struggling for their own liberation.⁴ Therefore, praxis means specifically the praxis of liberating those who are materially poor. Today, in liberation theology, the notion of poverty has expanded and includes also those who suffer from social exclusion because of their gender, age, race, culture, sexual identity, and physical condition. For this reason, praxis involves also "the struggles of those who reject racism and machism . . . , as well as of those who oppose the marginalization of the elderly, children, and other 'unimportant' persons in our society."⁵

Liberation theologians also use the word "experience" to describe the first moment of their method. For example, in the introduction to the original edition of *A Theology of Liberation*, Gutiérrez says,

> This book is an attempt at reflection, based on . . . the *experiences* of men and women committed to the process of liberation in the oppressed and exploited land of Latin America. It is a theological reflection born of the *experience* of shared efforts to abolish the current unjust situation and to build a different society . . . Many in Latin America have started along the path of a commitment to liberation . . . ; whatever the validity of these pages, it is due to their *experiences*.⁶

Like the word "praxis," the term "experience" is often used by different theologies today. However, "experience" is a concept that is not easy to define, perhaps because it has different meanings, depending on the context in which it is used.⁷ In the context of liberation theology, experience might be defined as an event with the following characteristics. Firstly, experience

---

3. Boff, "Methodology of the Theology of Liberation," 10.
4. See Gutiérrez, *Theology of Liberation*, 54–57.
5. Ibid., xxx.
6. Ibid., xiii (emphasis mine).
7. See Mieth, "What is Experience?," 40.

is an event that happens in history. Secondly, it is not a "once and for all" event, but is rather a process. Thirdly, the person who has an experience can be active in the process (as long as he or she can cause the experience), passive (as long as he or she can undergo the experience), or both. Fourthly, it is an event that is immediate and concrete for the people who have the experience. Finally, the subject who has an experience can be an individual or a human group; in the latter sense, it is possible to talk about a collective experience.[8] The experience upon which liberation theology reflects is the experience of liberation of the poor.

In some way, "praxis of liberation" and "experience of liberation" are not exactly the same. The notion of praxis indicates only the active dimension of liberation, whereas the notion of experience might entail both the active and the passive dimensions of liberation. On the one hand, praxis means action. The praxis of liberation means that an individual or a group does something for the liberation of the poor. Thus, the concept of praxis does not connote passivity. On the other hand, experience suggests both activity and passivity. The experience of liberation might indicate both that an individual or a group does something for the liberation of the poor, and that an individual or a group is liberated. Since liberation theologians use both "praxis" and "experience," I will employ the two terms as well.

The experience upon which liberation theology reflects is the praxis of liberation. However, this is a *Christian* praxis. As I said above, when liberation theology talks about praxis, it refers especially to the social and political action of popular movements that were strong during the sixties and the seventies of the last century in Latin America. It was a time of proliferation of groups and organizations that were committed to the liberation of the poor. It was not a movement exclusively of or in the church, but a movement of the Latin American people as a whole.[9] However, many Christians participated in this movement forming groups that were concerned about social justice and had an explicit Christian identity.[10] In this sense, the *Comunidades Eclesiales de Base* (Base Ecclesial Communities) were paradigmatic.[11] According to Gutiérrez, they were the womb from which

8. See ibid., 44–49; O'Collins, "Theology and Experience," 280–85.

9. Gutiérrez, *We Drink from Our Own Wells*, 21, 28.

10. According to Pilario, Christian groups that were social justice-oriented in Latin America were, for instance, "Christians for Socialism, ISAL (*Iglesia y sociedad para América Latina*) . . . *Sacerdotes para el tercer mundo* (Priests for the Third World), SAL (*Sacerdotes a favor de Latino-América*)" (Pilario, *Back to the Rough Grounds*, 283).

11. For some historical, sociological, and ecclesiological comments on the Base Ecclesial Communities, see Boff, *Ecclesiogenesis*, 1–40; Boff, *Church*, 7–10, 115–37; Comblin, *Called for Freedom*, 5–6, 84–90; Comblin, *People of God*, 118–19, 140–41; McGovern, *Liberation Theology and Its Critics*, 197–223; Dawson, "The Origins and Character of the Base Ecclesial Community," 109–28.

liberation theology emerged.[12] However, the life of these communities was concerned not only with political action, but also with prayer.[13] They combined, as it were, contemplation and praxis. They found in the Word of God an inspiration for their praxis, and in turn, their political action led them back to prayer as a source of strength for their praxis. This integration between praxis and prayer is an essential characteristic of the "spirituality of liberation"[14]—understanding "spirituality" as a "form of following of Jesus" or a "way of Christian life."[15] For this reason, sometimes Gutiérrez claims that the first moment of the method of liberation theology is not merely praxis, but a specific way of Christian life, i.e., a life that integrates both praxis and prayer.[16]

The main subjects of the praxis of liberation are the poor themselves. As Gutiérrez says, the poor are the "protagonists of their own liberation."[17] However, there are "non-poor people," if we may call them this way, who are positively involved in the liberation of the poor. Some lay people, religious, priests, and bishops, who are not "the poor," are in solidarity with the poor and actively support their liberation.[18] In this sense, these non-poor people are also subjects of the praxis of liberation, but in a secondary way. "Secondary" does not mean unimportant. Rather it means that their role is to second or to support the poor in the process of liberation. This secondary role applies to the liberation theologians, who might have suffered poverty or social exclusion in their own lives, and, in this case, they can speak out of their own experience. However, if they have not personally suffered poverty or social exclusion, they can endorse the liberation of the poor precisely through their theological reflection.

In fact, participation in the process of liberation of the poor is a necessary condition for doing liberation theology. As Boff says, the first step for doing liberation theology is pre-theological, in the sense that, before doing theology in the strict sense of the word, the theologian needs to be actively

---

12. Gutiérrez, *Theology of Liberation*, xxxiii.

13. Gutiérrez, *We Drink from Our Own Wells*, 22.

14. Ibid., 113. For different but complementary approaches to the spirituality of liberation, see Gutiérrez, *We Drink from Our Own Wells*; Sobrino, *Spirituality of Liberation*; Casaldáliga and Vigil, *The Spirituality of Liberation*; Jaén, *Hacia una Espiritualidad de la Liberación*.

15. Gutiérrez, *Theology of Liberation*, xxxii; Gutiérrez, *We Drink from Our Own Wells*, 27–28,

16. See Gutiérrez, *Theology of Liberation*, xxviii, xxxi–xxxiv; Gutiérrez, *We Drink from Our Own Wells*, 35–38, 52–53.

17. Gutiérrez, *Theology of Liberation*, 67.

18. See ibid., 59–62.

committed to the liberation of the poor. This commitment demands some conditions from the theologian. First, it requires that the theologian sees the reality of the poor. Therefore, in order to do liberation theology, it is necessary to have what Johann Baptist Metz calls a "mysticism of open eyes," that is, a "mysticism that obligates us to perceive more acutely the suffering of others."[19] However, a person who wants to do liberation theology does not or should not see the world of the poor from afar. Rather, he or she knows the reality of the poor from inside. That is to say, to do liberation theology demands an insertion in the world of the poor. This immersion may vary from person to person. But the challenge of doing liberation theology is that it requires from the theologian at least a minimal insertion in the reality of the poor.[20] Second, commitment to the liberation of the poor involves solidarity with them. However, as Jon Sobrino reminds us, solidarity "is not a matter of one-way flow of aid but of mutual giving and receiving."[21] In other words, solidarity implies a relationship of reciprocity and equality with the poor. Furthermore, authentic solidarity involves real love for the poor. As Gutiérrez says, "The solidarity is not with 'the poor' in the abstract but with human beings of flesh and bone. Without love and affection . . . , there can be no true gesture of solidarity." Love for the poor "is not possible apart from a certain integration into their world and apart from bonds of real friendship with those who suffer despoliation and injustice."[22] Precisely, friendship with the poor is the third requirement. As Gutiérrez states, "If there is no friendship with them and no sharing of the life of the poor, then there is not authentic commitment to liberation."[23] Therefore, participation in the process of liberation is a necessary condition for doing liberation theology.[24] This participation demands from the theologian seeing the reality

---

19. Metz, *Passion for God*, 69. As Martinez says, for Metz, "What most characterizes the political role of the Christians is their ability to see more, to see with the eyes of their faith . . . the invisible, unnoticed, inopportune suffering in every society and in the destitute countries in the world. Christians contribute to the transformation of society by making known what they see, by bringing it to the public eye, especially through their own solidary praxis. In this respect, Christianity is for Metz a *Schule des Sehens* (school of seeing)" (Martinez, *Confronting the Mystery of God*, 80). For a comparative interpretation of the theologies of Metz and Sobrino as supportive of a mysticism of open eyes, see Eggemeier, "Mysticism of Open Eyes," 43–62.

20. Boff, "Methodology of the Theology of Liberation," 7, 10–11.

21. Sobrino, *Principle of Mercy*, 146.

22. Gutiérrez, *We Drink from Our Own Wells*, 104.

23. Gutiérrez, *Theology of Liberation*, xxxi.

24. Christopher Rowland rightly observes, "The key thing is that one first of all *does* liberation theology rather than learns about it. Or, to put it another way, one can only learn about it by embarking on it. To ask the question, 'What is liberation theology?' and

of the poor, an insertion in their world, solidarity with them, and friendship with them.

The second moment of the method of liberation theology is reflection. At this stage of the method, the theologian reflects upon the reality of the poor and their experience of liberation. This second moment involves four instruments or mediations for reflection, namely, the perspective of the poor, sociological analysis, interpretation in the light of faith, and the use of an ideological suspicion.

Firstly, the moment of reflection includes the perspective of the poor. To reflect upon the reality of the poor, the theologian needs to hear what the poor say about their own reality. The poor know better than anybody else about their own reality, and the theologian should try to understand how they interpret their own world. Furthermore, the theologian should pay attention to the way in which the poor live and understand their Christian faith. In this way, the professional theologian will be able to communicate in theological categories what the poor live as Christians. This continuity between the reflection of a professional liberation theologian and the way in which the poor live their faith is possible only if the theologian has a personal contact with the poor. This is why the first step of the method, i.e., participation of the theologian in the process of liberation of the poor, is a necessary condition for doing liberation theology.[25]

Secondly, the moment of reflection involves sociological analysis. In order to understand the reality of the poor, and in order to liberate them from their situation of poverty, it is necessary to identify the causes of such a situation. Confronted by the reality of poverty, the theologian should ask: Why this poverty? What are its causes?[26] This is why Gutiérrez defines liberation theology not simply as reflection on praxis, but as *critical* reflection on praxis. It is critical because it enquires into the causes of poverty. Originally, liberation theologians found in Marxist theory and in the theory of dependence appropriate instruments to analyze the reality of poverty.[27] However,

---

think that one can answer without commitment and the understanding which emerges from it is to miss out on the central ingredient of liberation theology. This experience cannot adequately be communicated except by committing oneself and taking the first step along the road of solidarity and action. Therein lies the root of understanding" (Rowland, "Introduction," 4).

25. See Boff, "Methodology of the Theology of Liberation," 1, 9, 14–15; Gutiérrez, *Theology of Liberation*, xxix–xxx.

26. See Gutiérrez, *Theology of Liberation*, xxiii; Gutiérrez, *We Drink from Our Own Wells*, 107; Boff, "Methodology of the Theology of Liberation," 11.

27. See Boff, "Methodology of the Theology of Liberation," 12–13. See also Gutiérrez, *Theology of Liberation*, 51–54; Boff, *Liberating Grace*, 67–72; McGovern, *Liberation Theology and Its Critics*, 117–89.

today some liberation theologians recognize that these tools are limited and even inadequate to interpret the reality of the poor.[28] In addition, today the notion of poverty includes not only those who are socio-economically poor, but also those who suffer from social exclusion because of their gender, age, race, culture, sexual identity, and physical condition. The realization of this complex reality, Gutiérrez says, has led liberation theology "to incorporate beneficial perspectives and new sources of knowledge from the human sciences (psychology, ethnology, anthropology) for its study of a reality that is intricate and shifting."[29] Therefore, in liberation theology, the moment of reflection includes socio-economic, psychological, anthropological analyses, and other types of analysis that study different dimensions of the reality of the poor.

Thirdly, the moment of reflection involves interpretation of the liberation of the poor in the light of faith. This hermeneutical mediation is strictly speaking the *theological* moment in the method of liberation theology. As Boff says, this is "the specific moment by virtue of which a discourse is formally theological discourse."[30] What does "interpretation in the light of faith" mean? Boff answers, "Once having understood the concrete situation of the oppressed [by means of sociological analysis], the theologian must proceed to ask: What does the word of God say about this situation . . . ?" He continues, "It is a matter, then, of seeing the process of oppression/liberation in the light of faith. And what is the light of faith . . . ? The light of faith is concretely found in holy scripture. Thus, the light of faith and the light of the word of God are the same thing."[31]

Furthermore, interpretation of the liberation of the poor in the light of faith includes the Christian tradition. According to Boff, liberation theology "seeks to maintain a bond of basic continuity with the living faith tradition of the Christian people." With that goal in mind, liberation theology has a double approach to Christian tradition. On the one hand, it adopts an "attitude of criticism, as it becomes aware of the limits and insufficiencies of the production of the past, the inevitable tribute, in part, to be paid to the particular age in which a theology took shape." On the other hand, liberation theology adopts an "attitude of rehabilitation, as it reincorporates forgotten, fertile theological threads that can enrich us, and even call us to account."[32]

---

28. See Gutiérrez, *Theology of Liberation*, xxiv; Gutiérrez, "Task and Content of Liberation Theology," 23.

29. Gutiérrez, *Theology of Liberation*, xxiv.

30. Boff, "Methodology of the Theology of Liberation," 15.

31. Ibid., 15.

32. Ibid., 18.

The interpretation of the experience of the poor in the light of faith is not one-directional, but two-directional. The question is not only "What does the word of God say about this situation [i.e., the reality of the poor]?" but also liberation theology "interrogates the word of God" from the viewpoint of the poor.[33] In other words, not only is the experience of the poor interpreted in the light of both Scripture and tradition, but also Scripture and tradition are interpreted in the light of the present situation of the poor.

Finally, the interpretation of the word of God in the light of the experience of the poor involves the use of what Segundo calls "ideological suspicion,"[34] which consists in the suspicion that "anything involving ideas, including theology, is bound up with the existing social situation, in at least an unconscious way."[35] According to Segundo, it is naive to think that the word of God is "immune to the ideological tendencies" of the world today.[36] There is no such a thing as a neutral interpretation of the Bible. Every interpretation of the Bible is a partisan interpretation, even when it believes or pretends to be neutral. Thus, "there is no such thing as an autonomous, impartial, academic theology floating free above the realm of human options and biases. However academic it may be, theology is intimately bound up with the psychological, social, or political status quo though it may not be consciously aware of that fact."[37] Therefore, a theology that endorses the cause of the poor should free itself from pretended neutralities. Theology should be liberated "from its atavism and its ivory tower, toppling the naive self-conception it entertains at present: i.e., that it is a simple, eternal, impartial interpretation . . . of the word of God."[38] Consequently, the hermeneutic of ideological suspicion in the method of liberation theology includes a conscious and explicit partiality for the poor.[39]

The third moment of the method of liberation theology is praxis again. In fact, the second moment of the method—i.e., the moment of reflection—is not for the sake of reflection itself. Rather, in liberation theology, theoretical reflection seeks to energize the praxis of liberation. As Gutiérrez says, "If theological reflection does not vitalize the action of the Christian community in the world by making its commitment to charity fuller and more

---

33. Ibid., 15–16.

34. Segundo, *Liberation of Theology*, 9. The word "ideology" is understood here in a broad sense, that is, as a set of ideas that works as a support for the interests and the actions of an individual person or a human group. See ibid., 102.

35. Ibid., 8.

36. Ibid., 7.

37. Ibid., 13; see ibid., 74–75.

38. Ibid., 19.

39. Ibid., 13.

radical . . . , then this theological reflection will have been of little value."[40] If we recall the basic structure of the method of liberation theology—that is, praxis-reflection-praxis—we should be able to understand Boff when he states, liberation theology "emerges from action and leads to action." However, the theologian does not propose a specific program of political action. That is not his or her role as a theologian. Rather, a theologian "can only open grand perspectives for action."[41]

This methodological process of praxis-reflection-praxis is called the "hermeneutical circle," which Segundo defines as "the continuing change in our interpretation of the Bible which is dictated by the continuing changes in our present-day reality, both individual and societal . . . And the circular nature of this interpretation stems from the fact that each new reality obliges us to interpret the word of God afresh, to change reality accordingly, and then to go back and interpret the word of God again, and so on."[42] Gutiérrez describes the hermeneutical circle as a "circular relationship" between orthopraxy and orthodoxy.[43] The praxis of liberation leads to the "right" understanding of Christian faith, which, in turn, demands the "right" praxis of liberation, and so on.[44] In reality, this hermeneutical process is not a circle, but a spiral or an ascending helix, since the goal of the process is not to return to the same point where we were before, but to advance both in the process of liberation and in the interpretation of the Bible. According to Boff, "there is a hermeneutic circle, then, or 'unceasing interplay' between the poor and the word of God . . . The primacy in this dialectic, however, belongs undeniably to the sovereign word of God—the primacy of value, at any rate, if not necessarily methodological priority."[45] Likewise, Gutiérrez asserts, "The ultimate norms of judgement come from the revealed truth that we accept by faith and not from praxis itself."[46]

SOME ESSENTIAL TENETS OF LIBERATION THEOLOGY

Liberation theology is a kind of theodicy, which is, in a broad sense, an attempt to talk about God in view of the existence of suffering and evil. Gutiérrez asks the theodicy question with the following words: "Among us

40. Gutiérrez, *Theology of Liberation*, 174.
41. Boff, "Methodology of the Theology of Liberation," 20.
42. Segundo, *Liberation of Theology*, 8.
43. Gutiérrez, *Theology of Liberation*, xxxiv.
44. Gutiérrez, *We Drink from Our Own Wells*, 50
45. Boff, "Methodology of the Theology of Liberation," 16.
46. Gutiérrez, *Theology of Liberation*, xxxiv.

the great pastoral, and therefore theological, question is: How is it possible to tell the poor, who are forced to live in conditions that embody a denial of love, that God loves them? This is equivalent to asking: How can we find a way of talking about God amid the suffering and oppression that is the experience of the Latin American poor?"[47] It is important to highlight three points that are implicit in Gutiérrez's statement. Firstly, liberation theology does not deal with the problem of suffering and evil *in general*. Liberation theology addresses specifically the evil of material poverty and the suffering of the poor that is caused by social injustice. Secondly, the purpose of liberation theology is not about "defending" God against the objections that might be raised in view of the existence of suffering and evil. The goal of liberation theology is about telling the poor that God loves them. Finally, liberation theology is not interested in theoretically speculating about the origin of suffering and evil. Liberation theology is interested in removing the unjust suffering from the lives of the poor.[48] In other words, as a theodicy, liberation theology has a practical purpose: to support the liberation of the poor.

In this section, I will explain some essential tenets of liberation theology, including its understanding of God, Jesus Christ, and the Holy Spirit. This analysis will be based on the theologies of Gustavo Gutiérrez, Jon Sobrino, Leonardo Boff, and José Comblin. I have chosen these four theologians for the following reasons. Firstly, among the liberation theologians, Gutiérrez is generally considered the "father of liberation theology," for he is the one who systematically presents fundamental concepts of liberation theology, especially in his classic book *A Theology of Liberation*. Secondly, Sobrino is the liberation theologian that develops a Christology of liberation in a more systematic way. In my judgment, Sobrino is an interesting interlocutor for a critical analysis of liberation Christology. Finally, Leonardo Boff and José Comblin are those who develop a pneumatology of liberation. Furthermore, it is appropriate to choose these four theologians since liberation theology is not the endeavor of a single person, but a collective enterprise. The term "liberation theology" generally refers to the theology done by a group of theologians based in Latin America at the end of the last century.[49] In a general sense, these theologians share the same theological

47. Ibid., xxxiv.

48. See Sobrino, *Principle of Mercy*, 29.

49. We talk about liberation theologians *in Latin America*, and not about *Latin American theologians*, because not all of them were born in such a territory. Besides, it is not easy to delimit the territory called "Latin America." Probably the expression "Latin American and the Caribbean" would be more appropriate. However, liberation theologians generally just use the term "Latin America." Thus, this is the term that I will employ in this study.

ideas. However, it is more accurate to say that each of these theologians has produced *a* theology of liberation. Therefore, on the one hand, there is no such a thing as *the* theology of liberation. On the other hand, it is possible to speak of "theology of liberation" if it is understood as a collective enterprise.[50]

Definition of Two Key Terms: "Liberation" and "the Poor"

It is appropriate to begin our analysis with the clarification of two essential concepts in liberation theology, namely, "liberation" and "the poor." When liberation theology talks about "the poor," it means first of all those who suffer from what is called "material poverty," that is, "the lack of economic goods necessary for a human life worthy of the name."[51] Some of these basic goods for living are "land, work, food, house, health, education."[52] If material poverty is the lack of what is necessary for living, then "poverty means death."[53] In this sense, the poor are those who suffer a situation that leads them to a "premature and unjust death."[54] However, the meaning of the word "poverty" has become more complex in liberation theology. At the beginning, as it was already said, liberation theology emphasized the economic dimension of poverty. Today, liberation theology pays attention to other dimensions of material poverty.[55] According to Richard, now liberation theology defines "the poor and the excluded not only with socio-economic categories of social class, but also with categories of gender (man-woman), generation

---

50. Gutiérrez recognizes a "spatial extension" of liberation theology in the last decades. See Gutiérrez, *Theology of Liberation*, xix. This extension includes not only the development of liberation theologies in non-Latin American countries, but also the creation of new kinds of liberation theologies, such as Black theologies and feminist theologies, in Catholic and non-Catholic traditions.

51. Gutiérrez, *Theology of Liberation*, 163. In her analysis of Schillebeeckx's theology, McManus defines the poor as "those who suffer" (McManus, *Unbroken Communion*, 135). To my mind, McManus' definition of the poor is not completely adequate for a theology of liberation, since it is too general. It is true that the poor suffer. Nevertheless, the question is, from what do they suffer? What are the causes of their suffering? According to liberation theology, the poor are those who suffer especially from material poverty and from social exclusion. Again, liberation theology does not deal with the problem of suffering in general, but addresses a specific kind of suffering, that is, the suffering of the poor that is caused by social injustice.

52. Richard, *Fuerza Etica y Espiritual de la Teología de la Liberación*, 72 (translation mine).

53. Gutiérrez, *Theology of Liberation*, xxi; Gutiérrez, *We Drink from Our Own Wells*, 9.

54. Gutiérrez, *We Drink from Our Own Wells*, 2, 28, 94, 100.

55. See Gutiérrez, *Theology of Liberation*, xxi–xxiii.

(young-adult), race and culture (white-black-indigenous), including also among the excluded those who are 'different' because of their sexual identity and those whom the system considers 'disabled.'"[56] Therefore, the notion of the poor includes not only those who are socio-economically poor, but also those who suffer social exclusion because of their gender, age, race, culture, sexual orientation, and physical conditions, among other aspects of human reality. To include these other dimensions of material poverty, I will use the term "social outcasts" in this study. The advantage of this term is that it includes both those who are socio-economically poor, for they are always marginalized from society, and those who have been excluded because of their gender, age, race, culture, sexual orientation, and physical conditions.

But socio-economic poverty is still the paradigmatic form of material poverty in liberation theology. All those who are socio-economically poor are oppressed and marginalized precisely because they are poor. This phenomenon does not happen with the other aspects of human reality that were mentioned above. For instance, according to Boff, not all women and black people are oppressed and excluded from society: "A black taxi driver and a black soccer star are not the same thing. Similarly, a female domestic servant and the first lady of the land are not the same." However, Boff observes, "the oppressions of a noneconomic type aggravate pre-existing socio-economic oppression. The poor are far more grievously oppressed when, besides being poor, they are black, Indian, women, or elderly."[57] In these cases, Gutiérrez says, the poor are "doubly oppressed and marginalized."[58]

When liberation theology talks about "liberation," it means the liberation of social outcasts. If poverty means death, then liberation means "to give life."[59] Gutiérrez often describes liberation as a historical process that has three different levels or dimensions.[60] Here I will explain the first two levels of liberation, leaving the third for later. The first level is economic, social, and political liberation. As Boff asserts, "*liberation* in liberation theology denotes first of all *social liberation*. This is *the* question of our time. And this was the question from which liberation theology sprang."[61] Most people relate liberation theology with this first level of liberation.

---

56. Richard, *Fuerza Etica y Espiritual de la Teología de la Liberación*, 35 (translation mine).
57. Boff, "Methodology of the Theology of Liberation," 14.
58. Gutiérrez, *Theology of Liberation*, xx.
59. Ibid., xxxvii; Gutiérrez, *We Drink from Our Own Wells*, 3.
60. See Gutiérrez, *Theology of Liberation*, xxxviii, 24–25, 56, 103, 137.
61. Boff, "Methodology of the Theology of Liberation," 4.

A Critical Analysis of Liberation Theology 21

However, there is a second level of liberation, which is the level of personal freedom. Unfortunately, most people do not associate liberation theology with this second level of liberation; perhaps that is why Gutiérrez calls it the "humblest level."[62] To talk about this second level, Gutiérrez uses the expression *"liberación del hombre"* (liberation of the human being).[63] This liberation of the human being is the process by which a person becomes the "artisan of its own destiny,"[64] and "the oppressed reject the oppressive consciousness which dwells in them."[65] In other words, at the second level, men and women are liberated from oppressive structures that exist in their own consciousnesses or minds. They are liberated from structures of oppression that exist not "outside," but "inside" them. Gutiérrez says: "modern human aspirations include not only liberation from exterior pressures which prevent fulfillment as a member of a certain social class, country, or society. Persons seek likewise an *interior liberation*, in an individual and intimate dimension; they seek liberation not only on a social plane but also on a psychological. They seek an *interior freedom*."[66] Seventeen years after the first publication of *A Theology of Liberation*, in the new introduction to his book, Gutiérrez states clearly, "it is not enough that we be liberated from oppressive socio-economic structures; also needed is a *personal transformation* by which we live with profound *inner freedom* in the face of every kind of servitude, and this is the second dimension or level of liberation."[67] Therefore, the second level is about personal freedom. According to Comblin, this "true liberation of the 'self'" lies at the heart of liberation theology.[68] The "call to freedom" takes place in the daily struggles of men and women who try to liberate themselves from the constraints and dependencies that condition their lives.[69] "When human beings seek to overcome their limits . . . , basic liberation is taking place."[70]

However, Comblin writes, "the conquest of freedom is both individual and collective."[71] Freedom is personal, but always in relationship with

---

62. Gutiérrez, *Theology of Liberation*, xl.
63. Gutiérrez, *Teología de la Liberación*, 91, 224.
64. Gutiérrez, *Theology of Liberation*, 56.
65. Ibid., 57.
66. Ibid., 20 (emphasis mine).
67. Ibid., xxxviii (emphasis mine).
68. Comblin, *Called for Freedom*, 201.
69. Ibid., 31.
70. Ibid., 199.
71. Ibid., 30.

others.⁷² Therefore, the first and second levels of liberation are interrelated. On the one hand, "Only men and women who accept this vocation [for freedom] will be able to authentically assume the tasks of [socio-political] liberation."⁷³ On the other hand, real personal freedom exists only "within an overall emancipation of the entire human race."⁷⁴ Both levels are part of a single event called liberation.

Comblin acknowledges, nevertheless, that unfortunately "Liberation theology has gone along its way paying practically no attention to the theology of freedom."⁷⁵ Therefore,

> The greatest reproach that can be made against liberation theology is that it has not devoted enough attention to the true drama of human persons, to their destiny, to their vocation, and consequently to the ground of the issue of freedom. This does not mean that in their own life or in their action as persons the theologians have not paid enough attention to it, but it does not come out clearly enough in their writings. This lack has made it possible for their followers or hasty activists to spread a superficial notion of Christianity that reduces it to a strategy of political or social struggle.⁷⁶

For this reason, it is necessary to recover the concept of personal freedom in liberation theology, or to be more precise, it is necessary to re-establish the relationship between personal freedom and social liberation.

God the Liberator

The experience of liberation is an experience of God's love for social outcasts. Gutiérrez says: "'God first loved us' (1 John 4:19). Everything starts from there."⁷⁷ Regarding God's love, liberation theology makes the distinction between the order of reality, and the order of knowing.⁷⁸ On the one hand, men and women know God through God's actions in history (epistemological order). On the other hand, God's being is the basis of God's action

---

72. Ibid., 30, 37.
73. Ibid., 199.
74. Ibid., 30.
75. Ibid., 48. According to Comblin, some liberation theologians have mistrusted the idea of freedom because, for them, freedom is associated with liberalism. See ibid., 27.
76. Ibid., 197.
77. Gutiérrez, *We Drink from Our Own Wells*, 109.
78. See Gutiérrez, *God of Life*, 2.

in history (ontological order). However, God's being and God's actions are one in God.[79] The point here regarding God's love is that human beings know God's love through God's actions of love in history.

An essential characteristic of God's love for human beings is its gratuitousness. God's love is a gift that God freely gives to men and women. This does not mean that God gives "something" to them. It rather means that God is giving God's self to human beings. As Karl Rahner asserts about God, "the giver himself is the gift."[80] God does not love human beings because they are good, but because God is good. Human beings do not merit God's love, that is, they do not receive divine love as a reward for their rituals or their good deeds. Human beings cannot manipulate or blackmail God with their actions.[81]

God loves human beings by sharing divine life with them. Loving someone means willing the good of the beloved person. The supreme good that God wills for human beings is God's own life. Therefore, God's love for human beings is manifested by giving them life. This notion of God as giver of life is expressed in the images of God as mother and father, both of which are present in the Bible.[82]

Even though God's love is for all human beings, God has a preferential option for the poor. This preferential option of God does not mean that the non-poor are excluded from divine love. As Gutiérrez asserts, the "word 'preference' denies all exclusiveness."[83] Why does God have a preferential (but not exclusive) option for social outcasts? If loving someone entails both willing the good of the beloved person, and acting in such a way that the beloved person may have a worthy life, then it makes sense that God opts preferentially for the poor, since they are the ones who do not have a worthy life. An analogy might be helpful to understand God's preferential option for social outcasts. God is like a mother (or a father) who has two sons.[84] In a fight that the mother unsuccessfully tries to prevent, the oldest son attacks the younger son to the point that the latter ends up badly injured. The mother takes her youngest son to the hospital and stays with him as long as necessary. With this action of staying with the youngest son, she is showing a preferential option for him. This action does not mean that she does not

---

79. See Aquinas, *Summa Theologiae* I 19.2.

80. Rahner, *Foundations of Christian Faith*, 120.

81. See Gutiérrez, *We Drink from Our Own Wells*, 110.

82. See Gutiérrez, *God of Life*, 1.

83. Gutiérrez, *Theology of Liberation*, xxv.

84. Cf. Goizueta, *Caminemos con Jesús*, 176; Goizueta, "Theo-Drama as Liberative Praxis," 71.

love her older son. This action simply shows the justice of the mother, i.e., it is *just* to be with the son who has been badly beaten. In the same way, God has a preferential option for the poor not because the poor are good, but because God is good and just.[85]

God's preferential option for the poor involves God's reaction to their suffering. This statement entails that liberation theology gets away from the notion of an apathic God.[86] In fact, God is a God who reacts both with indignation and with compassion when he sees the affliction of those who are oppressed. On the one hand, God reacts with indignation. The prophet's denunciations in the Old Testament, for instance, are expressions of God's indignation.[87] On the other hand, God reacts with compassion, which means suffering with the people who suffer.[88] Etymologically, passion comes from the Latin word *passio*, which means suffering. Com-passion means suffering with. The words of God in the book of Exodus, for example, express God's compassion: "I have observed the misery of my people who are in Egypt; I have heard their cry on account of their taskmasters. Indeed, I know their sufferings, and I have come down to deliver them from the Egyptians, and to bring them up out of that land to a good and broad land" (Exodus 3:7-8).[89] God's double reaction of indignation and compassion leads God to act.

God's action of love is called salvation. To love someone is to will the good of the beloved person. Therefore, loving someone means saving the

---

85. See Gutiérrez, *God of Life*, 163; Gutiérrez, *Theology of Liberation*, xxviii. God's justice is different from what many people envisage. A bad interpretation of the law of retribution is an example of the notion of justice that many people have. The law of retribution can be summarized in two phrases: the righteous should be rewarded and the wicked should be punished. A correct interpretation of the law of retribution is that God is not indifferent to human actions. God rejoices at the good actions of the righteous, and God rages at the bad actions of the wicked. However, the law of retribution has its limitations, and it can be misinterpreted in many different ways. The book of Job deals with this problem. A wrong interpretation of the law of retribution, for instance, is the following: if God rejoices at the good actions of the righteous, then the righteous person must be blessed by God because he or she has been good. In other words, many people think that if they are good, it is just to receive God's blessing. However, this notion of justice is not God's notion of justice. Again, human beings do not merit God's love. They cannot demand anything from God, for God is free. For a very fine commentary on the book of Job from the perspective of liberation theology, see Gutiérrez, *On Job*. See also Harrington, *Why Do We Suffer?*, 15-49.

86. See Gutiérrez, *God of Life*, xiii.

87. See Gutiérrez, *Theology of Liberation*, 165-68.

88. Cf. Sobrino, *Principle of Mercy*, 16-18.

89. For liberation theologians, the Exodus is a paradigmatic event of liberation. See Gutiérrez, *God of Life*, 3-6; Gutiérrez, *Theology of Liberation*, 88-89; Gutiérrez, *We Drink from Our Own Wells*, 73-79.

beloved person from what is evil. God's action of love for human beings is, then, a saving action from what is evil. If the supreme good that God gives to human beings is life, then the supreme evil from which God saves human beings is death. God saves human beings in history. This salvation, however, will be complete only at the end of time. Salvation is here already, but not yet complete. Therefore, salvation has two dimensions, namely, one historical and the other eschatological. As Gutiérrez says, salvation is an intra-historical reality that guides history to its fulfillment.[90]

The liberation of those who are social outcasts is an expression of God's saving action in history.[91] For liberation theology, "there are not two histories, one profane and one sacred, 'juxtaposed' or 'closely linked' . . . The history of salvation is the very heart of human history . . . There is only one history."[92] In this sense, in the light of faith it is possible to say that the process of liberation of social outcasts is a manifestation of both God's saving action in history and God's preferential option for the poor.

God liberates social outcasts in an integral way. This integral liberation has three dimensions. I already mentioned two of them, namely, social liberation and personal freedom. The third and deepest level is the liberation from sin. According to Gutiérrez, sin is a power in human beings that breaks the friendship with God and with other human beings. Sin is the deepest cause of social injustice.[93] The three dimensions of liberation are interrelated. As I said above, the poor will not have social liberation if they are not interiorly freed, and vice versa, the poor will not have personal freedom if they are not socially liberated. Furthermore, neither social liberation nor personal freedom is possible if there is no liberation from sin, and vice versa, the liberation from sin is manifested in both social liberation and personal freedom. All three levels of liberation are part of a single process.

God's liberating action demands a human response. Human beings are free to accept or reject God's love, which is another way to say that human beings are free to accept or reject salvation. This acceptance or rejection of life is an option that every person faces in his or her existence. In this sense, Gutiérrez suggests, "human existence, in the last instance, is nothing but a yes or no to the Lord."[94] A negative human response to God's love is called sin. A positive human response to God's saving action includes both

90. Gutiérrez, *Theology of Liberation*, 86.
91. Gutiérrez, *We Drink from Our Own Wells*, 2.
92. Gutiérrez, *Theology of Liberation*, 86.
93. Gutiérrez, *Theology of Liberation*, xxxviii, 24. The affirmation that sin is the source of social injustice is a theological interpretation of the historical reality of poverty. This is why I have kept the explanation of the third level of liberation until this point.
94. Ibid., 84.

passivity and activity. On the one hand, salvation is a gift of God. A positive human response means openness to and acceptance of that gift. This is the *passive* dimension of the human response to God's love. On the other hand, salvation involves an invitation from God to human beings to collaborate with God in the history of salvation. As Leonardo Boff says, "God's love does not do violence to [human freedom]. Instead it invites a loving response from human beings. It does not subjugate anyone. Instead it invites all to undertake a journey where God and human beings unite to make history. This is the history of salvation, the fruit of two freedoms at work and the product of two loves."[95] A positive human response to God's love means to collaborate with God in the history of salvation. This is the *active* dimension of the human response to God's love. For liberation theology, a positive human response to God's love means participation in the process of liberation. As Gutiérrez says, "the process of liberation is the saving work that God calls us to share."[96]

In this relationship between God and human beings in the process of liberation, on the divine side, God is the one who has the initiative to liberate social outcasts, and God is the one who invites human beings to participate in the process of liberation. On the human side, men and women are the ones who respond positively to God's initiative by accepting the gift of liberation (passive dimension), and by participating in the process of liberation (active dimension). Gutiérrez expresses this relationship between God and human beings in at least three different ways. Firstly, he talks about the relationship between *gratuitousness* and *effectiveness*. As was already said, God's love for human beings is gratuitous. God's love is a gift that God freely gives to men and women. They need an attitude of contemplation to be aware of God's gift in their lives (passive dimension). Quoting Bernanos, Gutiérrez says, "contemplation disposes us to recognize that 'everything is grace.'"[97] Once human beings are aware of God's love in their lives, they can respond positively to that love by means of effective action (active dimension). The relationship between gratuitousness and effectiveness is not one of balance. For Gutiérrez, "gratuitousness is an atmosphere in which the entire quest for effectiveness is bathed."[98]

Secondly, Gutiérrez talks about *spiritual poverty* or *spiritual childhood*.[99] The notion of "poor in spirit" appears in Matthew 5:3. For Gutiér-

---

95. Boff, *Liberating Grace*, 110.
96. See Gutiérrez, *Theology of Liberation*, xxxix.
97. Gutiérrez, *We Drink from Our Own Wells*, 111.
98. Ibid., 109.
99. Gutiérrez distinguishes three different meanings of the word "poverty," namely,

rez, spiritual poverty is not simply detachment from material goods. In a deeper sense, spiritual poverty means having no other sustenance in one's life than God's love. It means both the attitude of openness to God and the attitude of welcoming God in one's life.[100] Spiritual poverty is also called spiritual childhood, which is the "outlook of the person who accepts the gift of divine filiation [passive dimension] and responds to it by building fellowship [active dimension]."[101] Salvation is "God's gift of definitive life to God's children, given in a history in which we must build fellowship. Filiation and fellowship are both a grace and a task to be carried out; these two aspects must be distinguished without being separated."[102]

Finally, Gutiérrez states that human beings have been freed to love. As Paul says: "For freedom Christ has set us free" (Galatians 5:1). Thus, there is a distinction between freedom *from* and freedom *for*. In Jesus Christ, God frees human beings *from* sin and death in all their historical manifestations, for example, material poverty, injustice, oppression, and social exclusion. This freedom is a gift of God (passive dimension). However, this is not the end of the process. Human beings are freed *for* love and *for* communion with others, which is the final stage in the process of liberation. However, loving others and building communion with others are the tasks of human beings (active dimension).[103] In fact, by loving, human beings respond to the initiative taken by God to love.[104] By liberating social outcasts, human beings respond to the initiative taken by God to liberate.

Therefore, who is God according to liberation theology? God is the liberator of social outcasts. God is love; hence, God gives life. Therefore, anything that means death, including material poverty, is against God's will. Thus, God has a preferential option for the poor because they are afflicted by an unjust situation that is leading them to death. In view of the suffering of social outcasts, God reacts with indignation and compassion, and this double reaction leads God to act in history. The process of liberation of the poor is a manifestation of God's action in history on behalf of social outcasts, and this action is God's initiative. However, God's liberating action in history demands a human response. On the one hand, liberation is a gift from God. A positive human response entails acceptance of the gift of

---

"real poverty as an evil—that is something that God does not want; spiritual poverty, in the sense of a readiness to do God's will; and [poverty as] solidarity with the poor" (Gutiérrez, *Theology of Liberation*, xxv).

100. See Gutiérrez, *Theology of Liberation*, 169–71.
101. Gutiérrez, *We Drink from Our Own Wells*, 127.
102. Gutiérrez, *Theology of Liberation*, xxxix.
103. See ibid., 24; Gutiérrez, *We Drink from Our Own Wells*, 92.
104. Gutiérrez, *We Drink from Our Own Wells*, 110.

liberation. On the other hand, the process of liberation involves an invitation from God to human beings to collaborate with God in that process. A positive human response implies participation in the process of liberation.

Jesus Christ the Liberator

The experience of liberation is a manifestation of God's love for social outcasts, a love that has its greatest expression in Jesus Christ. This section explains critically a Christology of liberation. I will explain only those aspects of liberation Christology that will be correlated with theological aesthetics in the following chapters. As I said above, my analysis will focus mostly on Sobrino's Christology. I will explain four aspects of his Christology: the historical Jesus, the kingdom of God, Jesus' death on the cross, and the resurrection of Jesus Christ.

The Historical Jesus

For liberation Christology, the "historical Jesus" is the starting point of an account of the whole reality of Jesus Christ. This reality involves two interrelated aspects. As Sobrino says, "Jesus Christ is a whole that . . . consists of a historical element (Jesus) and a transcendental element (Christ), and the most characteristic feature of faith as such is the acceptance of the transcendental element: that this Jesus is more than Jesus, that he is *the* Christ."[105] Both elements are interrelated. Without the Jesus of history, it is impossible to know who the Christ of faith is. Without faith in Christ, it is impossible to fully understand the history of Jesus. However, as Sobrino asserts, every theologian has to face a methodological problem: where does one start the account of the whole reality of Jesus Christ? Liberation Christology opts to start with the reality of the historical Jesus as a point of access to the whole reality of Jesus Christ.[106]

Sobrino has a distinct understanding of the term "historical Jesus," which is very rich in meaning. Firstly, the historical Jesus means the earthly life of Jesus. Sobrino says: "I have chosen as my starting point the reality of Jesus of Nazareth, his life, his mission and his fate, what is usually called the 'historical Jesus.'"[107] Secondly, the historical Jesus refers to the praxis of Jesus. In other words, among the different aspects of the earthly life of Jesus,

---

105. Sobrino, *Jesus the Liberator*, 36–37.
106. See ibid., 36.
107. Ibid., 36.

Sobrino focuses on the actions of Jesus. Sobrino claims: "the most historical aspect of the historical Jesus is his practice . . . By 'practice' I mean the whole range of activities Jesus used to act on social reality and transform it."[108] Thirdly, the historical Jesus means the "history of Jesus"[109] that has been handed over to his disciples so that they may imitate Jesus, especially in his praxis. Sobrino says:

> The historical dimension of Jesus does not mean, therefore, from a formal point of view what is simply datable in space and time, but what is handed down to us as a trust for us to pass on in our turn. This implies treating the texts of the New Testament in general and the Gospel texts in particular as narratives published to keep alive through history a reality started off by Jesus. This reality, after the resurrection, is responsible for passing on faith in Christ, but in terms of Jesus' own intention its original task was to pass on his practice, in Jesus' own words, discipleship, considered primarily as a continuation of his practice.[110]

Therefore, the historical Jesus means the narratives about the life of Jesus, especially the account of his praxis. In this sense, Sturla Stålsett rightly suggests that, instead of the "history of Jesus," the expression the "story of Jesus" suitably expresses what Sobrino wants to convey by the term "historical Jesus."[111] Finally, the word "historical" in the expression "historical Jesus" means "what sets history in motion."[112] The history (or story) of Jesus has been handed over to his disciples so that they may transform reality as Jesus did through his praxis. Therefore, not only the praxis of Jesus has an impact on history, but the praxis of his disciples has a transformative effect on history as well. To understand this idea that "historical" is what sets history in motion, it is helpful to remember that liberation theology is a reflection on the *historical* praxis of liberation. To say that the praxis of liberation is historical does not simply mean that such praxis occurs in a specific space and time. It also means that such praxis has an impact on the history of society.

Therefore, Sobrino's notion of the historical Jesus "transcends the positivism of historical facts," as Robert Lassalle-Klein avers.[113] It is not that Sobrino disregards the question about what Jesus really did and said two thousand years ago; however, he definitely goes beyond that question.

108. Ibid., 51.
109. Ibid., 50.
110. Ibid., 51.
111. Stålsett, *The crucified and the Crucified*, 212.
112. Sobrino, *Jesus the Liberator*, 51.
113. Lasalle-Klein, "Jesus of Galilee and the Crucified People," 347.

Some people may ask: is it legitimate on Sobrino's part to employ the term "historical Jesus" if he is not using it in the way that, for instance, many biblical scholars use it? In my opinion, it is legitimate. Considering the "poverty of our vocabulary," using Thomas Aquinas' expression,[114] I think there is no other term that articulates more properly what Sobrino wants to say with the term the "historical Jesus." In fact, the biblical scholar Daniel Harrington claims that Sobrino correctly eschews the "narrow version of historical criticism" found in many authors and formulates a "more adequate and fruitful way of treating the ancient sources," which "involves taking seriously the historical data about Jesus and trying to do theology on the basis of and in the light of these data."[115]

The Kingdom of God

For liberation Christology, a fundamental aspect of the praxis of Jesus is the kingdom of God. In the gospels, Jesus does not appear proclaiming himself. Rather, he appears announcing the "kingdom of God."[116] What does Jesus mean by the term "kingdom of God"? First of all, the kingdom of God means God's action of reigning.[117] "The term 'reign' of God," Sobrino says, "is actually more appropriate than 'kingdom' of God."[118] The kingdom is *of God*. It is God who wills to reign not outside this world, but in this world.[119] Furthermore, the kingdom of God is the transformation of this world. God reigns in this world to transform it according to God's will. In Sobrino's words, "God's 'kingdom' is what comes to pass in this world when God truly reigns: a history, a society, a people transformed according to the will of God."[120] Since the will of God is that all human beings have life, the kingdom of God is the reign of life.[121]

The kingdom of God has two dimensions, namely, one historical and the other eschatological. On the one hand, the kingdom of God occurs in history. God is already reigning in history to transform the world. On the other hand, the kingdom of God will be complete only at the end of time.

114. Aquinas, *Summa Theologiae* I 37.1 c.
115. Harrington, "What Got Jesus Killed?," 80–81.
116. Sobrino, *Jesus the Liberator*, 67.
117. See ibid., 71.
118. Ibid.
119. "The 'kingdom of heaven,'" says Harrington, "was Matthew's typically Jewish substitute expression. As a sign of reverence Jews avoided using the name of God" (Harrington, *Jesus*, 21).
120. Sobrino, *Jesus the Liberator*, 71.
121. Ibid., 84.

Therefore, the kingdom of God "is" already, but not yet. In other words, the kingdom of God is a process or event that occurs in history, but that will reach its completeness only at the end of time.[122]

An essential characteristic of the kingdom of God is its gratuitousness. To reign in history is God's initiative. As Sobrino says, the kingdom "cannot be forced by human action. The coming of the kingdom is, then, shot through with gratuitousness; God comes out of gratuitous love, not in response to human actions."[123] However, the kingdom of God demands a human response. Human beings are free to respond in a positive or a negative way. A negative human response is called sin. As Gutiérrez says, sin is "to resist welcoming the kingdom of God."[124] A positive human response includes both a passive and an active dimension. On the one hand, the kingdom of God is a gift of God. As such, a positive human response means openness to and welcoming of the kingdom of God. This is the passive dimension of a positive human response. On the other hand, the kingdom of God includes an invitation from God to human beings to collaborate with God in the work of transforming the world. As such, a positive human response means active participation in the transformation of the world. Gutiérrez describes this active dimension with the following words: "The kingdom of God brings with it the demand for certain kinds of behaviour . . . The acceptance of the kingdom finds expression both in thanksgiving to God and in deeds done for our brothers and sisters . . . The kingdom requires us to change our present reality, reject the abuses of the powerful, and establish relationships that are fraternal and just. When we behave thus, we are accepting the gift [of the kingdom of God]."[125] Therefore, the kingdom of God is not separated from human action. On the contrary, the gratuitousness of the kingdom of God demands the effective action of human beings.[126]

However, some liberation theologians do not always express adequately this relationship between God's kingdom and human action. In my opinion, Sobrino's way of expressing this relationship is often inadequate. For instance, Sobrino claims that human beings should "build" the kingdom of God.[127] Likewise, Sobrino says that the kingdom of God "obliges us to make

122. See Sobrino, *Jesus the Liberator*, 129–30; Gutiérrez, *God of Life*, 101–2.

123. Sobrino, *Jesus the Liberator*, 76. See Sobrino, "Central Position of the Reign of God," 65.

124. Gutiérrez, *We Drink from Our Own Wells*, 97.

125. Gutiérrez, *God of Life*, 102.

126. See Gutiérrez, *Theology of Liberation*, 132; Gutiérrez, *We Drink from Our Own Wells*, 108.

127. See Sobrino, *Jesus the Liberator*, 102, 127, 128; Sobrino, "Central Position of the Reign of God," 72.

it present through historical mediations and to bring it about at all levels of historical reality."[128] To my mind, it is misleading to use expressions such as "building the kingdom," "making the kingdom present," or "bringing the kingdom" to talk about the role of human beings in the kingdom, because if human beings are the ones who build the kingdom, then it is not the kingdom *of God*, but the kingdom of human beings.[129] For this reason, it is more appropriate to say that the kingdom of God is always God's initiative, and human action is always a response to God's initiative. Perhaps it is possible to say that human beings "build" the kingdom of God provided that they are understood as "collaborators" of God in the transformation of the world.[130] However, this collaboration between God and human beings is not that of equals, since God is not a being among other beings in the world. Rather, the collaboration is that of a God who works in and through the free actions of human beings.

The kingdom of God is a gift for all human beings; however, the poor are the principal recipients of the kingdom of God.[131] "Blessed are you who are poor," Jesus says, "for yours is the kingdom of God" (Luke 6:20). According to Sobrino, in the gospels, the poor includes two groups. First, the poor are those who are materially poor, for instance, those who suffer from hunger, sickness, and imprisonment. Second, the poor are those who are sociologically poor, that is, those who are despised in society, for instance, prostitutes. Therefore, the poor are "those close to the slow death poverty brings . . . , and those who are also deprived of social dignity."[132] If poverty means unjust and premature death, then poverty is incompatible with the kingdom of life. God reigns in the world so that human beings may have a worthy life. Therefore, it makes sense that the poor are the preferential addressees of the kingdom of God, since they are the ones who lack a worthy life. That the kingdom of God has a historical dimension means that God is already working now in history in order to transform the world into a place where the poor may have a worthy life. Furthermore, the kingdom of God includes an invitation from God to all human beings, especially the poor, to collaborate with God in the transformation of the world on behalf of the poor. "Accepting the kingdom of God," then, "means refusing to accept

---

128. Sobrino, *Jesus the Liberator*, 129.

129. Sobrino's theology has been criticized as a kind of Pelagianism probably because he does not explain well the relationship between God's saving work and human action. See, for instance, Piar, *Jesus and Liberation*, 134 n. 4.

130. See 1 Corinthians 3:5–11.

131. See Sobrino, *Jesus the Liberator*, 80–81; Gutiérrez, *God of Life*, 115–17; Gutiérrez, *Theology of Liberation*, 168, 171

132. Sobrino, *Jesus the Liberator*, 81.

a world that instigates or tolerates the premature and unjust deaths of the poor."[133]

Jesus proclaims the kingdom of God by means of his praxis. Jesus' praxis includes actions such as performing miracles of healing, welcoming sinners, denouncing social injustices, and having controversies with some groups that have socio-economic and religious power, such as the rich, the scribes, the Pharisees, and the priests. For Sobrino, on the one hand, the miracles and the welcome of sinners are only "signs" of the kingdom because they do not bring about social transformation, but only demand individual conversion. On the other hand, the denunciations and the controversies are the actions that really bring the kingdom of God, because in those actions Jesus addresses social and religious groups, and by doing so, his actions transform the whole society.[134] Here, Sobrino shows that his understanding of the kingdom of God is mostly focused on, or limited to, its social dimension. Without denying the social dimension, I suggest that the kingdom of God also produces transformation at the personal level. God wills to reign in all the dimensions of human reality. Jesus manifests this all-embracing quality of the kingdom of God when he addresses social groups as well as individuals. Therefore, I consider Jesus' actions of healing the sick and welcoming sinners to be not mere "signs" of the kingdom, but real manifestations of the kingdom of God at the personal level.

Therefore, Jesus' praxis of healing the sick and welcoming sinners are manifestations of the kingdom of God at the personal level. According to Sobrino, the miracles of healing showed Jesus' compassion. In the face of the suffering of the sick, Jesus reacted with compassion, that is, he suffered with those who suffer. His compassion for the sick led Jesus to act, that is, to heal them. Likewise, the action of welcoming sinners showed Jesus' compassion. Here, "sinners" mean those who were considered as such according to the religious beliefs at the time of Jesus, for instance, prostitutes. Not only were sinners despised by society; they had also adopted the idea that God himself despised them. This sense of being rejected by everyone was a cause of suffering for sinners. In view of the suffering of these people, Jesus had a double reaction. He reacted with compassion for these sinners, and with indignation against the society that despised them. This double reaction led Jesus to act, i.e., to welcome sinners, which meant being close to them, or more simply being a friend to them.[135] Therefore, Jesus' praxis of healing the sick and of welcoming sinners showed God's compassion for social outcasts.

133. Gutiérrez, *God of Life*, 102.
134. See Sobrino, *Jesus the Liberator*, 160–61.
135. See ibid., 95–97.

Jesus' praxis of denouncing social injustices, and of getting into controversy with powerful socio-economic and religious groups, are manifestations of a kingdom of life that is in conflict with a kingdom of death. In the gospels, Jesus appears facing the power of evil, which is at work in human beings and in society to destroy both the relationships among human beings and the relationship of human beings with God. The power of evil, which causes death, is against the kingdom of God, which is the source of life. Hence, an essential aspect of Jesus' praxis, as a manifestation of the kingdom of God, is his struggle against the power of evil. Jesus confronts the power of evil, for instance, when he meets persons with unclean spirits or demons. Jesus' action of casting out demons shows the power of God over the power of evil.[136] Jesus also confronts the power of evil in history when he confronts some groups that have socio-economic and religious power, for instance, the rich, the scribes, the Pharisees, and the priests.[137] Some of these groups, instead of protecting the poor, oppress them, and instead of serving God, serve wealth. The text in Matthew 6:24 and Luke 16:13, "You cannot serve God and wealth," preserve the Aramaic word *mammon* to refer to wealth. The word *mammon* helps to personify wealth as a master. In this way, the text conveys the idea of wealth as an idol. Idolatry means that people put their trust in something or someone who is not God. By putting their trust in wealth, people reject God, and they cling to their wealth instead of sharing it with the poor. In this way, idolatry causes the unjust and premature death of the poor.[138] This reality is a manifestation of the historical power of evil that is against the kingdom of God. That is why Jesus' denunciations of social injustices and his conflicts with different groups are manifestations of a kingdom of life that is against the kingdom of death.

The terminology that Sobrino uses to express this conflict between the kingdom of life and the kingdom of death is misleading. Sobrino says: "History contains the true God (of life), God's mediation (the kingdom), and its mediator (Jesus) as well as the idols (of death), their mediation (the anti-kingdom) and mediators (oppressors)."[139] I argue that Sobrino's parallelism—between God and the kingdom of God, on the one hand, and idols and the anti-kingdom, on the other hand—is misleading. First of all, as Stålsett indicates, the term "anti-kingdom" does not appear in the New Testament. The notion of "Satan's kingdom" in Matthew 12:26 and Luke 11:18

---

136. See ibid., 93–95.

137. See ibid., 170–78.

138. See Sobrino, *Jesus the Liberator*, 180–89; Gutiérrez, *God of Life*, 48–49, 55–56.

139. Sobrino, *Jesus the Liberator*, 162. By "oppressors," Sobrino means those who oppress the poor. At the time of Jesus, these "oppressors" are the rich, the scribes, the Pharisees, and the priests. See ibid., 170–78.

might serve as an equivalent to Sobrino's idea of the anti-kingdom. However, Sobrino never uses the term "the kingdom of Satan," perhaps because it does not clearly express the historical dimension of the power of evil.[140] However, the main problem with Sobrino's parallelism is not the absence of the term "anti-kingdom" in the New Testament. The principal problem is the understanding of evil in an ontological way.[141] Some statements of Sobrino point in that direction. Sobrino claims, for example, that the Evil One is "not higher than God or stronger than God, but the reverse."[142] Sobrino says the Evil One is a "trans-historical reality."[143] It is not clear what Sobrino means when he states that the Evil One is the reverse of God or a trans-historical reality, but his statement can be understood as indicating that the Evil One is a transcendental being, which is an opponent of God. Furthermore, to talk about the idols of death, Sobrino uses the expression "divinities of death." According to Sobrino, "we speak of idols in a real, not figurative, sense as divinities of death."[144] Commenting on the verse in the gospels, "You cannot serve God and wealth," Sobrino says, "Jesus poses the question of God dialectically from the existence of various gods among whom we must choose and . . . makes clear what this choice means: to serve one master means hating the other. In plain terms, Jesus asks people not only if they believe in God, but what god they do not believe in 'and' what god they 'hate.' Jesus calls these gods that must be hated, not just ignored, 'masters,' and, by setting them against God, calls them gods."[145] Therefore, Jesus knows about the "struggle of the gods."[146] Sobrino concludes by asking: "Who is God, then, for Jesus? . . . The conclusion, in technical language, is the following: *This* God-Father is antagonistic to and in conflict with the other gods."[147] It is not clear what Sobrino means when he states that the idols are real divinities or gods, but his statement can be understood as saying that the idols are divine beings, which are opponents of God. In fact, putting God and the Evil One side by side, or putting God and the idols side by side, is very problematic. The Evil One and the idols are not "beings" like God "is." As Segundo says, idolatry is the "worship of a nonexistent god."[148]

---

140. Stålsett, *The crucified and the Crucified*, 291.
141. See ibid., 367–68.
142. Sobrino, *Jesus the Liberator*, 94.
143. Ibid., 170, 179.
144. Ibid., 185.
145. Ibid., 187.
146. Ibid.
147. Ibid., 191.
148. Segundo, *Liberation of Theology*, 47.

It might be argued that what Sobrino is trying to say is that *at the time of Jesus* people believed in the existence of many gods and demons. This is precisely what is not clear in Sobrino's argumentation. I am not saying that Sobrino believes in the existence of evil in an ontological way. What I am saying is that the way he explains the conflict between the reign of life and the reign of death is misleading.[149]

Jesus' Death on the Cross

Liberation Christology distinguishes three different aspects of the event of Jesus' death on the cross.[150] The first aspect is the historical dimension of Jesus' death, which can fall under the heading: "Why is Jesus killed?" The second aspect is the theological dimension: "What can we say about God vis-à-vis Jesus' death?" The third aspect is the dimension of the poor: "What is the relationship between the poor and Jesus' death?" These three aspects are interrelated. This section explains each of these dimensions.

The first aspect of the event of Jesus' death on the cross is the historical dimension. Jesus' death is not a fortuitous event. It is the outcome of a historical process. As I explained in the previous section, the denunciation of social injustices and the controversies with some social and religious groups are part of Jesus' praxis. Those groups find in Jesus' praxis a threat to their power. For this reason, they seek and find the way to put Jesus to death. Therefore, Jesus' death is not something that happens by accident. Jesus' death on the cross is something that is intentionally planned and inflicted upon him by those who feel threatened by his message.[151]

However, Jesus does not die as a resigned victim. Jesus knows that his enemies are plotting against him. Seeing his life in danger, Jesus could have retired somewhere to avoid the conflict. However, Jesus does not shrink back. Jesus persists in proclaiming the kingdom of God because he is faithful to the cause of liberation of the poor as the cause of God. In this sense, Jesus freely gives his life. This is not to say that Jesus seeks death. On the contrary, Jesus is afraid of suffering a violent death. However, he does not draw back because he is faithful to God and to the poor until the end.[152]

---

149. Instead of Sobrino's opposed terms "kingdom" and "anti-kingdom," I prefer Gutiérrez's expressions "kingdom of life" and "kingdom of death," which implicitly appear in Romans 5:17. See Gutiérrez, *We Drink from Our Own Wells*, 60–61.

150. See Sobrino, *Jesus the Liberator*, 195.

151. See ibid., 196–200.

152. See ibid., 200–201.

Therefore, Jesus' death has both a passive-negative aspect and an active-positive aspect. On the one hand, Jesus is killed by those groups that reject his proclamation of the kingdom of God. Jesus' death is something that is unjustly inflicted on him. In this sense, Jesus' death has a passive-negative element. On the other hand, Jesus freely gives his life. Jesus could have drawn back in view of the danger of being killed. However, he is faithful to the mission he has received from God of proclaiming God's kingdom. In this sense, Jesus' death has an active-positive element. These two aspects of Jesus' death should always be distinguished and held in tension.

The second aspect of the event of Jesus' death on the cross is the theological dimension. God does not want Jesus' death on the cross. What God wants from Jesus is to stay faithful to his mission of proclaiming God's kingdom. The death on the cross is not a necessary outcome, but a possible consequence of such a proclamation. In fact, the announcement of God's kingdom involves a call for conversion. As part of his praxis, Jesus invites "sinners" to convert. Here "sinners" include those who have socio-economic and religious power and oppress the poor. When Jesus denounces the injustices committed by those social and religious groups, and when he enters into controversy with them, Jesus does not seek to condemn them, but to save them. Conversion, though, is a necessary condition for salvation. Jesus hopes until the end that those who have socio-economic and religious power can change, i.e., they can stop oppressing the poor.[153] Nevertheless, the gospels tell us that the oppressors not only reject Jesus' call to conversion, but also find a threat in his call. For this reason, they put him to death. Therefore, not God, but human beings are responsible for Jesus' death. Again, God does not want Jesus' death on the cross. What God wants from Jesus is to remain faithful to his mission of proclaiming the kingdom of God, hoping until the end that human beings will welcome Jesus' message.

Therefore, I disagree with Sobrino, who suggests that God is ultimately responsible for Jesus' death on the cross. Sobrino says: "Jesus is God's initiative, and so is—scandalously—the cross."[154] Sobrino provides three arguments to support the idea that God wants Jesus' death on the cross. Firstly, this is part of God's mysterious plan. Secondly, it shows what God wants human beings to be. Finally, it manifests the credibility of God's love.

---

153. See ibid., 96–97. Perhaps it is naive to think that the oppressors can convert. However, if we think the opposite, i.e., that it is impossible for them to change, then we are saying that human beings are not free. Thinking that it is impossible for human beings to convert would involve a deterministic and pessimistic view of humanity.

154. Ibid., 230.

Firstly, Jesus' death on the cross as part of God's mysterious plan:[155] on this, Sobrino quotes two verses from the New Testament. The first is the question that Jesus asks the disciples of Emmaus: "Was it not necessary that the Messiah should suffer these things?" (Luke 24:26). The second verse refers to the words that Peter addresses to the crowd in the Acts of the Apostles: "This man [Jesus], handed over to you according to the definite plan and foreknowledge of God" (Acts 2:23).

Secondly, Jesus' death on the cross shows what God wants human beings to be. According to Sobrino, there must be something good in the cross as long as it is part of God's plan. The cross is something good because it has a saving effect on human beings. However, Sobrino has in mind a specific notion of salvation. Among the different models of salvation in the New Testament, he prefers the model of sacrifice. The notion of sacrifice does not mean that suffering itself produces salvation. What the notion of sacrifice indicates is that the sacrifice should be pleasing to God in order to be accepted by God. In this sense, the notion of sacrifice applies to Jesus because his life of love was pleasing and accepted by God. Therefore, what is pleasing to God is not just one aspect of Jesus, let us say, his death. What is pleasing to God is the whole life of Jesus. However, Jesus' life was a life of love, and it is historically proved that "love has to go through suffering."[156] The point here is that the paradigm of what is pleasing to God has appeared on earth. Therefore, if human beings follow this paradigm, they will be pleasing to God. They will be accepted and saved by God. In other words, Jesus is the example of what a true human being is. In Jesus, God reveals what God wants human beings to be.[157]

Finally, Jesus' death on the cross manifests the credibility of God's love for human beings. On this point, Sobrino quotes the verse in the gospel of John: "For God so loved the world that he gave his only Son" (John 3:16). He interprets this verse in the following way: "Not sparing the Son is the way of saying that there is no restraint on God's love for human beings." Sobrino continues: "if human beings do not understand that, by preferring us to his own Son, God wanted to show us his love, nothing will convince them of it."[158] Furthermore, Jesus' death on the cross shows that God is powerless. By preferring human beings instead of his own Son, God tells human beings that God is there "for us," that God is "at our mercy."[159]

---

155. See ibid., 220–21.
156. Ibid, 228.
157. See ibid., 221–30.
158. Ibid., 231.
159. Ibid., 231–32.

I disagree with Sobrino's three arguments. In his first argument, to support the idea that Jesus' death is God's initiative, Sobrino quotes the biblical text, "Was it not necessary that the Messiah should suffer these things?" (Luke 24:26). In my interpretation, what was necessary was that Jesus remain faithful to the mission of proclaiming the kingdom of God when his life was threatened by those in power. The suffering of the cross was not a necessary outcome, but a possible consequence of his mission, since those in power were free to accept or reject Jesus' proclamation. Sobrino also quotes the words that Peter addresses to the crowd in the Acts of the Apostles: "This man [Jesus], handed over to you according to the definite plan and foreknowledge of God" (Acts 2:23). To my mind, this verse does not claim that Jesus' death is part of God's plan. The foreknowledge and plan of God is not the killing of Jesus, but the handing over of Jesus. Indeed, God gives Jesus to human beings, and God hopes that human beings will welcome Jesus. However, human beings are free to accept or reject Jesus. Ultimately, they decided to reject Jesus. Therefore, human beings, and not God, are responsible for the unjust death of Jesus. The aforementioned verse of the Acts of the Apostles explicitly points out this human responsibility. Sobrino quotes only the first part of the verse, but it continues: "This man, handed over to you according to the definite plan and foreknowledge of God, you crucified and killed by the hands of those outside the law" (Acts 2:23).

In his second argument, Sobrino suggests that Jesus' life of love is pleasing to God, but "love has to go through suffering."[160] Therefore, Jesus' suffering, as a necessary element of a life of love, is pleasing to God. I disagree with Sobrino's idea that suffering is a necessary component of a life of love. As I said above, the suffering of the cross is not a necessary outcome, but a possible consequence of a life of love.

In his third argument, Sobrino suggests that God is responsible for Jesus' death as long as God preferred us to his Son. To support this idea, Sobrino quotes the biblical text, "For God so loved the world that he gave his only Son" (John 3:16). To my mind, this verse does not prove that God, out of love for us, gives his Son to be killed. What the verse says is that Jesus is a gift from God to all humanity—a gift that human beings are free to accept or reject. Therefore, the text is not talking about a "choice" that God has to face, ultimately preferring us to his Son, as Sobrino suggests. Besides, Sobrino's idea of a powerless God who is at our mercy is wrong and dangerous. If God were powerless, then God would not be able to liberate the poor from those who oppress them. For all these reasons, I disagree with Sobrino's idea that God is responsible for Jesus' death on the cross.

---

160. Ibid., 228.

Before we consider the third dimension of the cross, i.e., the perspective of the poor, it is important to point out a gap between the first and second dimensions in Sobrino's Christology. Moving from the historical to the theological dimension of Jesus' death, Sobrino shifts from the idea of the "struggle of the gods" to the notion of sacrifice. As Stålsett asserts, "Whereas Jesus is killed because of the struggle of the gods, the explanation for his actually dying is sought with reference to God alone."[161] In fact, to explain the historical dimension of Jesus' death, Sobrino uses a dualistic interpretation of reality: two powers are fighting in history. These two powers are the kingdom and the anti-kingdom, God and the Evil One, or God and the idols. However, to explain the theological dimension of the cross, Sobrino focuses on God as the one ultimately responsible for Jesus' death. In his theological interpretation of the cross, Sobrino puts aside, or forgets about, both the historical oppressors (the rich, the scribes, the Pharisees, the priests) and the trans-historical oppressor (the Evil One). In fact, Sobrino does not posit any relationship between the historical and the theological dimensions of Jesus' death. This disconnection is bewildering because a basic understanding of liberation theology is that the theological dimension occurs in and through the historical dimension of our reality.[162]

The third and final aspect of Jesus' death on the cross is the dimension of the poor. It is important to remember that Jesus' death has a passive-negative and an active-positive dimension. On the one hand, the passive element is that the cross is something inflicted on Jesus. Those who have socio-economic and religious power put Jesus to death because they reject Jesus' proclamation of a God who reigns on behalf of the poor. On the other hand, the active element is that Jesus freely gives his life in faithfulness to the cause of the poor as the cause of God.

Today, the process of liberation of social outcasts can be an analogical expression of the cross if it reproduces both the passive and active dimensions of Jesus' death. The poor are the main subjects of the process of liberation, and they can suffer the cross in an analogical way. In its passive dimension, the poor can suffer the cross in the sense that, as they struggle for their own liberation, the poor can be killed by their oppressors. In this sense, the poor suffer an unjust death, which is inflicted on them. The poor

---

161. Stålsett, *The crucified and the Crucified*, 406.

162. See ibid., 408–10. Probably Sobrino cannot make the link between the historical and theological dimensions of Jesus' death because it would imply a contradiction, for, on the one hand, he claims that the anti-kingdom, the idols of death, the Evil One are the ones who put Jesus to death, and on the other hand, he says that God is responsible for Jesus' death. To link both dimension would mean that God works through the anti-kingdom, which is both self-contradictory and theologically incorrect.

can suffer also the cross in its active dimension. Facing the danger of being killed by their oppressors, if they remain faithful to the cause of their own liberation, they are freely giving their lives. Thus, the poor can be called "crucified people" only if they experience in an analogical way the passive and active dimensions of the cross. The same analogy applies to those who are not materially poor, but who are in solidarity with the poor. As they support the process of liberation of the poor, many lay people, religious, priests, and bishops can suffer the cross as well. As they accompany the poor in the process of liberation, they can be threatened and killed by the oppressors of the poor. If they remain faithful to the cause of the poor as the cause of God, they are freely giving their lives. In this sense, they can be called "crucified people" as long as they experience the passive and active dimensions of the cross in an analogical way.

Sobrino explains the notion of the "crucified people" via the figure of the Suffering Servant in the Old Testament. The Suffering Servant is a prefiguration of Jesus on the cross as well as an analogy of the poor today. Therefore, through the figure of the Suffering Servant, Jesus and the poor share some characteristics. The Suffering Servant has the following two characteristics. First, the Servant is killed for establishing justice. Likewise, Jesus is killed for establishing justice. Can we say the same thing about the poor? Here Sobrino distinguishes an active and a passive dimension of the Servant:

> In fact today too many die formally like the Servant for trying actively to establish justice: all kinds of prophets, priests and bishops, nuns and catechists, peasants and workers, students and lecturers. They try to establish right and justice and end up like the Servant. Their death is formally like the death of Jesus. But among the crucified people there are also many—the majority—who end up like the Suffering Servant but not directly for what they actively do, simply for what they are. They are killed *passively*, for just being what they are.[163]

The active Servant and the passive Servant are interrelated: "Without the active Servant, the passive Servant would have no voice and unless the passive Servant exists, the active Servant would have no reason to exist."[164]

Second, the Servant is chosen by God to bring salvation to the world. Likewise, Jesus is chosen by God to bring salvation to the world. Can we say the same thing about the poor? Here Sobrino refers to what the Latin American Episcopal Conference that met in Puebla called the "evangelizing

163. Sobrino, *Jesus the Liberator*, 258.
164. Ibid., 259.

potential" of the poor: "For the poor challenge the church constantly, summoning it to conversion; and many of the poor incarnate in their lives the evangelical values of solidarity, service, simplicity and openness to accepting the gift of God."[165] Therefore, the poor bring salvation to the world in two different ways. First, the poor call human beings to conversion. In Sobrino's words, "the crucified people demonstrate the existence of enormous sin and demand conversion because of it. But they also offer the possibility of conversion as nothing else in the world can. If the crucified people are not able to turn hearts of stone into hearts of flesh, nothing can."[166] Second, the poor offer an example of Christian life if they embody values such as solidarity, service, and simplicity. Sobrino acknowledges that not all the poor offer this example of Christian life. However, it is also true that many of them do exemplify those values.[167] In this way, the poor bring salvation to the world. In my view, the expression "the poor bring salvation" is theologically misleading, since the one who brings salvation to the world is God. It would be more appropriate to say that the poor are mediations or instruments of God's saving action. Finally, I have a reservation about Sobrino's notion of the crucified people. To say that the crucified people are chosen by God to bring salvation to the world does not mean that God wants the poor to suffer as victims of social injustice to bring salvation to the world. In other words, God brings salvation to the world through the poor not thanks to the fact that they have suffered from injustice and oppression, but in spite of that fact.

The Resurrection of Jesus Christ

The resurrection of Jesus Christ is essentially related to his death. Sobrino defines the resurrection of Jesus Christ with the following words: "Put it in terms of what must be denied, it is said that death was not the end of Jesus' life. Put it in terms of what must be affirmed, it is said that Jesus goes on possessing a proper entity in the present (not only in the memory of his followers), a reality that is positive, insuperable, and definitive."[168] However, the resurrection of Jesus Christ is fully understood only if it is seen in relationship with the cross: "The cross is the prime *locus theologicus* for understanding the resurrection."[169] In relationship with the cross, the resur-

---

165. CELAM, *Puebla*, 1147; quoted in Sobrino, *Jesus the Liberator*, 21.
166. Sobrino, *Jesus the Liberator*, 262.
167. Ibid., 263.
168. Sobrino, *Christ the Liberator*, 20.
169. Ibid., 14.

rection manifests, as Gutiérrez asserts, that "life, not death, has the final word."[170] To understand this assertion, liberation Christology distinguishes three different aspects of the resurrection. The first aspect is the theological dimension of the resurrection, which can be put under the heading: "What does the resurrection of Jesus Christ say about God?" The second aspect is the historical-eschatological dimension of the resurrection, with the heading: "What is the relationship between history and the eschatological dimension of the resurrection?" The third aspect is the dimension of the poor: "What is the relationship between the poor and the resurrection?" These three aspects are interrelated.

The first aspect is the theological dimension of the resurrection of Jesus Christ. Sobrino says, "In speaking of the resurrection of Jesus the first thing to stress is that what happened to Jesus is presented as direct action by God. The fact to which the New Testament first and foremost bears witness is that 'God raised [Jesus] from the dead' (Rom 10:9). This wording means that the resurrection of Jesus, while essentially affecting Jesus, is above all a theologal reality that directly expresses something new and decisive about God."[171] What does the resurrection say about God? Here it is important to remember the distinction between the passive-negative and the active-positive aspects of the cross. Thus, first, the resurrection expresses that God rejects the negative dimension of the cross, that is, God repudiates all kinds of injustice. Second, regarding the active-positive aspect of the cross, the resurrection manifests God's confirmation of Jesus' life as the true life. The resurrection confirms that a life like that of Jesus is what God wants from and for all human beings.[172]

The second aspect is the historical-eschatological dimension of the resurrection of Jesus Christ. The resurrection is an eschatological event. It indicates what will happen to human beings at the end of time. As such, the resurrection is not an intra-historical event. However, Sobrino argues, the resurrection is also a "reality that affects history in its present."[173] Therefore, the resurrection has a historical dimension as well. The effect that the resurrection has in the present is called "hope." The resurrection gives hope to those who suffer from injustice because it reminds them that God is more powerful than injustice.[174] In this way, the resurrection strengthens the

---

170. Gutiérrez, *We Drink from Our Own Wells*, 30. See Sobrino, *Jesus the Liberator*, 272.

171. Sobrino, *Christ the Liberator*, 19.

172. See ibid., 19.

173. Ibid., 12.

174. See ibid., 36, 42.

historical praxis of liberation by giving hope to those who struggle against social injustice.

The third aspect of the resurrection of Jesus Christ is the dimension of the poor. The resurrection is hope especially for the poor. The resurrection is the resurrection of a specific person, Jesus Christ, who is unjustly crucified, and whose crucifixion is the culmination of a life dedicated to the cause of the poor as the cause of God. Therefore, the resurrection of Jesus Christ is hope for all those who suffer the cross today in an analogical way. As Sobrino says, "Jesus' resurrection is hope, first of all, for those crucified in history. God raised a crucified man, and since then there is hope for the crucified. They can see the raised Jesus as the firstborn from among the dead, because they truly . . . see him as their elder brother. This gives them the courage to hope in their own resurrection, and they can now take heart to live in history."[175] To say that the resurrection is hope especially for the poor does not mean that the resurrection is only for the poor. On the contrary, the resurrection is hope for all humanity. However, in the face of the suffering of the poor, liberation Christology displaces the attention from one's own resurrection to the resurrection of those who suffer from poverty and social exclusion. Nevertheless, to have hope for the resurrection of the poor implies "taking an active part in that hope," that is, "being capable of making their hope ours, being ready to work for it."[176]

Sobrino always tries to "historicize" the different elements of Christian doctrine, that is, he tries to understand Christian faith in connection with historical praxis. In his effort to "historicize the resurrection,"[177] Sobrino suggests that human beings are and should be "raisers" of the crucified people.[178] To explain this statement, he makes an analogy between the kingdom of God and the resurrection. Using his typical terminology, Sobrino says: "the kingdom of God cannot be understood only as what is hoped for . . ., but also has to be viewed as what has to be built . . . Now this, even if in somewhat different and analogous terms, should be said of the concept of the resurrection."[179] Human beings are raisers of the crucified people, as they are builders of the kingdom of God. Human works for justice are "partial resurrections" that generate hope in the final resurrection, as well as

---

175. Ibid., 43.
176. Ibid., 44.
177. Ibid., 12.
178. Ibid., 47.
179. Ibid., 45–46. Cf. Sobrino, "Central Position of the Reign of God," 38–42.

being signs of the kingdom of God that generate hope in the possibility of the fullness of the kingdom.[180]

I have two objections to Sobrino's idea that human beings are raisers of the crucified people. My first objection is that only those who are dead can be raised, but the poor are not dead yet. Presumably Sobrino would reply that he is not talking about death in a literal sense, but in a metaphorical or analogical way, in the sense that the poor are living historical situations of death, or situations that will lead them to an unjust and premature death— using Gutiérrez's expression. Let us assume for a moment that this is what Sobrino is trying to express, i.e., that the poor are experiencing historical situations of death, and as such they should "be raised" from those situations. But then I have a second objection. In my view, the expression that human beings are raisers of the crucified people is misleading. Theologically speaking, we should say that the only one who can raise the poor from situations of death is God. Certainly, the poor can experience anticipations of the resurrection now in history. For instance, the experience of liberation can be interpreted as such. However, those experiences of liberation, as anticipations of the resurrections, are done by God in and through the free actions of human beings. In other words, God is the one who raises the poor in and through the mediation of human beings. Perhaps, instead of saying that human beings are raisers of the crucified people, it would be more accurate to say that human beings can be mediations or instruments of a God who raises the poor from their situations of death.

This objection to Sobrino's expression "human beings are raisers" is similar to my objection to Sobrino's idea that "human beings build the kingdom of God." Sobrino is aware of this problem. He acknowledges that his "reflections [about the resurrection and the kingdom of God] have been misunderstood as an expression of human hubris, of trying to do in history what God alone can do . . . I hope it is clear that I am not talking of repeating God's action . . . What I do insist on is giving signs—analogously—of resurrection and the coming of the kingdom."[181] Thus, what Sobrino is saying is that human actions are signs of the resurrection and the coming of the kingdom. These human actions are analogous to God's saving action. However, in my view, the idea that human actions are analogous to God's action does not explain well the relationship between God's saving action and human action in the history of salvation. Sobrino does not express well the fact that God is the subject of salvation, and we, human beings, are mediations of God's saving action. Perhaps I am nagging about something which is just

180. Sobrino, *Christ the Liberator*, 49.
181. Ibid., 48.

a matter of terminology. However, I suggest, Sobrino's way of expressing the relationship between God's saving work and human works can lead to theological inaccuracies.

Therefore, to summarize this section on Christology, we ask, who is Jesus Christ according to liberation theology? Jesus Christ is the liberator of all social outcasts. Jesus Christ is the greatest manifestation of God's love for the poor. We have explained four essential aspects of liberation Christology, namely, the historical Jesus, the kingdom of God, Jesus' death on the cross, and the resurrection of Jesus Christ. For liberation Christology, the historical Jesus is the starting point of an account of the whole reality of Jesus Christ. The historical dimension of the earthly life of Jesus refers especially to his praxis. Jesus' proclamation of the kingdom of God includes his praxis of healing the sick, welcoming sinners, and denouncing social injustices. Those who have social and religious power do not welcome Jesus' message, and put him to death. Jesus' death on the cross has a passive-negative dimension, as long as it is something unjustly inflicted on him, and it has an active-positive dimension, inasmuch as Jesus freely gives his life in fidelity to the cause of the poor as the cause of God. The resurrection of Jesus Christ indicates that life, not death, has the final word, and this is a source of hope for social outcasts.

The Liberating Holy Spirit

The experience of liberation is a manifestation of God's love for social outcasts, which is none other than the experience of the Holy Spirit, the Spirit of God, or the Spirit of Christ.[182] This section explains some essential aspects of a pneumatology of liberation that will be correlated with theological aesthetics in the following chapters. As I said above, my analysis will

---

182. The term "Spirit of Christ" is less used in the New Testament, compared to other expressions such as "the Holy Spirit," "the Spirit of God," or simply "the Spirit." See Johnson, *She Who Is*, 294 n. 18. However, the Spirit is in close connection with Christ. In fact, for Christians, "the Holy Spirit is the enduring presence of the risen Jesus in the world" (Boff, *Liberating Grace*, 195). According to Comblin, we know Jesus through the experience of the Spirit: "The Holy Spirit was sent to lead us to Christ, and Christ leads us to the Father" (Comblin, *Holy Spirit and Liberation*, 163). Nonetheless, the development of pneumatology is a necessary correction of the "christomonism" that exists in the Western theological tradition. Comblin defines christomonism as "a theological system placing exclusive value on Christ's mission in the salvation of humanity to the detriment of the Holy Spirit" (Comblin, *Holy Spirit and Liberation*, 187). Likewise, Johnson suggests that the Spirit has been neglected in Christian theology. See Johnson, *She Who Is*, 128–31.

be based on Comblin's pneumatology, and it will be expanded with Boff's theology of grace.

In Latin America, Comblin says, the "experience of the Spirit is not something much talked about in the base communities. Yet they all speak of a new experience of God, and what is this if not an experience of the Spirit?"[183] The task of liberation theology is precisely to articulate this experience of the poor. The very meaning of the name "Spirit" indicates its relationship with the liberation of social outcasts, as we will see. In Hebrew, the word for "spirit" is *ruah*; in Greek, it is *pneuma*; in Latin, it is *spiritus*. The word "spirit" means wind, which is something that we cannot grasp or hold. The wind is always free. An essential characteristic of the Spirit is its freedom and its elusiveness.[184] The word "spirit" also means breath, which is a characteristic of a living being. The apostle Paul says, "The Spirit is life" (Romans 8:10). We cannot see the wind itself, but we can perceive it in what it does, for instance, we can recognize it in the movement of the leaves of a tree. Similarly, we cannot see the Spirit itself, but we can discern its action in human beings, in society, and in the world. Freedom, life, and action, all these words are related to the process of liberation: the *praxis* (action) of liberation seeks to *free* the poor from everything that oppresses them so that they may have *life*. The wind is powerful. It can move the blades of a windmill, or it can create the waves of the sea. However, the wind is gentle as well. On a very hot day, there is nothing more comforting than the caress of the wind. Likewise, the Spirit gives strength to the poor in their struggle for liberation, and it gives consolation to the oppressed in their suffering. Therefore, just by analyzing the meaning of its name, we can detect a connection between the Spirit and the process of liberation.

The Spirit is actively present in the world. The Spirit works not outside this world, but within this world.[185] Therefore, the Spirit works in the history of human beings, societies, and the world. Nevertheless, how can Christians distinguish what events in history are actually works of the Spirit and what events are not? For liberation pneumatology, *life*—and especially a worthy

183. Comblin, *Holy Spirit and Liberation*, 9. See Comblin, "Holy Spirit," 146. Johnson observes, "whenever people speak in a generic way of God, of their experience of God or of God's doing something in the world, more often than not they are referring to the Spirit" (Johnson, *She Who Is*, 127).

184. Johnson points out, the notion of divine elusiveness is expressed in all the images that Scripture uses to talk about the Spirit: "blowing wind, flowing water, burning fire, light. None of these elements has a stable definite shape, nor can they be grasped; yet each has a clear impact on the world it touches" (Johnson, *She Who Is*, 131).

185. As long as the whole world is potentially a mediation of God's Spirit, Johnson says, "there is no exclusive zone, no special realm, which alone may be called religious" (Johnson, *She Who Is*, 124).

life for the poor—is the main criterion to discern the presence of the Spirit in the world. Everything in history that sustains, promotes, and leads to life is a work of the Spirit.[186] Moreover, for Christians, it is necessary to detect the "signs of the Spirit"[187] in the world. This is how Pope John XXIII and Vatican II interpret the Lord's invitation to read the "signs of the times."[188] From the perspective of a pneumatology of liberation, "the time of the Spirit is always the time of the irruption of the poor."[189]

The Spirit is involved in the creation of life. In the opening lines of the book of Genesis, the author says: "In the beginning when God created the heavens and the earth, the earth was a formless void and darkness covered the face of the deep, while a wind [Spirit] from God swept over the face of the waters" (Genesis 1:1–2). Therefore, the Spirit is present in the process of creation that occurs in history until it reaches its culmination at the end of time. In fact, the Spirit is always re-creating in history. The Spirit is present in the renewal of human beings, society, and the world. As the psalmist says: "When you [God] send forth your spirit, they are created; and you renew the face of the ground" (Psalm 104:30). The historical process of liberation is precisely a process of re-creation or renewal. On the one hand, the liberating praxis seeks to transform all human beings into a new humanity, i.e., persons who are free from all that oppresses them. The apostle Paul asserts, "Where the Spirit is, there is freedom" (2 Corinthians 3:17). On the other hand, the liberating action looks for the creation of a new society, i.e., a place where love, justice, and peace prevail. The process of liberation—as a process of creative renewal of human beings, societies, and the world—is a manifestation of the action of the Holy Spirit in history.[190]

The Spirit works in the history of the world through human beings. In the process of liberation, the Spirit works especially through the poor and the excluded from society. The Spirit is the one who moves them to action. The Spirit is the one who inspires them to denounce injustice and to claim their rights as human beings. The Spirit is the one who empowers the poor

---

186. See Johnson, *She Who Is*, 127.

187. Comblin, *Holy Spirit and Liberation*, 161.

188. See John XXIII, *Humanae Salutis*, 4; Vatican II, *Gaudium et Spes*, 4.

189. Comblin, *Holy Spirit and Liberation*, 182. Liberation theologians described the movement of liberation in Latin America as an "irruption of the poor," because it was a sudden, visible, and active presence of those who were for very long "absent" in society. Gutiérrez suggests that the irruption of the poor in history is in the final analysis an irruption of God in the lives of human beings. See Gutiérrez, *Theology of Liberation*, xx; Gutiérrez, *We Drink from Our Own Wells*, 28

190. See Comblin, *Holy Spirit and Liberation*, 46–49; Comblin, "Holy Spirit," 155; Johnson, *She Who Is*, 135–39.

to liberate themselves and to struggle against everything that causes their premature and unjust death. As long as the praxis of liberation promotes justice and a worthy life for the poor, there is no separation between what the Spirit does and what the poor do, because the Spirit works through them.[191]

The Spirit is the gift of God's love.[192] As Paul says, "God's love has been poured into our hearts through the Holy Spirit that has been given to us" (Romans 5:5).[193] As such, the principal recipients of the gift of the Spirit are the poor.[194] However, the gift of the Spirit demands a response from human beings. They can accept or reject the gift of the Spirit. To say that the Spirit works in the world through human beings does not mean that the Spirit treats them like puppets. The Spirit respects the freedom of human beings. The Spirit inspires them to bring justice and peace to the world. However, human beings can accept or reject the inspirations of the Spirit.

The relationship between the gift of the Spirit and the response of human beings can be seen through the notion of grace. The Spirit and grace are closely linked. As Comblin says, "God's grace comes to us through the work of the Holy Spirit,"[195] or in the words of Boff, "when we talk about the experience of grace, we should always remember it is an experience of the Holy Spirit and his activity in the world . . . To experience grace means to allow ourselves to be overtaken by the presence of the Spirit."[196]

Grace is the encounter and the relationship between God, who communicates God's self to human beings, and human beings, who are open to God's self-communication.[197] Therefore, on the one hand, grace is God's self-communication to human beings. This dimension of grace has already been alluded to in this chapter through the notion of gratuitousness—for instance, the gratuitousness of both God's love and God's kingdom. In fact, the words "gratuitous" and "grace" have the same root in Latin. To say that something is a grace always refers to something that is gratuitously given. In Christian faith, that "thing" is God's self. Grace is God giving God's self to

---

191. See Comblin, *Holy Spirit and Liberation*, 61–76; Comblin, "Holy Spirit," 156.

192. See Aquinas, *Summa Theologiae* I 36.1, I 37.1, I 38.2.

193. See Comblin, *Holy Spirit and Liberation*, 175–77; Johnson, *She Who Is*, 142–43.

194. Johnson writes, "the Spirit's renewing presence is always and everywhere partial to her beloved creatures suffering from socially constructed harm" (Johnson, *She Who Is*, 137).

195. Comblin, "Grace," 210.

196. Boff, *Liberating Grace*, 51.

197. Ibid., 15.

human beings. As Boff states, "grace is not a quality of God; it is the essence of God. God does not possess grace; he is grace."[198]

On the other hand, grace is the openness of human beings to God's self-communication. Grace has effects on human beings. A crucial effect of God's grace is the openness of human beings to God. This openness is manifested in a longing for the infinite. Men and women want to be completely fulfilled. However, nothing in this world seems to satisfy this yearning. "Only God seems to be the satisfactory pole toward which their interior compass points," says Boff. "Only in God will they find rest."[199] However, it is God's love that produces this desire in our human hearts. In other words, this longing for God is an effect of God's grace in human beings.

Therefore, everything is grace in the lives of human beings as long as God is the one who gives them life and freedom. In this sense, God is the power that sustains human beings in their free decisions. As Boff declares, "freedom is not some last human instance apart from grace, some ultimate residue that belongs exclusively to human beings. It, too, is immersed in the movement of grace; the latter makes the former more truly itself, more truly free."[200] Therefore, the free acceptance of God's grace makes human beings more free, whereas the rejection of God's grace makes them less free. That is why sin—i.e., the rejection of God's grace—is an absolute contradiction in itself. When they sin, human beings are using their freedom to be less free. To say that God is the power that sustains human beings in their free decisions, even as they choose to sin, does not mean that God is the one who is responsible for their evil acts. Human beings are the ones who are responsible for their own evil acts.[201]

From the perspective of liberation, grace—i.e., the gift of the Spirit—is what dynamizes the process of liberation. As Gutiérrez says, "the longing for liberation that wells up from the hearts of the poor and oppressed of this world . . . is a sign of the active presence of the Spirit."[202] Indeed, God's grace is what sustains the process of liberation of the poor. Boff writes, "The grace of God is not present in the liberation process as some parallel reality. It is not that the liberation process stands over here while grace stands over there. The liberation process itself, seeking to produce a human life that is more fraternal and open to God, already constitutes the presence

---

198. Ibid., 4.
199. Ibid., 43.
200. Ibid., 58.
201. See ibid., 59.
202. Gutiérrez, *Theology of Liberation*, xxxviii.

of liberating grace in the world. God's liberating grace is incarnated in the pain-filled but liberative course of human beings."[203]

In this sense, what we call "charisms" are at the service of the liberation of the poor. The term "charism" comes from the Greek word *charis* or *chairein*, which mean favor, grace, benevolence, and gift. Paul uses the term "charism" to talk about the gifts that come from the Spirit.[204] Charisms are concrete, ordinary functions that each individual exercises in the community for the good of all. These functions in the community depend on the qualities and the talents of each person. However, it is God who gives these talents, as the parable tells us.[205] Therefore, theologically speaking, human abilities, skills, and professions are not merely the result of human effort, but are seen as gifts from God. Each individual is called to employ his or her talents as a way of self-realization and as a way of serving the community.[206] In this sense, each individual is also called to put his or her charisms at the service of the liberation of social outcasts.

Therefore, who is the Holy Spirit according to liberation theology? It is the liberating Spirit of God who is actively present in the process of liberation of the poor. The Spirit works in and through human beings, inspiring them to collaborate with God in the process of liberation. In this sense, the charisms that the Spirit gives to every human person are meant to be at the service of the liberation of social outcasts.

LIBERATION THEOLOGY AND AESTHETICS

Having explained the method of liberation theology and some of its essential tenets, now we can ask, is there any relationship between liberation theology and aesthetics? Is it possible to find a connection between art and the method of liberation theology in which praxis has a priority? Can art be involved somehow in the liberation of social outcasts? Can we understand the active presence of the Spirit of God in the process of liberation with aesthetic categories? Can we make a correlation between the experience of art and liberation Christology? These are some of the fundamental questions that we will explore in the following chapters.

To be fair, the question about the relationship between liberation and aesthetics is not completely absent in liberation theology. In general, it is true, liberation theology has not paid attention either to the aesthetic

203. Boff, *Liberating Grace*, 154.
204. See 1 Corinthians 12:1–11; Romans 12:6–8.
205. Matthew 25:14–30.
206. See Boff, *Church*, 156–62.

dimension of liberation or to the liberating quality of aesthetics.[207] For instance, considerations about aesthetics are largely, if not totally, absent in the theological corpus of Sobrino. However, it is fortunate and remarkable that aesthetics is very present in the writings of at least one of the founders of liberation theology in Latin America, namely, Gustavo Gutiérrez.

Gutiérrez's theology is infused with aesthetics, especially with the spirit of poetry. The literary production of some of his compatriots, such as José María Arguedas and César Vallejo, permeates some of the writings of the Peruvian theologian.[208] Gutiérrez resorts to the art of literature for several theological reasons. Firstly, theology should engage a dialogue with the culture in which it is developed. According to Gutiérrez, a theology made from the grassroots always articulates the wisdom of a people, that is, their culture, which includes their religion. In this sense, theology has the "flavor" of the culture in which it is developed. Since art and literature are expressions of culture, theology should engage in a conversation with them. In this sense, Gutiérrez writes, "In the contributions that I myself have been able to make to liberation theology, my frequent references to Felipe Guamán Poma de Ayala, César Vallejo, José Carlos Mariátegui, and José María Arguedas, among others, have had the purpose precisely of communicating some of this 'savor.'"[209]

Secondly, literary works can give theological insight. Gutiérrez claims, César Vallejo's "witness has helped me to understand the Book of Job and relate it more fully to my own experience."[210] As Gaspar Martinez observes, Vallejo is "a crucial, in a way unsurpassed, partner in Gutiérrez's journey into the mystery of God. Although Gutiérrez has not written any work on this Peruvian poet, Vallejo is always present whenever Gutiérrez's God-talk reaches its mysterious and painful depth." Martinez continues, "Gutiérrez finds not only powerful intuitions in Vallejo but also the language of poetry as one of the best languages to express the inexpressible, to point to reality beyond reality, to achieve disclosure through mystery."[211]

---

207. Farley, for instance, criticizes that beauty is nowhere "to be found in contemporary exhortations to praxis, social liberation and world change." We do not find the concept of beauty "in what may be the most globally widespread theological movement of the late twentieth century, the praxis or political theologies of liberation" (Farley, *Faith and Beauty*, 7–8).

208. See Gutiérrez, *Density of the Present*, 190–93, 200; Gutiérrez, *God of Life*, 41, 90–91, 97, 189; Gutiérrez, *On Job*, xi, xv–xvi, 111 n. 2, 120 n. 8.

209. Gutiérrez, *Theology of Liberation*, xxxv.

210. Gutiérrez, *God of Life*, 158.

211. Martinez, *Confronting the Mystery of God*, 247.

Thirdly, literary art can help us "seeing" and "hearing" the poor. According to Gutiérrez, liberation theology "tries to give a visible, audible presence to the poor, to those we think of as insignificant." Some works of Latin American literature, especially in poetry, try to do the same, since "only poetic language, made of silence and words, is capable of making present those who sometimes seem absent to us."[212]

Fourthly, as we said before, for Gutiérrez, liberation theology is a way of speaking about God and of saying to the poor: "God loves you." However, "How can we speak of love without poetry? Love is the thing that has always given rise to poetry."[213] Therefore, poetry is an artistic mediation to express God's love for the poor.

Finally, Gutiérrez remarks on the importance of aesthetics, especially the dimension of beauty, for liberation theology. Gutiérrez quotes Gonzalo Rose, a Peruvian poet, who says, "Why should I have loved the rose and justice? Yet this is what we are called to do in Latin America: to love justice and beauty. God is the source of both. Our language about God, that is, our theology, must take both of these aspects into account."[214] Gutiérrez points out that the creation story in Genesis "tells us that at the end of the first week 'God saw all that he had made, and indeed, it was very good' (Gen 1:31). The word used here for good also means beautiful. Theology is about the good and the beautiful in the work of God, in human life. For that reason theology cannot overlook that which breaks the beauty of the world and strangles the expression of human joy and happiness."[215] In this sense, liberation theology should pay attention to "the aesthetic dimensions of a process of liberation which seeks to take into account all aspects of what it is to be human." For instance, liberation theology should advocate the "right to beauty" for the poor, which is an "expression (more pressing than some suppose) of the right to life."[216]

As we can see, Gutiérrez appreciates the aesthetic dimension and he tries to incorporate it into his theology. As Martinez notes, "Gutiérrez, as a person of exquisite aesthetic sensibility and an admirer of literary language and of the sublimity of poetry as a quasi-supernatural language, has been influenced by Arguedas to an extent still not fully analyzed."[217] Indeed,

---

212. Gutiérrez, *Density of the Present*, 206.
213. Ibid., 144–45.
214. Ibid., 145.
215. Ibid., 194.
216. Gutiérrez, "Task and Content of Liberation Theology," 36. For a fine explanation of what the "right to beauty" involves, see McCormick, *God's Beauty*, 38–76.
217. Martinez, *Confronting the Mystery of God*, 144–45.

it would be interesting to study not only the influence of Arguedas, but the influence of aesthetics in general on Gutiérrez's theology. The present work does not intend to make such an analysis, partly because the focus of our present study is on painting, while the theological work of Gutiérrez is more related to literary art; but also because a theological aesthetics of liberation cannot be developed based only on the few ideas that Gutiérrez has about aesthetics. We need the help of other theologians to develop such a theology. Indeed, in the following chapter we will ask if the theological aesthetics of Hans Urs von Balthasar and of Karl Rahner are useful for the development of a theological aesthetics of liberation. Nevertheless, Gutiérrez has sensed and pointed out some essential elements of a theological aesthetics of liberation, for instance, the power of art to let us see and hear the poor, and the connection between beauty and justice. We will expand these theological intuitions more fully in the following chapters.

Chapter 2

Von Balthasar or Rahner?
Towards a Theological Aesthetics of Liberation

Having clarified what liberation theology is in the previous chapter, the goal of this chapter is to explore what theological aesthetics is, in order to establish a possible correlation between liberation theology and theological aesthetics in the following chapters. First of all, it is necessary to state the obvious: theological aesthetics is theology. This statement means that theological aesthetics is not primarily about beauty or art. The object of theological aesthetics is God in relationship with the world. In other words, theological aesthetics is reflection about God and his saving action in the world from the perspective of aesthetics. However, this leads us to the question, what is aesthetics? After providing a brief overview of the development of aesthetics as an intellectual and experiential discipline, Richard Viladesau concludes that aesthetics involves three interrelated dimensions: first, the study of sensation, imagination, and feeling, as non-conceptual types of knowledge; second, the study of beauty; and third, the study of art in general and/or of the fine arts in particular.[1] Consequently, "theological aesthetics will consider God, religion, and theology in relation to sensible knowledge (sensation, imagination, and feeling), the beautiful, and the arts."[2] In other words, theological aesthetics includes a theology of perception, a theology of beauty, and a theology of art.

---

1. Viladesau, *Theological Aesthetics*, 6–8.
2. Ibid., 11.

Theologians have undertaken theological aesthetics in different ways. Following David Tracy's threefold classification of theological disciplines, Viladesau argues that it is possible to do theological aesthetics in the way of fundamental theology, systematic theology, or practical theology.³ Viladesau claims that Hans Urs von Balthasar's theological aesthetics is a systematic theology, while he (Viladesau) develops a fundamental theology in his book *Theological Aesthetics*.⁴ The theological aesthetics that I will develop in the following chapters is a practical theology. The point here is that there are different ways of doing theological aesthetics. Brown states something similar about the possibility of doing theological aesthetics in various ways: "it makes no sense to speak of a single, uniform relation between aesthetics and theology, as if every theology would need or want to engage in aesthetics in the same manner . . . Aesthetics may be one thing when done in the context of an academic ecumenical liberal North American systematic theology and quite another thing when done in the context of a Catholic liberation neo-orthodox Central American practical theology."⁵

In spite of the different and valid ways of tackling theological aesthetics, today most people associate this discipline only or mostly with von Balthasar's work. This narrow vision of theological aesthetics is unfortunate. Von Balthasar's theology is only one way among others of doing theological aesthetics. However, his work has some importance in theology and in the life of the Catholic Church today, and for that reason it should not be dismissed. Nevertheless, there are other ways of doing theological aesthetics. Karl Rahner, whose theology is generally considered opposed to von Balthasar's,⁶ has some ideas about art from which a theological aesthetics can be developed. In the following pages, I will explore the theological aesthetics of both von Balthasar and Rahner, paying attention to the pos-

---

3. For Tracy's threefold classification of theological disciplines, see Tracy, *Analogical Imagination*, 54–58. Tracy mentions the "complementary" emphases of these three theological disciplines, and the need of "collaboration" between them. See Tracy, *Analogical Imagination*, 79. Matthew Lamb suggests, "it seems Tracy is also attempting to establish mutually critical correlations between the subdisciplines of fundamental, systematic, and practical theologies" (Lamb, "David Tracy," 682). In this sense, the theological aesthetics of liberation that I will develop here intends to correlate theological aesthetics, which is generally under the categories of fundamental and systematic theologies, and liberation theology, which is a type of practical theology.

4. Viladesau, *Theological Aesthetics*, 37–38. Karen Kilby argues that von Balthasar's theological aesthetics includes both a fundamental and a dogmatic theology. See Kilby, *Balthasar*, 50.

5. Brown, *Religious Aesthetics*, 37.

6. For a comparative analysis of the theologies of von Balthasar and Rahner, see Williams, "Balthasar and Rahner"; Kilby, "Balthasar and Karl Rahner," 262–65.

sibilities and the limitations of their theologies for the development of a theological aesthetics of liberation.

EXPLORING VON BALTHASAR'S THEOLOGY AS A POSSIBLE MODEL FOR A THEOLOGICAL AESTHETICS OF LIBERATION

In this section I will explore some dimensions of von Balthasar's theology, its possibilities and its limitations for the development of a theological aesthetics of liberation. Firstly, I will explain some essential aspects of his theological aesthetics. Secondly, I will explore his *Theo-Drama*, and the possibility of finding in it any kind of social concern. Thirdly, I will explain his opinions about liberation theology. Finally, I will make some summary and critical remarks about von Balthasar's theology in relationship to the possibility of using his theology as a model for a theological aesthetics of liberation.

Von Balthasar's Theological Aesthetics

In von Balthasar's own words, theological aesthetics is an attempt "to develop a Christian theology in the light of the third transcendental, that is to say: to complement the vision of the true and the good with that of the beautiful."[7] In fact, von Balthasar's theological aesthetics, which he develops in his multivolume *The Glory of the Lord*, is just the first part of a theological trilogy. He explains to his readers: "In order to maintain the right balance, a 'theological aesthetics' should be followed by a 'theological dramatics' and a 'theological logic' . . . Only then would the *pulchrum* appear in its rightful place within the total ordered structure, namely as the manner in which God's goodness (*bonum*) gives itself and is expressed by God and understood by man as the truth (*verum*)."[8] Therefore, each part of the trilogy takes a transcendental as a hermeneutical concept to look at the mystery of God: beauty in *The Glory of the Lord*, goodness in *Theo-Drama*, and truth in *Theo-Logic*. To be sure, when von Balthasar speaks of beauty, goodness, and truth, he is not mainly referring to the beauty, goodness, and truth of the world. As transcendentals, beauty, goodness, and truth are attributes of Being. Hence, from a Christian perspective, beauty, goodness, and truth are attributes of God.

---

7. Balthasar, *Glory of the Lord*, 1:9.
8. Ibid., 11.

For von Balthasar, it is necessary to recover the notion of beauty in Christian faith and in theology. In a world without beauty, the good "loses its attractiveness, the self-evidence of why it must be carried out. Man stands before the good and asks himself why *it* must be done and not rather its alternative, evil."[9] In a world without beauty, "the proofs of the truth have lost their cogency. In other words, syllogisms may still dutifully clatter away like rotary presses or computers which infallibly spew out an exact number of answers by the minute. But the logic of these answers is itself a mechanism which no longer captivates anyone . . . And if this is how the transcendentals fare because one of them has been banished, what will happen with Being itself?"[10] Thus, beauty has the power to attract or captivate. Without beauty, Christian faith, and the object of faith itself (i.e., God), would attract nobody. Without beauty, theology has the danger of becoming overly speculative (i.e., a theology full of perfect syllogisms, but that, at the end, does not communicate the mystery of God to people), and runs the risk of becoming merely utilitarian (for instance, a theology that is at the service of a particular form of human action).[11]

Therefore, for von Balthasar, theological aesthetics is a theology of beauty. However, a theology of beauty includes a theology of perception as well: "If all beauty is located at the intersection of two moments which Thomas calls *species* and *lumen* ('form' and 'splendour'), then the encounter of these is characterized by the two moments of beholding and of being enraptured. The doctrine of the beholding and perceiving . . . of the beautiful . . . and the doctrine of the enrapturing power of the beautiful are complementarily structured, since no one can really behold who has not also already been enraptured, and no one can be enraptured who has not already perceived."[12]

Thus, of the three dimensions that Viladesau finds in theological aesthetics—namely, a theology of beauty, of perception, and of art—von Balthasar develops the first two, and to a lesser degree the third. In fact, if someone expects to find a theology of art in *The Glory of the Lord*, in all likelihood he or she will be disappointed. It is not that von Balthasar completely lacks ideas about art. Indeed, he has a few, and we will study some of them later. However, as Brown comments, Balthasar's "treatment of issues normally dealt with in aesthetics [for instance, issues about art]

---

9. Ibid., 19.
10. Ibid.
11. See ibid., 147.
12. Ibid., 10.

is nonetheless spotty and erratic."[13] One of the reasons why Balthasar does not develop a theology of art is that, as I said above, he is not very interested in the beauty of the world, as we find it in art for instance. Rather, he is interested in beauty as an attribute of God.

Theological Method and the Analogy of Being

Von Balthasar's theology is generally described as a theology "from above" (distinct from a theology "from below," such as the theology of Rahner).[14] The expression "a theology from above" means a theology whose starting point is the mystery of God. In fact, as I mentioned above, when von Balthasar speaks about beauty, he is not talking principally about the beauty of the world, but about the beauty of absolute Being, i.e., God. Therefore, as he develops a Christian theology from the viewpoint of the third transcendental, it is clear that he is doing a theology from above, that is, a theology that begins with God, or more precisely with the beauty of God. In this sense, von Balthasar declares, "by theological aesthetics we mean a theology which does not primarily work with the extra-theological categories of a worldly philosophical aesthetics . . . , but which develops its theory of beauty from the data of revelation itself with genuinely theological methods."[15] Therefore, Brown observes, von Balthasar appears to believe that "only an aesthetics directly derived from revelation will be useful to theology."[16]

For von Balthasar, the problem today is that people understand beauty only in earthly terms, and not as an attribute of divine Being: "The assumption throughout is that the world of the beautiful originally belongs to man, and that it is he who determines its content and boundaries. The native country of the beautiful would then be the world or, at most, 'Being' itself, but only in so far as is not divine but 'creaturely' . . . In this event, the decision has implicitly been taken that beauty is not a 'transcendental' like oneness, truth, and goodness, or, what amounts to the same thing, that beauty [does] need not to be predicated of God in its proper sense."[17] In other words, the problem today is what might be called the "secularization of beauty," in which beauty is understood as totally devoid of any transcendental or religious dimension. For some people, "aesthetics" is an independent science, which studies perception, beauty, and art, only in a worldly sense, without

13. Brown, *Religious Aesthetics*, 195 n. 1.
14. See O'Hanlon, "Jesuits and Modern Theology," 27–31.
15. Balthasar, *Glory of the Lord*, 1:114.
16. Brown, *Religious Aesthetics*, 19.
17. Balthasar, *Glory of the Lord*, 1:67–68.

any reference to religion or God. If beauty is an independent worldly object, without any transcendental or religious dimension, then the attempt to do theological aesthetics is impossible and nonsensical.

However, divine beauty is not disconnected from earthly beauty. On the contrary, there is "a genuine relationship between theological beauty and the beauty of the world."[18] To explain this relationship, von Balthasar begins with a sort of reflection "from below." He accepts that "those who have been once affected inwardly by the worldly beauty of either nature, or of a person's life, or of art," have an idea of what beauty is.[19] He suggests that there is continuity from the beauty of this world into the beauty of the supernatural world. Similar to Rahner in his understanding of the human subject (as we will study later), von Balthasar accepts that earthly beauty has a dimension that calls for the totality of the human spirit. Thus it is possible that, beginning from the beauty of this world, "the way must also lead into the religious dimension which itself includes man's definitive answer to the question about God."[20] If this is so, "then an inner analogy between both forms or stages of beauty [i.e., the natural and the supernatural] ought not to be immediately dismissed."[21] Therefore, by virtue of the relationship and continuity between both forms of beauty, it is theologically correct to make an analogy between worldly beauty and divine beauty. Von Balthasar claims, "The fundamental principle of a theological aesthetics, rather, is the fact that, just as this revelation is absolute truth and goodness, so also is it absolute beauty; but this assertion would be meaningless if every transposition and application to revelation of human categories from the realms of logic, ethics ('pragmatics'), and aesthetics, if every analogical application of these categories, were simply forbidden. And why should the validity of such analogies be recognised in practice by scholarship for the first two fields . . . while being refused *a limine* for the third field?"[22]

---

18. Ibid., 78.

19. Ibid., 36.

20. Ibid., 34. We should not think that Balthasar does a theology "from below" just because he has this *provisional* reflection on beauty from the perspective of the subject. He insists that beauty is not principally a subjective experience, but an attribute of the object. He clearly states that "if the subjective ability to experience finds the reason and justification for its existence in an experienceable object, then without this object that experiential ability can by no means be demonstrated in its totality nor indeed be made comprehensible. For this reason, in the course of our inquiry we have pointed to this object by way of anticipation; but our object can be correctly understood only when it has been visible in itself. Even our anthropological considerations did not have their meaning in themselves" (ibid., 419).

21. Ibid., 35.

22. Ibid., 590.

In the analogy between divine beauty and worldly beauty, the primacy is always on God's side. God, and not the world, is the normative standard of beauty. According to von Balthasar, "if beauty is conceived as transcendentally, then its definition must be derived from God himself. Furthermore, what we know to be most proper of God—his self-revelation in history and in the Incarnation—must now become for us the very apex and archetype of beauty in the world."[23] Therefore, if we are to use the analogy correctly, God should never be measured by the standards of worldly beauty, but it is the world that should be measured by the standards of God's beauty. Von Balthasar says, "We can post as many question marks and warnings signs as we will all along the length and breadth of this analogy, but they will only apply to the ever-present possibility of misusing the analogy, and not to its rightful use. Misuse of the analogy consists in simply subjugating and subordinating God's revelation with its own form, to the laws not only of metaphysics and of private, social, and sociological ethics but also of this-worldly aesthetics, instead of respecting the sovereignty which is manifested clearly enough in God's work."[24]

Furthermore, if we are to use the analogy correctly, we should have a correct understanding of what beauty is, even in its worldly dimension. For von Balthasar, beauty is in the object, and not in the subject. He longs for those days "when human art and Christian revelation met in an encounter which saw the creation of icons, basilicas and Romanesque cathedrals, sculptures and paintings." However, von Balthasar continues, "since then too many misunderstandings and too many terrible things have occurred for us still to be in a position to insist more on the similarity of the two spheres than on their dissimilarity. Man's habit of calling beautiful only what strikes *him* as such appears insurmountable."[25] Von Balthasar opposes any kind of aesthetics that understands beauty merely as an emotional experience that occurs in the subject. The experience of the beautiful is not an experience to satisfy the subject's needs.[26]

> The young experience this subjective aspect with particular intensity and tend to generalise it. Since they have not yet acquired objective criteria for the evaluation of works of art, and because they have not yet learned to distinguish by seeing and listening, they compensate with the "enthusiasm" proper to their age . . . People who cling to this view of the subjective nature of taste's

23. Ibid., 68.
24. Ibid., 36.
25. Ibid., 37.
26. See ibid., 312, 452.

judgment have remained immature adolescents. By developing his soul according to the images of the objectively beautiful, the maturing person gradually learns to acquire the art of discrimination, that is, the art of perceiving what is beautiful in itself. In the process of development, the subjective elements of perception . . . more and more pass into the service of objective perception.[27]

In this sense, von Balthasar distinguishes "theological aesthetics" from "aesthetic theology." Theological aesthetics is a theology that understands beauty as an attribute of divine Being, whereas aesthetic theology is a theology that understands beauty in worldly and subjective terms.[28] By making this distinction, as Brown observes, "von Balthasar warns against the dangers of an aesthetic theology."[29]

But here we find a tension, if not a contradiction, in von Balthasar's theological method. On the one hand, for von Balthasar, there is an analogy between worldly beauty and theological beauty. On the other hand, he argues that the theological notion of beauty should be derived only from revelation itself, and not from worldly aesthetics. In other words, theological aesthetics should never "deteriorate into an 'aesthetic theology' by betraying and selling out theological substance to the current viewpoints of an inner-worldly theory of beauty."[30] If we want to interpret von Balthasar in a benevolent way, we can say that it seems that for him the analogy between worldly beauty and theological beauty works only to some extent, or that there is more difference than similarity in the analogy between worldly beauty and divine beauty. In any case, the truth is that von Balthasar's method has a conflict within itself. Karen Kilby has detected this tension too. She writes, "There is a real intellectual knot here, for [von] Balthasar is committed on the one hand to a 'sharp contrast' between worldly and revealed beauty, and on the other hand to an important *analogy* between them: his capacity to coherently negotiate the tension between these two commitments is in fact a key issue running through the whole of the *Theological Aesthetics*."[31]

---

27. Ibid., 172–73.
28. Ibid., 37, 77.
29. Brown, *Religious Aesthetics*, 19.
30. Balthasar, *Glory of the Lord*, 1:37.
31. Kilby, *Balthasar*, 51.

A Theory of Beauty and Perception

I said above that of the three dimensions that theological aesthetics generally cover—namely, beauty, perception, and art—von Balthasar analyses especially the first two, and to a lesser degree the third. I also indicated that, regarding his ideas about art, Balthasar's treatment is uneven. However, it turns out that his presentation about aesthetic issues is patchy not only when he talks about art, but also when he talks about beauty and perception. Kilby rightly observes,

> [Von] Balthasar does not attempt to define beauty, nor does he offer any kind of methodological analysis of what is involved in perceiving it, nor again any careful tracing of the history of ideas such as those of beauty or art. The first volume of *The glory of the Lord* begins not with any attempt at careful or systematic examination of ideas in aesthetics, but with a variety of ruminations on beauty, the perception of it, and the importance of both. The experience of beauty is for the most part evoked and alluded to rather than described, analyzed, or argued over.[32]

In this section, I will try to collect some of von Balthasar's ideas about beauty and perception, and to present them in an organized way. Von Balthasar claims that in aesthetics we should distinguish and relate to each other "two elements in the beautiful which have traditionally controlled every aesthetics and which, with Thomas Aquinas, we could term *species* (or *forma*) and *lumen* (or *splendor*)—form (*Gestalt*) and splendour (*Glanz*)."[33] "Form" (*Gestalt*) or "figure" (*Gebilde*) "can be understood only as a revelation of the mystery of Being."[34] In fact, Being can be materially grasped through its form. Without the form, the "depths of reality" would remain beyond our reach and our vision.[35] "The appearance of the form, as revelation of the depths, is an indissoluble union of two things. It is the real presence of the depths, of the whole of reality, *and* it is a real pointing beyond itself to these depths... Both aspects are inseparable from one another, and together they constitute the fundamental configuration of Being."[36] Therefore, form "not only 'points' to an invisible, unfathomable mystery"; it is also "the apparition of this mystery." Furthermore, "the content (*Gehalt*) does not lie behind the form (*Gestalt*), but within it." Consequently, "whoever is not capable of

---

32. Ibid., 43.
33. Balthasar, *Glory of the Lord*, 1:115.
34. Ibid., 19, 487.
35. Ibid., 115.
36. Ibid., 115–16.

seeing and 'reading' the form will, by the same token, fail to perceive the content."[37]

In its form, the beautiful has a light or splendor that comes from within. "The beautiful is above all a *form*, and the light does not fall on this form from above and from outside, rather it breaks forth from the form's interior." Therefore, von Balthasar continues, "*species* and *lumen* in beauty are one, if the *species* truly merits that name (which does not designate any form whatever, but pleasing, radiant form)."[38] Thus, "we see form as the splendour, as the glory of Being."[39]

The beautiful has the power to captivate in and through its radiant form. "Only that which has form can snatch one up into a state of rapture."[40] This state consists in that "before the beautiful—no, not really *before* but *within* the beautiful—the whole person quivers. He not only 'finds' the beautiful moving; rather, he experiences himself as being moved and possessed by it . . . Such a person has been taken up wholesale into the reality of the beautiful and is now fully subordinate to it, determined by it, animated by it."[41] However, this experience of being enraptured "never happens in such a way that we leave the (horizontal) form behind us in order to plunge (vertically) into the naked depths."[42] Rather, it is through its radiant form that the depth of reality is revealed to us in such a way that it draws us into its mystery.

This theory of beauty applies to the experience of worldly beauty, which we find in nature, in a person's life, and in art. About the beauty of art, von Balthasar says, "artistic form has an exterior which appears and an interior depth, both of which, however, are not separable in the form itself."[43] Therefore, the "vertical" dimension of reality is manifested in and through the "surface" of the artistic form. This holds true "even in those abstract constructions which reduce the dimension of depth to a minimum by attempting to express everything at the horizontal level of surface, colour, and rhythm."[44] For von Balthasar, the beauty of a work of art is in the object itself. In other words, the beauty of an artistic work has in itself an "interior

---

37. Ibid., 146–47.
38. Ibid., 146.
39. Ibid., 116.
40. Ibid., 32.
41. Ibid., 240–41.
42. Ibid., 116.
43. Ibid., 147.
44. Ibid., 431.

rightness and evidential power."[45] The validity of its beauty comes from the artistic work itself.[46] Therefore, in order to perceive the beauty of a work of art, "a person must become interior to the work, must enter into its spell and radiant space, must attain to the state in which alone the work becomes manifest in its being-in-itself."[47]

Before we move to von Balthasar's theological understanding of this theory of beauty, it is important to pause for a moment to reflect on what might be called the "ivory-tower" character of von Balthasar's theology, or using García-Rivera's expression, the "caged spirit" quality of von Balthasar's thought.[48] Kilby makes the following point in her introduction to von Balthasar's theology. Regarding his theory of beauty, Kilby asks, "is this in fact the way beauty is? This is a kind of question that [von] Balthasar's writing does not particularly encourage . . . [Von] Balthasar does not so much analyze or develop arguments about the nature of beauty as offer wide-ranging ruminations; in the course of these ruminations, the concept of beauty that emerges is presented not as *one* conception of beauty which might perhaps be argued to be superior to *other* possible conceptions, but rather as an unavoidable account of the way things are."[49]

George Pattison has a similar critique. Von Balthasar, Pattison suggests, "offers us too much too soon. Instead of the grand anticipation of a 'theological aesthetics' . . . , theology (I suggest) would do better to linger, to spend time, to risk wasting time, with the world, with artists' . . . efforts—fumbling and inadequate as they no doubt often are—to open up that world."[50] In other words, in his writings, von Balthasar appears as someone who knows too much—and offers us too much—about aesthetics, when, in fact, his theory is just one understanding of aesthetics among many. If we ask artists (not to mention art historians, art critics, and philosophers of art) about the concept of beauty, probably we will find that they have valid answers which are different from von Balthasar's understanding. For this

---

45. Ibid., 453.

46. See ibid., 597.

47. Ibid., 600.

48. García-Rivera, who truly admires von Balthasar, nevertheless writes: "Von Balthasar inspires but gives precious little insight on how a theological aesthetics might take concrete form and become viable for us today. Inspiring as it is, von Balthasar's theological aesthetics becomes a caged spirit unless it can be shown how it engages the concrete challenges raised by the powerful nihilism of our day" (García-Rivera, *Community of the Beautiful*, 94–95).

49. Kilby, *Balthasar*, 45–46.

50. Pattison, "Is the Time Right for a Theological Aesthetics?," 114.

reason, von Balthasar—and anyone who wants to do theological aesthetics—should spend more time with artists to hear what they say.

Presumably, von Balthasar would reply that he does not need to listen to artists for two reasons. First, he would say that he is not doing aesthetic theology, but theological aesthetics, that is, a theology that derives its truths from revelation. However, here we find an argument that, according to Brown, is "specious." The idea that revelation shows us the nature of all truth, and therefore the truth about beauty and art, is false. Christian revelation is not "the sufficient means by which we can discover all other basic truths, such as those pertaining to art and aesthetics."[51] Second, von Balthasar contends that beauty is wrongly perceived in the modern world.[52] Therefore, Balthasar would dismiss the aesthetic ideas of others because, he would say, they have lost the sense of what beauty truly is, and therefore their opinions are invalid. In fact, as Kilby observes, "The would-be questioner, then, very easily finds himself wrong-footed: perhaps if one is not able to acknowledge that beauty is a matter of form and splendor, it is because one has lost the feeling for it, the ability to perceive it."[53]

Whether von Balthasar's theory of beauty is correct or not, the point here is that his thought is locked in an ivory tower, unable and unwilling to have a conversation with other ways of thinking, firstly because he presumes that he already knows the truth, which God has revealed to him, and secondly because he presumes that the opinions of others are wrong because they have lost the sense of beauty. Here we are talking about his ideas about aesthetics, beauty, and art in general. However, we will find the same pattern in his theological understanding of such ideas, which is what we will study in the next sections.

Jesus as the Form of Divine Revelation

Von Balthasar applies analogically the theory of beauty, which we have just outlined, to what Christianity calls revelation and faith. As Sherry says, von Balthasar "draws an analogy between carefully attending to a work of art and contemplating the Christian mystery: in both cases we behold what is presented to us."[54] Or as Dillenberger claims, for von Balthasar, "the means

---

51. Brown, *Religious Aesthetics*, 20.

52. Von Balthasar regrets that "We no longer dare to believe in beauty," that the world "can no longer see [beauty] and reckon with it" (Balthasar, *Glory of the Lord*, 1:18–19).

53. Kilby, *Balthasar*, 46.

54. Sherry, *Spirit and Beauty*, 16.

of contemplating God is like the contemplation of art."[55] Kilby suggests an image that visually grasps the theory of beauty that we analyzed in the previous section. The image is that of "a spectator standing transfixed before a great work of art—a painting, perhaps, or a statue—who is caught up, taken out of himself or herself, by its beauty."[56] This image works analogically in von Balthasar's theology: "we are to think of God's revelation on the analogy with a work of art, and the act of faith on the analogy of the person who stands before a work of art, gazing upon it and being transported by it."[57]

Thus, according to von Balthasar, the supreme object of theological aesthetics is "the form of divine revelation in salvation-history."[58] God "who is formless takes form in the world and in history, and can be encountered and experienced by the whole man in this form which he himself has chosen and put on."[59] On his own initiative, "God takes form and allows himself to be seen, heard, and touched."[60] Jesus Christ is the "central form of God's revelation,"[61] and "from this form there shines forth God's objective glory."[62] As a form, Jesus is the "appearance of divine depth."[63] On the one hand, "Christ is the form because he is the content."[64] This means that "Jesus is what he expresses—namely, God."[65] On the other hand, the Son is the form, but the Father is the content.[66] In this sense, Jesus "is not whom he expresses—namely, the Father."[67]

Jesus is the "primal form" not only of God, but also of the world and of humanity. His form is "beyond autonomy and heteronomy since it unites

---

55. Dillenberger, *Theology of Artistic Sensibilities*, 225.

56. Kilby, *Balthasar*, 42.

57. Ibid., 48. Another metaphor that von Balthasar's uses to explain analogically what Christianity calls revelation and faith is the image of a musical instrument. Due to the limits of the present study, and due the fact the present work focuses more on painting than on music, I cannot delve into the theological significance of such a metaphor. For some paragraphs in which von Balthasar writes about the image of a tuned instrument, see Balthasar, *Glory of the Lord*, 1:214, 236, 244, 456–57.

58. Balthasar, *Glory of the Lord*, 1:28.

59. Ibid., 293–94.

60. Ibid., 303.

61. Ibid., 149.

62. Ibid., 198.

63. Ibid., 149.

64. Ibid., 451.

65. Ibid., 29.

66. Ibid., 594.

67. Ibid., 29.

God and man in an unimaginable intimacy."[68] In Jesus "what is demonstrated to be the true God at the same time reveals to us the image of true man, and vice versa."[69] Therefore, Jesus is the "perfection of the form of the world,"[70] and as such he is the "measure for all other worldly and human measures."[71] It is Christ who is the measure of the world, and not the world the measure of Christ. In fact, he cannot be measured by any standards outside of himself. "If we were to speak of measure and form in the case of Christ, this could not be in the sense that he could be measured with an alien standard from without: if he is the 'Unique One,' then no external measure suffices to measure him; he can be measured only by himself."[72]

Christ, as the form of divine revelation, has an objective self-evidence, which does not depend on the appreciation of the beholder. For von Balthasar, "the subjective condition of the possibility of seeing an object for what it is" does not "intrude upon the constitution of the object's objective evidence." Likewise, then, Jesus, as the form of divine revelation, is not dependent on the subjective conditions of the beholder who sees his form.[73] "The fact that Christ 'says nothing to me' in no way prejudices the fact that Christ says everything to everyone."[74]

The possibility for the subject to perceive Christ as the form of divine revelation is ultimately a grace of God.[75] That the subject can by the grace of God see the manifestation of divine depth in Jesus' form means two interrelated things. On the one hand, "That we are able to speak here of 'seeing'" shows that there is "something to be seen and grasped." It shows that "something is 'offered' to man by God, indeed offered in such a way that man can see it, understand it, make it his own, and live from it."[76] In other words, if the subject can see the appearance of divine depth in the form of Christ, it is because God has offered to human beings the possibility of seeing God in Jesus' form. On the other hand, for von Balthasar, "The mere light of reason clearly does not suffice to illumine this work" of God. "But the light of God which faith *sees* the form as it is, and, indeed, it can demonstrate that the evidence of the thing's rightness emerges from the thing itself and sheds its

68. Ibid., 25.
69. Ibid., 546.
70. Ibid., 422.
71. Ibid., 456.
72. Ibid.
73. Ibid., 453.
74. Ibid., 452.
75. Ibid., 149.
76. Ibid., 118.

light outwards from it."⁷⁷ In other words, "The decisively illumining factor must lie in the phenomenon itself, and this in two senses. First, in the sense that the figure which Christ forms has in itself an interior rightness and evidential power . . . And, second, in the sense that this rightness, which resides within the reality of the thing itself, also possesses the power to illumine the perceiving person by its own radiant light . . . Now, the evidential power . . . lies in the phenomenon itself and demands a theological act of seeing the form."⁷⁸

Thus, if the subject can perceive the revelation of divine depth in Jesus' form, it is because he or she has received the light of God's grace to see the form, a light that comes from within the form itself. Therefore, although "seeing" seems to be an activity of the human subject, in reality it rather means an active passivity or receptivity of the subject. Von Balthasar claims, "God possesses the full initiative in the creature's relationship to him. It is God who says who he is and how one should properly relate to him. For these reasons, in the creature's primary aprioristic structure, . . . passivity has precedence over activity. But this passivity, if it is rightly understood, will be seen to be that of a being which from the outset is active in its very receptivity, . . . a being whose fundamental act consists precisely in its ability to receive."⁷⁹ Therefore, as García-Rivera asserts, "'Seeing' is, paradoxically, an *act* of *receptivity*." Seeing the form is not a "controlling act, but an act of surrender to that which is 'seen.'"⁸⁰ According to von Balthasar, as the human subject beholds the form of Christ, he or she is enraptured and transported into the depths of divine mystery. "As we pass through Jesus' finitude and enter into its depths we encounter and find the Infinite, or rather, we are transported and found by the Infinite."⁸¹ For von Balthasar, "love" is the word that best describes the whole dynamics of seeing the form of divine beauty in Christ and being transported by it:

> There is a good reason why the word used here is *amor* . . . For what is at stake here is the movement effected by seeing what God has shown. This is a movement of the entire person, leading away from himself through the vision towards the invisible God . . . The transport of the soul, however, must here again be understood in a strictly theological way. In other words, it must be understood not as a merely psychological response

77. Ibid., 166–67.
78. Ibid., 453–54.
79. Ibid., 239.
80. García-Rivera, *Community of the Beautiful*, 88–89.
81. Balthasar, *Glory of the Lord*, 1:150.

to something beautiful in a worldly sense which has been encountered through vision, but as the movement of man's whole being away from himself and towards God through Christ, a movement founded on the divine light of grace in the mystery of Christ. But the whole truth of this mystery is that the movement which God (who is the object that is seen in Christ and who enraptures man) effects in man (even in his unwillingness and recalcitrance, due to sin) is co-effected willingly by man through his Christian *eros* and, indeed, on account of the fact that the divine Spirit en-thuses and in-spires man to collaboration.[82]

What happens if a person maintains that he or she cannot see Jesus as the form of divine revelation? For von Balthasar, "anyone who rejects the form of Christ has objectively misapprehended it, either in whole or in part. Not only has he not contributed the necessary subjective enthusiasm for the form . . . , but it can be objectively proven to him that, in considering the form, he has overlooked essential aspects of it."[83] Therefore, if someone cannot see the form of divine revelation in Christ, it is not because God's grace is lacking in that person; rather it is because he or she has not looked either at some essential parts of the form of Christ or at the wholeness of the form of Christ. In other words, if someone cannot see the form of divine revelation in Christ, it is not God's fault, but the fault of the human subject.

However, this idea that it is the person's fault if he or she cannot see the form "should make us wary," using Kilby's expression in her study of von Balthasar's theology.[84] Von Balthasar's notion of "seeing the form," Kilby points out, has an "all-or-nothing quality": "One sees the form, as [von] Balthasar presents it, or one fails to do so."[85] This all-or-nothing feature is another dimension of the "caged spirit" character of von Balthasar's thought, that is, his lack of openness for a theological dialogue. According to Kilby, von Balthasar's theology allows for "the possibility of an author to stand above his reader: the author, who has already 'seen the form,' who is already in possession, as it were, of this central aesthetic experience . . . does what he can to indicate this central beauty to the readers, who in turn themselves either see or fail to see." If von Balthasar has already seen the form, he already possesses the truth—or has been possessed by the truth—and therefore he does not need to hear other opinions. Thus, his approach "seems to envisage

---

82. Ibid., 118.
83. Ibid., 496.
84. Kilby, *Balthasar*, 2; see ibid., 15, 167.
85. Ibid., 55.

little room for disagreement."⁸⁶ Moreover, to disagree with von Balthasar appears as opposition to Christian faith itself, because if he has seen the form, if he knows the truth of the gospel, then to disagree with him is like arguing against the gospel itself. As Kilby says, "there always lurks the danger of an implication that not to accept [von] Balthasar's theology is simply to fail to see, to lack the eyes of faith."⁸⁷ In fact, the logic of von Balthasar's work has the danger of not allowing "any distinction between resistance to his own theological position and resistance to the gospel as such."⁸⁸

The Cross as the Manifestation of God's Glory

The cross is central in von Balthasar's theological aesthetics. He claims "we ought never to speak of God's beauty without reference to the form and manner of appearing which he exhibits in salvation-history." God has chosen to reveal God's self in the form of Jesus, especially in his death on the cross and his descent into hell, that is, "the most abysmal ugliness of sin and hell by virtue of the condescension of divine love, which has brought even sin and hell into that divine art."⁸⁹ For von Balthasar, "the Passion is

---

86. Ibid., 55. One of the main points of Kilby's critique of von Balthasar is that he "writes as though from a position above his materials—above tradition, above Scripture, above history—and also, indeed, above his readers. He frequently seems to presume . . . a God's eye view." The problem then is that von Balthasar's theology "seems to transgress the usual bonds of theology, to speak with too much confidence, to know more than can be known" (ibid., 13, 114). In other words, von Balthasar lacks theological humility. It is ironic that John McDade, who praises von Balthasar's theology as "the last great theological synthesis in which there is the full flowering of European Christian humanism," says that von Balthasar "seems to float, angel-like, above the particularity of human history" (McDade, "Catholic Theology in the Post Conciliar Period," 429). Probably McDade does not realize that von Balthasar's floating like an angel *above* human history implies his presuming to have a God's eye view.

87. Kilby, *Balthasar*, 56.

88. Ibid., 58. Rahner had also detected this all-or-nothing quality of von Balthasar's theology. According to Herbert Vorgrimler, Rahner described von Balthasar's thought as an "Either you have this vision and insight or you don't." Rahner wondered, "from where von Balthasar had obtained his knowledge [for instance] of the inner life of the deity." It is well known that the mystical visions of Adrienne von Speyr were one of the sources of von Balthasar's theology. For Rahner, the problem is that a theology that relies on mystical visions that are not available to other people has the danger of being gnostic (Vorgrimler, *Understanding Karl Rahner*, 125). Therefore, von Balthasar's theology is locked in an ivory tower because he appears as someone who already knows the truth, a truth that is a kind of esoteric knowledge as long as it is known only by a few people. For some critical remarks about von Speyr's mystical visions as a source of von Balthasar's theology, see Kilby, *Balthasar*, 9, 26–30, 156–60.

89. Balthasar, *Glory of the Lord*, 1:121.

something which happens in the Son on authority from and as a work of the Father."[90] The Father manifests and glorifies himself in the form of the servant Son: "In the form of humiliation of the son who does nothing but obey, the Father expresses his paternal lordship and glory." Therefore, the humiliation of the Son—i.e., Jesus' passion, death on the cross, and descent into hell—"is already in essence the glorification of the Father, and, hence, also of the Son himself." The resurrection "can only ratify the extent to which a love that goes unto death has already glorified itself interiorly."[91]

Therefore, according to von Balthasar, Jesus' "formlessness" or "deformity" on the cross is the form of manifestation of God's glory. "His bearing of the world's sin . . . , his being made sin for us . . . is understandable only as a function of the glory of love, before and after and, therefore, also during his descent into darkness: what we have before us *is* pure glory, and even though it is really a concealment and really an entering into darkness (embracing even the descent into hell), it is always but a function of its opposite."[92] *Kenosis* and *doxa* are not "two images alongside each other, as in a diptych consisting of two complementary halves."[93] Rather, both aspects form a unity.

Here it is important to point out a connection between von Balthasar's and Sobrino's Christologies. It seems that von Balthasar had an influence on Sobrino's theology of the cross. Indeed, talking about his own Christology, Sobrino writes: "No doubt, this, like any other christology, is influenced more by some traditions than others, but the fundamental influence comes from the real crucified world. I do not think one has to have read a word of Paul or Luther or [Hans] Urs von Balthasar or Moltmann—although undoubtedly their writings help us to conceptualize the cross in a particular way—to understand this scandal if one lives in the world where historical crosses are everyday events."[94] In fact, Paul Ritt finds a similarity between Sobrino and von Balthasar: "Each author connects the idea of Jesus' lordship with abasement or kenosis."[95] Likewise, de Gruchy detects a "convergence in Balthasar's and Sobrinos's Christologies, notably with regard to *kenosis*."[96] Whether or not von Balthasar had an influence on Sobrino's Christology, certainly both give a positive meaning to Jesus' suffering on the cross. In

---

90. Ibid., 600–601.
91. Ibid., 595–96.
92. Ibid., 448.
93. Ibid., 463.
94. Sobrino, *Jesus the Liberator*, 235.
95. Ritt, "Lordship of Jesus Christ," 725.
96. Gruchy, *Christianity, Art and Transformation*, 135.

chapter 1, we explained how Sobrino understands the cross as something good, as something pleasing and willed by God. Here we have seen how von Balthasar understands the cross as something positive as long as it is the manifestation of God's glory. Indeed, as Kilby says, in von Balthasar's theology, there is a "proclivity to cast suffering in a positive light," which one can see "first of all in [von] Balthasar's treatment of the Cross, and its extension in Holy Saturday."[97]

According to von Balthasar, Christian beauty includes what "a worldly aesthetics . . . discards as no longer bearable."[98] In other words, God manifests his beauty precisely in what the world considers ugly, namely, the passion and the cross of Jesus. In this sense, the divine principle of beauty contradicts the worldly principles of beauty. The masterpiece of divine imagination, i.e., Jesus' death on the cross, reduces the works of human imagination to nothing.[99] "If the Cross radically puts an end to all worldly aesthetics, then precisely this end marks the decisive emergence of the divine aesthetic."[100] In this sense, there is no analogy between divine beauty and worldly beauty.[101] However, von Balthasar argues, "even worldly aesthetics cannot exclude the element of the ugly, of the tragically fragmented, of the demonic, but must come to terms with these. Every aesthetic which simply seeks to ignore these nocturnal sides of existence can itself from the outset be ignored as a sort of aestheticism. It is not only the limitation and precariousness of all beautiful form which intimately belongs to the phenomenon of beauty, but also fragmentation itself, because it is only through being fragmented that the beautiful really reveals the meaning of the eschatological promise it contains."[102] Therefore, it is not theologically possible to make an analogy between divine beauty and worldly beauty as long as worldly aesthetics ignores the element of the ugly, i.e., as long as worldly

---

97. Kilby, *Balthasar*, 115. For a critical analysis of von Balthasar's theology of Holy Saturday, see Pitstick, *Light in the Darkness*. Pitstick concludes in her study that von Balthasar's "*descensus* theology cannot be true, nor is it an expression of the Catholic Faith" (Pitstick, *Light in the Darkness*, 346). A remarkable feature of Pitstick's analysis is that she takes non-liturgical sacred art as a theological source (see ibid., 74–84). Considering theologically what iconographic and non-iconographic representations of the Descent in Eastern and Western art present, Pitstick claims, "the Descent's significance shown in images is exactly the opposite of what [von] Balthasar thinks its reality was. Thus [von] Balthasar's interpretation seems forced and his dismissal of the traditional reading of the icon unsound" (ibid., 330).

98. Balthasar, *Glory of the Lord*, 1:121.

99. Ibid., 167.

100. Ibid., 448.

101. See ibid., 121, 602.

102. Ibid., 448–49.

aesthetics remains as pure aestheticism. Still, the challenge is to perceive God's beauty in the "image which the primal Maker of Images has created for us," that is, the image of the "Humiliated Fool, an image which captivates no one." For von Balthasar, "such challenge is perhaps only possible for the Christian," as long as he or she is someone who receives from God the eyes to behold the "primal image" of divine beauty.[103]

Before we move to the next section, it is important to pause to reflect on what von Balthasar says about worldly aesthetics. He declares two things. First, the analogy between divine beauty and worldly beauty does not work here, as long as divine beauty includes the ugly, while worldly beauty excludes the ugly. Second, worldly aesthetics neglects the reality of ugliness, tragedy, and evil. Is what von Balthasar says true? If we look at the history of art, we will find that artists have often included the dimension of the ugly in their works of art. Perhaps, as we said above, von Balthasar should spend more time listening to artists to realize that, indeed, worldly aesthetics has paid a lot of attention to the ugly. Finally, it is important to indicate that the all-or-nothing character of von Balthasar's theology is shown again here in the idea that *only the Christian* can see God's beauty in the image of a Humiliated Fool; for what he is saying is: if someone fails to see divine beauty in the figure of the crucified Jesus in the way that he (von Balthasar) is presenting it, then that person is not Christian.

The Form of Christ Imprinted on the Christian

Seeing the form of Christ by the power of the light that comes from within the form itself transforms the whole existence of the beholder.[104] Von Balthasar asks,

> What is a person without a life-form, that is to say, without a form which he has chosen for his life, a form into which and through which to pour out his life, so that his life becomes the soul of the form and the form becomes the expression of his soul? For this is no extraneous form, but rather so intimate a one that it is greatly rewarding to identify oneself with it. Nor is it a forcibly imposed form, rather one which has been bestowed from within and has been freely chosen . . . But if man is to live in an original form, that form has first to be sighted.[105]

103. Ibid., 25–26, 176.
104. Ibid., 454.
105. Ibid., 23–24.

In this sense, "to be a Christian is precisely a form."[106] Being a Christian is a possibility of existence opened up by God for every human being. This form of existence is illuminated by the archetype of Christ. A Christian fulfills his or her mission only if he or she becomes this form that has been instituted by Christ. "When it is achieved, Christian form is the most beautiful thing that may be found in the human realm."[107]

The Christian form consists in the fact that God impresses the form of Christ upon the believer, as long as the believer contemplates the form of Christ. "God does not impress upon the believer only one trait of his Son's, but rather his indivisible essential image . . . Constant contemplation of the whole Christ . . . transforms the beholder as a whole into the image of Christ."[108] In other words, this is a "metamorphosis of the beholder into the image he beholds . . . The image unfolds *into* the one contemplating it, and it opens out its consequences in his life. It is not I who draw my consequences from what I have seen; if I have really seen it in itself, it is the object of my vision which draws its implications in me." This metamorphosis, i.e., "the impress in us of the only valid image of God," "occurs the more impressively, in the literal sense, the less resistance the impress of the image encounters."[109]

The Christian form, then, is "God's work, and the work of man in so far as he makes himself available to the divine action without opposition, acceptingly, allowing God to act, concurring in his work." Christian existence is "the existence of a person who in faith has been divested of any intent to give himself shape, who makes himself available as matter for the divine action."[110] Therefore, Christian existence is the result of the cooperation between God and the individual, a collaboration that von Balthasar describes with the following words:

> the mystery of the "co-operation" . . . is both possible and necessary between God and creature, between Christ and his followers. In no person does Christ's image become impressed as a result of that person's power, but equally it never occurs without the person's will and cooperation. This collaboration, however, cannot consist in the fact that here two people are working alongside and with one another, for instance as a master painter sketches a painting and executes the chief strokes and then

106. Ibid., 27.
107. Ibid., 28.
108. Ibid., 236.
109. Ibid., 472–73.
110. Ibid., 35.

> leaves secondary aspects to his apprentices . . . Nowhere do God
> and man work together on the same plane.¹¹¹

Rather, in this collaborative relationship, God commands, and the creature obeys. Obedience is what characterizes the Christian existence, an existence that "embraces even death, indeed death on the Cross." To illustrate the relationship between God and creature, von Balthasar uses the metaphor of "the Lord who commands and the Handmaid who obeys." "With all the powers available to her," the handmaid "is always at the ready to be engaged in this or any other way, or even, if it should be the Lord's will, to be passed over, forgotten, neglected in a corner." An "active readiness" to obey is "the wet clay in which alone the Christ-form can become impressed."¹¹²

Therefore, the image or the metaphor that is operating here to explain the form of Christian existence is not only that of a spectator contemplating a work of art. Von Balthasar is employing here two other images. One is the metaphor of a sculpture in clay or of pottery, that is, a Christian should be like clay to be molded. The other is the image of wax that can be stamped or impressed. As Kilby says, "allowing to be molded and stamped by God . . . is, for [von] Balthasar, the perfection of faith." These images are meant to express those aspects of Christian existence, such as receptivity, self-abnegation, and humiliation, which "carry some sort of positive valuations for [von] Balthasar."¹¹³ Indeed, as Alyssa Pitstick remarks, "[von] Balthasar seems to ascribe a positive value to suffering and death in themselves in virtue of their likeness to the suffering Redeemer."¹¹⁴

According to von Balthasar, the Christian existence is molded by the form of the Son, who bears witness to what he has seen and heard of the Father:

> [Jesus] witnesses to what he says with himself—with his whole
> existence—so that the experience of God which he has had can,
> in turn, be repeated bodily . . . by those persons who associ-
> ate with him and believe in him . . . For just this reason, the
> experience of this existence on the part of the eyewitnesses can-
> not be an object of self-gratifying contemplation, but can only
> be had through the imitation of discipleship, which means by
> being conformed to Christ's functional attitude: the role of the

---

111. Ibid., 547.
112. Ibid., 547–48.
113. Kilby, *Balthasar*, 118.
114. Pitstick, *Light in the Darkness*, 133.

eyewitnesses is directly and necessarily functionalised for the sake of the community of all believers.[115]

Therefore, Christian witness should work for the sake of the community. In this sense, "The evangelical ethic of love of neighbour receives its meaning from the living archetype of Christ."[116] However, action, the good, and the ethic of love are categories that do not properly belong to von Balthasar's theological aesthetics, but to the second part of his theological trilogy, namely, his *Theo-Drama*, which we will examine in the following section.

Lack of Social Concern in von Balthasar's Theo-Drama

In her article about von Balthasar's theology of the sexes, Corinne Crammer comes to the conclusion that "social justice does not seem to be a central concern for [von] Balthasar."[117] Is this true? Other authors suggest the contrary. For instance, while acknowledging that von Balthasar's theology can be used to support an unjust status quo instead of promoting social transformation, de Gruchy wonders if this is an inevitable consequence of von Balthasar's theological aesthetics. De Gruchy's answer is that von Balthasar's "theological aesthetics does not encourage flight from the world but assumes Christian participation in God's mission to transform the world."[118] According to de Gruchy's interpretation of von Balthasar's theology, "social action is a response to the 'beauty reflected in the Christ-form.'"[119] Therefore, who is right? Does von Balthasar's theology include a concern for social justice or not? To answer this question, I will explain, first, some basic points of von Balthasar's *Theo-Drama*, which seems to be the right place in which to look in order to find a possible concern for social justice in his theological trilogy; and then, I will explain the critiques of von Balthasar's theology by Gerard O'Hanlon and Thomas Dalzell.

The second part of von Balthasar's theological trilogy, the so-called *Theo-Drama*, deals with God's action and human action in the world. If in his theological aesthetics von Balthasar takes the beautiful as the hermeneutical concept for theology, in his *Theo-Drama* he uses the good as the interpretative concept. For von Balthasar, what God does for man "is simply *good*. Theo-drama is concerned with the good. What God has done is to

---

115. Balthasar, *Glory of the Lord*, 1:322.
116. Ibid., 500.
117. Crammer, "One Sex or Two?," 107.
118. Gruchy, *Christianity, Art and Transformation*, 129.
119. Ibid., 135.

work salvation... The perception may be *beautiful* and the utterance *true*, but only the act can be *good*."[120] The good "cannot be contemplated in pure 'aesthetics' nor proved and demonstrated in pure 'logic,'" rather the "good is something *done*." Furthermore, the good—i.e., God's work of salvation—"takes place nowhere but on the world stage and its destiny is seen in the drama of a world history that is continually unfolding."[121]

To be sure, theological aesthetics and theological dramatics are distinguished, but not separated. Von Balthasar says, "Right at the heart of the *Aesthetics*, the 'theological drama' has already begun. 'Catching sight' of the glory... always involved being 'transported' by it... But this was all seen from within the aesthetic purview. Now we must allow the encountering reality to speak in its own tongue or, rather, let ourselves be drawn into its dramatic arena. For God's revelation is not an object to be looked at: it is his action in and upon the world, and the world can only respond, and hence 'understand,' through action on *its* part."[122]

Therefore, in order to explain the relationship between God's action and human action in the world, von Balthasar uses the analogy of drama and of theatre. He says: "What interests us here is the whole phenomenon of theatre... Our aim will be to show... how all the elements of the drama can be rendered fruitful for theology."[123] Likewise, "we are proposing to use the categories of drama to illuminate Christian theology."[124] However, von Balthasar points out that, in this analogy, the dissimilarity is greater than the similarity. For instance, the categories of secular drama cannot grasp or explain completely the theological reality that "God and man will never appear as equal partners. It is God who acts, on man, for man and then together with man; the involvement of man in the divine action is part of God's *action*, not a precondition of it."[125] Nevertheless, for von Balthasar, the model of drama and theatre is still "a more promising point of departure for a study of *theo-drama* than man's secular, social activity"[126] (as in the case, for instance, of liberation theology, in which the starting point is precisely the social action of human beings).

Regarding our enquiry about the possibility of finding a concern for social justice in von Balthasar's theology, the opening section of the first

120. Balthasar, *Theo-Drama*, 1:18.
121. Ibid., 19.
122. Ibid., 15.
123. Ibid., 9.
124. Ibid., 25.
125. Ibid., 18.
126. Ibid., 11–12.

volume of *Theo-Drama* is promising. He analyzes some approaches that are "trends of modern theology," such as "event," "history," "orthopraxy," and "political theology" (all these are certainly key concepts in liberation theology). According to von Balthasar, "Each of these attempts contains something right, even something indispensable. But none of them is adequate to provide the basis for a Christian theology. Each needs to be complemented. In part they complement each other, but when juxtaposed they do not attain the methodological clarity and *fullness* that their object requires. If they are seen in their positive contribution as well as in their partiality, they can all be shown to *converge* on what we have called *theo-drama*. Here, each of them can find what it lacks."[127] Therefore, in von Balthasar's mind, all these theological approaches that have a concern for social justice converge in his *Theo-Drama*; they find the fullness that their object requires in von Balthasar's theology.[128] As O'Hanlon asserts, for von Balthasar, "theological dramatics is capable of integrating many of the tendencies of contemporary theology . . . This is important because it means [von] Balthasar sees himself as engaged with the kind of issues which are relevant to a social theology."[129] However, in my judgement, the problem with von Balthasar's theology is that it never fulfills this expectation, i.e., he does not develop a theology that responds to the concerns of a social theology in a concrete way.

In his analysis of von Balthasar's *Theo-drama*, O'Hanlon seems to find both a social dimension and a lack of social concern in von Balthasar's theology. On the one hand, O'Hanlon suggests that there is a social dimension in von Balthasar's theology. As we already know from von Balthasar's own explanations, in his theology there is movement from aesthetics to dramatics, that is, from contemplation to action. In the words of O'Hanlon, "the contemplative theology of the aesthetics then turns into the combative, passionate theology of the dramatics."[130] However, already within the aesthetics, "we are asked not simply to contemplate Jesus but with Christian

---

127. Ibid., 25 (emphasis mine).

128. Thus, in the opening section of *Theo-Drama*, we find two patterns detected by Kilby in von Balthasar's theology: what she calls "fulfillment" and the "radiating circle." Both patterns are another version of von Balthasar's presumption that he knows the whole truth, and therefore, he can stand above other theological views. See Kilby, *Balthasar*, 71–93.

129. O'Hanlon, "Theological Dramatics," 94–95. By the term "social theology" O'Hanlon means "a theology which would reflect on our situation in the light of the gospel, and would attend to the social, economic, political and cultural, as wells as the personal, dimensions of that situation. It would . . . see itself as part of a process to bring about change" (ibid., 102).

130. Ibid., 93.

eros to follow him, be disciples,"[131] and discipleship, O'Hanlon suggests, "involves mission, and mission involves the ethic of justice and love that Jesus preached and lived... There is a primacy to be accorded to personal conversion, but there is also need of a conversion of structures."[132] In other words, "the Christian mission is to influence the world at both individual and social levels, with a primacy given to personal conversion in a work which also involves the changing of social structures."[133] This feature of von Balthasar's theology, O'Hanlon argues, encourages "in an obvious way the notion of social theology."[134] However, this encouragement to social transformation in von Balthasar's theology is not as obvious as O'Hanlon assumes. In my opinion, von Balthasar's theology *in itself* neither encourages an ethic of justice nor supports the change of social structures. All these are personal interpretations of O'Hanlon that he adds to von Balthasar's theology. Von Balthasar's theology *in itself* does not claim such things.[135]

Indeed, on the other hand, O'Hanlon himself suggests a limitation in von Balthasar's theology regarding a possible social concern in von Balthasar's thought. O'Hanlon finds in von Balthasar's theology a "dichotomy between human and theological hope," which is "based on the primacy of the spiritual... over the material."[136] In this sense, O'Hanlon asks von Balthasar about his notion of the kingdom of God: "Why not say... that one may hope for some visible approximations, anticipations, expressions of the Kingdom in both personal and social reality? Why make the distinction between human and theological hope into a disjunction which refuses to relate the latter to inner-worldly time and risks suggesting a separation between nature and grace?... It may be that despite formal statements to

131. Ibid., 94.
132. Ibid., 103.
133. O'Hanlon, "May Christians Hope for a Better World?," 179.
134. O'Hanlon, "Theological Dramatics," 103. Like O'Hanlon, Ritt suggests that, in von Balthasar's theology, social action derives from contemplation. However, such an action is secondary: "the effective exercise of [Jesus'] lordship does not depend on human performance, though his lordship calls for acknowledgment and action... Such action includes social praxis on behalf of those deprived of basic human rights. However, [von] Balthasar considers perception of Jesus' lordship to be the principal human response to the beauty reflected in the Christ-form; action that seeks to transform social reality into the kingdom of God is secondary or derivative in that it flows out of this initial faith perception of Jesus' lordship" (Ritt, "Lordship of Jesus Christ," 724).
135. Frederick Bauerschmidt makes a political interpretation of von Balthasar's *Theo-Drama*. However, he clearly states that such an interpretation implies "to move beyond [von] Balthasar's own work, to say what [von] Balthasar does not himself say" (Bauerschmidt, "Theo-Drama and Political Theology," 542). In other words, Bauerschmidt admits that von Balthasar's theology *in itself* is not a political theology.
136. O'Hanlon, "Theological Dramatics," 106.

the contrary [von] Balthasar, in his great appreciation of the transcendent, does undervalue the immanent, horizontal dimension."[137]

However, according to Thomas Dalzell, von Balthasar "does not undervalue the horizontal plane as such." In his theology, "neither the temporal nor the historical are ignored."[138] In fact, we should remember that, using von Balthasar's own words, the good—i.e., God's work of salvation—"takes place nowhere but on the world stage and its destiny is seen in the drama of a world history that is continually unfolding."[139] Therefore, the historical dimension is present in von Balthasar's theology. The problem though, Dalzell argues, is that he "tends to focus on the time and history of the individual subject," hence, "there is indeed a certain neglect of the social dimension in [von] Balthasar."[140]

According to Dalzell, "[von] Balthasar gives priority to personal conversion, to the transformation of the heart rather than to social structures."[141] In fact, "what one finds in his *Theo-Drama* is that the real drama takes place in the heart of the individual."[142] The notion of inter-subjectivity is present in von Balthasar's theology, but the inter-subjective level is not the same thing as the social level of reality. Indeed, von Balthasar's "dramatic theory formally allows for the interplay of various actors on the stage."[143] Thus, as O'Hanlon says, "it is no accident that running right through [von] Balthasar's theology is his use of the analogy of inter-subjectivity to speak about God, us, and the relationship between us and God."[144] However, Dalzell rightly asserts that the inter-subjective level should not be confused with the social level of reality. The "relationality" that von Balthasar prefers is more interpersonal than social, for in his theology "the accent falls on the relationship between two subjects."[145]

To be fair, in the midst of the thousands and thousands of pages written by von Balthasar on theological matters, there are at least two articles in which he addresses the social dimension of Christian faith in a positive way. Both articles are collected in *The von Balthasar Reader*. In one article, von

---

137. O'Hanlon, "May Christians Hope for a Better World?," 181.
138. Dalzell, "Lack of Social Drama," 458.
139. Balthasar, *Theo-Drama*, 1:19.
140. Dalzell, "Lack of Social Drama," 458. See Dalzell, *Dramatic Encounter of Divine and Human Freedom*, 227–85. See also Bauerschmidt, "Theo-Drama and Political Theology," 547–48.
141. Dalzell, "Lack of Social Drama," 461.
142. Ibid., 463. Cf. O'Hanlon, "Theological Dramatics," 107–8.
143. Dalzell, "Lack of Social Drama," 458.
144. O'Hanlon, "Theological Dramatic," 94.
145. Dalzell, "Lack of Social Drama," 472.

Balthasar seems to suggest that God is in solidarity with the poor. Therefore, "whoever is concerned with the struggle against injustice and the prosecution of rights in the world, does so in utter immediacy together with the God of revelation."[146] This is a remarkable, but unfortunately exceptional text in von Balthasar' theology. He does not develop this idea any further. In the other article, von Balthasar says, "theology has no direct competence in the realm of worldly structures; it simply sends Christians into the world with an image of the human whereby and according to which they are to organize its structures as responsibly and intelligently as they can."[147] Thus, on the one hand, von Balthasar says that social issues do not belong to the field of theology; on the other hand, he seems to suggest that Christians should get involve in the transformation of social structures, but the suggestion, to my mind, is too indirect and muted.

O'Hanlon thinks that "[von] Balthasar's distance from the socio-economic and political is much more a matter of personal sensibility than theological judgment. In this sense he is very much . . . a creature of his own milieu," that is, a "highly cultivated, educated Swiss milieu."[148] Along the same lines, Declan Marmion describes von Balthasar as a "refined aristocrat . . . , more at home with the arts than with politics."[149] In this sense, O'Hanlon finds that von Balthasar has a "detached, neutral stance" on socio-political issues—a stance that is "naive rather than merely politically innocent."[150] However, O'Hanlon regrets that von Balthasar does not engage in any kind of social analysis in his theological work: "After all, if art, music, drama, philosophy and so on may be dialogue partners for theology, why not economics and politics?"[151] As a consequence, von Balthasar's theology can "easily be hijacked to support an unjust *status quo*."[152] Therefore, O'Hanlon concludes, von Balthasar has a contribution to make to socio-political theologies, but his contribution is "unremarkable. It is correct . . . , but not too inspiring. It has the brake on, it is undramatic. What needs to happen is . . . a development of [von] Balthasar beyond himself."[153]

---

146. Balthasar, *The von Balthasar Reader*, 374.

147. Ibid., 370.

148. O'Hanlon, "Theological Dramatics," 108. See Mongrain, *Systematic Thought of Hans Urs von Balthasar*, 222–25.

149. Marmion, "Rahner and his Critics," 197.

150. O'Hanlon, "Theological Dramatics," 108.

151. Ibid., 109.

152. Ibid., 110.

153. Ibid.

Von Balthasar's Critique of Liberation Theology

The goal of this section is not to refute von Balthasar's critique of liberation theology.[154] The aim is more modest: to show that von Balthasar is very much at odds with liberation theology, and therefore, it is almost impossible to reconcile his thought with the theology of liberation. Although it is clear that von Balthasar knew about liberation theology, it is not clear that he understood it. As Sobrino says, von Balthasar had no idea how to respond to the emerging reality of the theology of liberation in Latin America.[155] Von Balthasar describes liberation theology with the following words,

> The theology of liberation is the theology of horribly suffering members of the Catholic Church who are crying for help . . . We are confronted by the southern hunger belt of humanity which, as it calls for help, accuses the richer brethren in Europe and the United States of capitalist exploitation and implores them to be mindful of the fundamental commands of the gospel and of the solidarity between all members of the Mystical Body of Christ. Practical help here means more than a handout. It means effectively striving for a worldwide order which would realistically observe both the laws of world economy and the laws of world Church, acting with Christian imagination and Christian determination to put an end to the worst abuses which cry out to heaven.[156]

Von Balthasar accepts that "the urgency of the practical concerns of liberation theology is not called into question."[157] However, he says in an almost patronizing tone, "I feel that the combined efforts of theology in the United States and Europe should also be directed toward helping the Latin American theology of liberation, which often becomes . . . confused. I mean helping to clarify it with a sympathetic understanding of its genuine claims."[158] Von Balthasar finds at least seven points that are "confusing" in liberation theology.

Firstly, liberation theology has reduced the realities of revelation and salvation to a mere socio-political liberation. For von Balthasar, "the totality of God's revelation to the world can in no way be reduced to political

---

154. For a summary of how Gutiérrez responds to the critiques of liberation theology, see McGovern, *Liberation Theology and Its Critics*, 99–101.
155. Sobrino, "Karl Rahner and Liberation Theology," 55.
156. Balthasar, "Current Trends in Catholic Theology," 84.
157. Balthasar, "Liberation Theology," 146.
158. Balthasar, "Current Trends in Catholic Theology," 84.

and social liberation, nor even to the general concept of liberation."[159] Von Balthasar accepts that Christians have a "duty to fight for social justice on behalf of the poor." However, "political and economic freedom can only be a relative freedom. 'Real freedom' is granted by God through the gift of his Holy Spirit, and even someone poor and oppressed can share in it and consciously live it, no less than the prisoner of the concentration camp and the Gulag."[160] In other words, for von Balthasar, liberation is not mainly about external, social, and political freedom, but principally about internal, personal, and spiritual freedom.

Secondly, the "greatest danger" of liberation theology is its tendency to link together "earthly action and the kingdom of God that comes down from God."[161] According to von Balthasar, liberation theology understands the kingdom of God as something that is achieved exclusively or mainly by human beings. Liberation theologians should learn, von Balthasar says, that the kingdom of God is a divine gift, and therefore, it "cannot be coerced into existence by any amount of social or political effort."[162] Therefore, if the possibility of a just society becomes a reality in history, even then such earthly society will not be "an immanent reflection or an anticipation of the kingdom of God."[163]

Thirdly, the main concern of liberation theology is not God, but human beings and their worldly project of liberation. Von Balthasar accuses liberation theology for being "self-seeking," i.e., for seeking only a human and worldly liberation. In von Balthasar's words, "liberation theology builds the gospel . . . into the temple of humanity it is trying to erect."[164] In other words, the liberationist interpretation of the gospel only seeks to promote a mere human project, that is, a socio-political liberation.

Fourthly, liberation theology emphasizes the efficacy of socio-political praxis; by doing so, the dimension of the cross becomes superfluous.[165] For von Balthasar, liberation theology fails to see that the Christian norm is not political efficacy, but the scandal of the cross, which includes Jesus' self-denying and obedience.[166] The cross consists in a love that suffers and

---

159. Balthasar, "Liberation Theology," 146.
160. Balthasar, *Theo-Drama*, 4:486.
161. Ibid., 482.
162. Balthasar, "Current Trends in Catholic Theology," 85.
163. Balthasar, "Liberation Theology," 142.
164. Balthasar, *Theo-Drama*, 4:66.
165. Ibid.
166. Balthasar, "Liberation Theology," 138.

endures everything, even death. Therefore, Christian faith is not about political efficacy, but about failure in worldly terms.[167]

Fifthly, liberation theology fails to see that "the promised Kingdom is to be universal." Von Balthasar accepts that Jesus sides with the poor; however, "Jesus' option does not constitute the founding of a party in opposition to the wealthy: these are not cursed, but rather invited to conversion."[168] Likewise, it is true that "the Church, too, must by preference side with the poor: But this option cannot compromise the universality of the Church's offer of salvation to all."[169]

Sixthly, liberation theology misinterprets Jesus' solidarity as "social solidarity," i.e., solidarity with the poor. According to this misinterpretation, the cross is simply the consequence of Jesus' social solidarity.[170] For von Balthasar, Jesus' solidarity is not about solidarity with the poor; rather it is an expression of his communion with our sinful human nature, a solidarity that reaches its maximum expression in the cross and in the descent into hell.[171]

Finally, there is no such a thing as "social sin," as liberation theologians claim. According to von Balthasar, "societal situations can be unjust, but in themselves they cannot be sinful. Only those persons can be sinful who are responsible for the existence of such situations and who continue to tolerate them even though they could abolish or ameliorate them."[172]

In conclusion, it is clear that von Balthasar is very critical of liberation theology. O'Hanlon more restrainedly asserts, von Balthasar has a "cool attitude towards liberation theology."[173] This is why de Gruchy's statement that there is "no reason why [von Balthasar's] theological aesthetics and theologies of liberation and transformation need to be regarded as antithetical to each other"[174] seems very odd. For de Gruchy, von Balthasar does not have a critical or cool attitude towards liberation theology, but rather an "ambivalent" approach: "[Von] Balthasar's recognition and affirmation of the 'practical concerns' of liberation theology is important, and is perhaps sufficient to demonstrate that his theological aesthetics did not imply any

---

167. See Balthasar, *Theo-Drama*, 4:483–85.
168. Balthasar, "Liberation Theology," 143.
169. Ibid., 144.
170. See Balthasar, *Theo-Drama*, 4:66, 268–69
171. Balthasar, *Mysterium Paschale*, 160–68.
172. Balthasar, "Liberation Theology," 145.
173. O'Hanlon, "The Legacy of Hans Urs von Balthasar," 406.
174. Gruchy, *Christianity, Art and Transformation*, 129.

withdrawal from the need to work for justice in the world."[175] I disagree with de Gruchy. In my judgment, von Balthasar's recognition of the practical concerns of liberation theology is not enough to show that his theology has any concern for social justice. His critique of liberation theology proves exactly the opposite.

Like de Gruchy, Roberto Goizueta also tries to argue that there is more similarity than difference between von Balthasar's theology and liberation theology. Goizueta says, "I draw on some fundamental insights that, I believe, these theologians have in common, even if often articulated with quite different emphasis." Goizueta continues, "If there is one statement that encapsulates this similarity, it is the Johannine assertion that 'God loved us first.'"[176] True, both von Balthasar and liberation theology maintain that God loved us first. However, in my view, a fundamental difference between von Balthasar and liberation theology lies precisely in the notion of God's love for us. While for liberation theology God's love for us is integral, that is, it includes the personal, the interpersonal, the social, the political dimensions of love, in von Balthasar's theology the socio-political dimension of God's love for the poor is practically absent. This difference is not simply a matter of emphasis, as Goizueta suggests. Rather, it is a different understanding of God's love for us. For this reason, it is almost impossible to reconcile both kinds of theology.

Is von Balthasar's Theology Helpful for a Theological Aesthetics of Liberation?

In this section, I will explain the reasons why von Balthasar's theology is not helpful for the development of a theological aesthetics of liberation.

Firstly, von Balthasar's division (although not a separation) between aesthetics and drama, or between contemplation and action, is not helpful for a theological aesthetics of liberation. Von Balthasar understands aesthetics only or mainly as contemplation, and not as praxis. Therefore, his theological aesthetics is not useful for the development of a theological aesthetics of liberation that considers aesthetics not only as contemplation, but also as praxis.

Secondly, the way in which von Balthasar uses analogy is not helpful for a theological aesthetics of liberation. He thinks that there is both a relationship and a continuity between divine beauty and worldly beauty (as long as we understand worldly beauty as a manifestation of being, and not

---

175. Ibid., 133.
176. Goizueta, *Christ Our Companion*, x.

as an emotional experience of the subject). Therefore, if there is a continuity between divine beauty and worldly beauty, it is possible and legitimate to make analogies between divine beauty and worldly beauty. However, the archetype is not worldly beauty, but God's beauty. Thus, the mystery of God can illuminate the reality of the human world, but the mystery of human existence cannot illuminate the reality of God. Therefore, the analogy between divine beauty and worldly beauty is not two-directional, but one-directional. Therefore, von Balthasar's way of using analogy is not appropriate for a theological aesthetics of liberation that uses a correlational mode of analogy.

Thirdly, von Balthasar's disdain for the subjective dimension of aesthetics is not helpful for the development of a theological aesthetics of liberation. According to von Balthasar, beauty is not about the subject who has an aesthetic experience, but is about the (beautiful) object itself that manifests being. Therefore, von Balthasar underestimates the subjective dimensions of aesthetics—such as the artist who creates a beautiful object and the recipient who has the experience of a work of art. Von Balthasar's disdain for the subjective dimension of aesthetics is not useful for the development of a theological aesthetics of liberation that pays attention not only to the objective side, but also to the subjective side of aesthetics, or to be more precise, to the relationship between the subject and the object.

Fourthly, von Balthasar's *Theo-drama* is not useful for the development of a theological aesthetics of liberation because it overlooks the socio-political dimension of reality. Since von Balthasar's theological aesthetics lacks the dimension of praxis, we turn our attention to his *Theo-drama*, which deals with categories such as the good, praxis, and action, with the expectation that we may find a concern for social justice there. However, what we find is that his theological dramatics, while focusing on the individual and on the inter-subjective interactions between God and human beings, practically lacks the socio-political dimension of reality. Therefore, von Balthasar's *Theo-drama* is not helpful for the development of a theological aesthetics of liberation that is interested not only in personal liberation, but also in socio-political liberation.

Fifthly, von Balthasar's underestimation of Jesus' solidarity with the poor is not helpful for a theological aesthetics of liberation. Von Balthasar's understanding of the dynamics of Christian faith is as follows. God is revealed in the radiant form of Jesus. Paradoxically, at least for the standards of the world, the revelation of God's glory finds its maximum expression both in Jesus' death on the cross and his descent into hell. Jesus' death on the cross is the result of his obedience to the Father. The Christian is someone who is enraptured by the vision as he or she contemplates Jesus as the form of divine revelation. As long as the Christian sees the form of God's revelation in Jesus, he or she will be imprinted by the form of Christ. The form of Jesus configures the life of the Christian. The problem with von Balthasar's theology is that it underestimates the notion of "social solidarity" in Jesus' ministry. For von Balthasar, Jesus' solidarity is not about solidarity with the poor, but about communion with our sinful human nature—a communion that finds an ultimate expression in his descent into hell. If the solidarity with the poor is not part of Jesus' form, then such social solidarity will not be imprinted in the lives of Christians. Therefore, von Balthasar's underestimation of Jesus' solidarity with the poor is not useful for the development of a theological aesthetics of liberation that considers Jesus' option for the poor as a central dimension of his ministry, and as a crucial aspect to understand his death on the cross. Furthermore, von Balthasar's idea that the beauty of God is revealed supremely in the death of Jesus, without giving any further explanation, qualification, or specification regarding the historical reasons of Jesus' crucifixion, is an "aestheticization of suffering," using Metz's expression.[177] This beautification of the cross, which gives positive meaning to unjust suffering, is not helpful for the development of a theological aesthetics of liberation that looks at the negative dimension of both Jesus' death on the cross and the suffering of the poor.

Finally, von Balthasar's critique of liberation theology shows that his theology is not helpful for the development of a theological aesthetics of liberation. His theology is so at odds with liberation theology, that it is theoretically and practically impossible to make a correlation between his theology and the theology of liberation. Furthermore, his theology is locked in an ivory tower, not open to dialogue with other theologies, either because he presumes that he already knows the whole truth, or because he presumes that those who differ from his view are wrong. Hence a dialogue between von Balthasar's theology and liberation theology is very difficult. The only way to establish both a dialogue and a correlation between theological aesthetics and liberation theology is by developing a theology beyond von Balthasar. Indeed, the theological aesthetics of liberation that I will develop in the following chapters has a non-Balthasarian approach since it assumes

---

177. Metz, *Passion for God*, 119. Regarding von Balthasar's neglect of the historical reasons of Jesus' crucifixion, Bauerschmidt observes: "[Von] Balthasar at times forgets his own admonition that while the cross 'was the goal of his whole existence, [it] was at the same time the crowning conclusion of an effort to realize the *polis* of God on earth.' No matter how much we stress the cross as the Son's obedience to the will of the Father [as von Balthasar does], no matter how seriously we take the unity of economic and immanent Trinity, no matter how much we stress that Jesus died *pro nobis*, we must not obscure the *political* significance of his cross as an execution of the just one by the unjust" (Bauerschmidt, "Theo-Drama and Political Theology," 550).

that many aspects of von Balthasar's theology are unhelpful, insufficient, and often inadequate for a theological understanding of God as the liberator of social outcasts.

EXPLORING RAHNER'S THEOLOGY AS A POSSIBLE MODEL FOR A THEOLOGICAL AESTHETICS OF LIBERATION

In this section I will explore some dimensions of Rahner's theology, its advantages and its limitations for the development of a theological aesthetics of liberation. Firstly, I will explain some essential aspects of his theological anthropology, which is the basis of his theological aesthetics. Secondly, I will describe some dimensions of his theological aesthetics. Thirdly, I will explore the social and historical dimensions of his theology, and his opinions about liberation theology. Finally, I will make some summary and critical remarks about Rahner's theology in relation to the possibility of using his theology as a model for a theological aesthetics of liberation.

Rahner's Theological Anthropology

The main theme of Rahner's theology is not God as an isolated divine Being, but rather God in relationship with human beings. In his own words, at the fundamental level of theology, "there is really only one question, whether this God wanted to be merely the eternally distant one, or whether beyond that he wanted to be the innermost center of our existence."[178] For Rahner, the answer to that question is that God willed to be the inmost core of our human existence. However, as every theologian, he faces the problem of where to begin to do theology, i.e., the question of method. For Rahner, the starting point of theological reflection is the graced human reality. "What is a human being?" is an essential question that all human beings can ask for themselves. To answer this question, we must do philosophy. However, Christianity has an answer to that question. To know and to understand the Christian answer to that question, we must do theology.[179] In fact, Christianity implies an anthropology, which is not merely philosophical, but also theological. Therefore, it is a mistake to think that the starting point of Rahner's theology is the plain human existence without any further

---

178. Rahner, *Foundations of Christian Faith*, 12.
179. Ibid., 11.

qualification. The starting point of his reflection is the graced reality of human existence, that is, a theological anthropology.

Theological Method and the Experience of Transcendence

Rahner's theology is often called "transcendental theology" for it employs a "transcendental method."[180] The starting point of his theology is what he calls "transcendental experience" or the "experience of transcendence."[181] This is the experience in which a subject experiences himself or herself as an "infinite possibility."[182] It is the experience of "the subject's openness to the unlimited expanse of all possible reality."[183] This experience is "transcendental" in the sense that the subject goes beyond what is being categorically or concretely experienced. However, it is important to understand from the outset that, for Rahner, "every transcendental experience is mediated by a categorical encounter with concrete reality in our world, both the world of things and the world of persons."[184] As Martinez says, "it is critical to understand the inner connection between 'transcendental' and 'categorial' [or categorical]. Both occur together; they belong to each other; they imply and require each other. The transcendental is the condition of possibility of the categorial, while at the same time, the transcendental only can appear and be revealed through the categorial."[185]

According to Rahner, transcendental experience is co-present in every act of both knowledge and freedom. At the level of knowledge, transcendental experience means that man "can place everything in question." Every answer that he finds is "always just the beginning of a new question." In this sense, man experiences himself as a being with an infinite horizon in knowledge. "The infinite horizon of human questioning is experienced as an horizon which recedes further and further the more answers man can discover."[186] At the deepest level, the question that rises up in human beings is the question about their own existence, and this is a transcendental question for it can never be completely settled.[187]

---

180. See Schüssler Fiorenza, "Method in Theology," 76–78.
181. Rahner, *Foundations of Christian Faith*, 20.
182. Ibid., 32.
183. Ibid., 20.
184. Ibid., 52.
185. Martinez, *Confronting the Mystery of God*, 7.
186. Rahner, *Foundations of Christian Faith*, 31–32.
187. Ibid., 32.

At the level of freedom, transcendental experience consists in the fact that a human person, in his or her actions, is responsible for himself or herself, for others, and for the world.[188] Transcendental freedom is not merely an "interior disposition."[189] Rather, "man's transcendental experience of his free subjectivity takes place only in his encounter with the world and especially with other people."[190] Transcendental experience in freedom is necessarily mediated through the encounter with other human beings because "the intercommunication of spiritual subjects in truth and in love and in society belongs to the realization of one's own existence."[191]

Transcendental experience is mediated in and through "the concrete reality of time and space, of man's materiality and his history."[192] Rahner asserts, "being in the world, being in time and being in history . . . are aspects of the free subjectivity of a person as such . . . His subjectivity and his free, personal self-interpretation take place precisely in and through his being in the world, in time, and in history, or better, in and through world, time and history."[193] Therefore, "Man as subject and as person is a historical being in such a way that he is historical precisely *as* a transcendent subject; his subjective essence of unlimited transcendentality is mediated *historically* to him in his knowledge and in his free self-realization. Hence man realizes his transcendental subjectivity neither unhistorically in a merely interior experience . . . , nor does he grasp this transcendental subjectivity by means of an unhistorical reflection and introspection."[194]

This mediation of human transcendence in and through history is "true not only of the individual history of an individual person, but also of the history of social units, of peoples and of the one human race," since "we are presupposing that in the origin, unfolding and goal of its history mankind forms a unity."[195] Since the self-interpretation of the human race takes place in and through history, it is "always still in progress until the final and definitive interpretation" at the end of history.[196]

---

188. Ibid., 41.
189. Ibid., 36.
190. Ibid., 51–52.
191. Ibid., 41.
192. Ibid., 36.
193. Ibid., 40.
194. Ibid., 140.
195. Ibid., 141.
196. Ibid., 41.

Transcendental experience permeates the everyday life of human beings.[197] It is "present precisely when a person experiences himself as involved in the multiplicity of cares and concerns and fears and hopes of his everyday world."[198] There are also "prominent moments" of transcendental experience, for instance, the experience of radical authenticity, of love, and of death.[199] However, the experience of transcendence is "always in the background," as a "secret ingredient."[200] For this reason, Rahner says, human beings can easily overlook the reality of transcendence in their daily life. Even more, they can ignore or evade the experience of transcendence.[201] For instance, a man can say to himself and to others that "one does well to suppress the question about the meaning of it all and to reject it as an unanswerable and hence meaningless question."[202]

According to Rahner, transcendental experience is the "a priori openness of the subject to being as such."[203] In fact, "man is a transcendent being insofar as all of his knowledge and all of his conscious activity is grounded in a pre-apprehension . . . of 'being' as such."[204] This pre-apprehension of being is "due to the working of that to which man is open, namely, being in an absolute sense. The movement of transcendence is not the subject creating its own unlimited space as though it had absolute power over being, but it is the infinite horizon of being making itself manifest." In other words, man experiences himself "as one who receives being."[205] In this sense, man's transcendence is a relationship that has not been established by the power of man; rather, it is experienced as something that has been established by another, by an absolute being.[206] Therefore, absolute being is both the ground of the experience of transcendence, and the end towards which man is oriented in transcendence.

"Holy mystery" is the term that Rahner preferably uses to name this absolute being, which is the source and the end of human transcendence. Rahner says that "we run the deadly risk that many contemporaries can hear the word 'being' as an empty . . . abstraction." For this reason, he prefers

197. Ibid., 32.
198. Ibid., 35.
199. Ibid., 132.
200. Ibid., 35.
201. Ibid., 32.
202. Ibid., 33.
203. Ibid., 35
204. Ibid., 33.
205. Ibid., 34.
206. Ibid., 42.

the term "holy mystery."[207] By "mystery," he means that such absolute being is ineffable. By "holy," he means that absolute being is not only the source and the end of human knowledge and freedom, but also and especially the source and the end of love. "Freedom is always the freedom of a subject who exists in interpersonal communication with other subjects . . . For a subject who is present to himself to affirm freely vis-à-vis another subject means ultimately to love." Therefore, "we must also take into account the character of the term and source of transcendence as love," since absolute being is "what opens up my own transcendence as freedom and as love." Thus, for Rahner, the name "holy" belongs to this infinite source and end of love, for "love in the presence of the incomprehensible and the ineffable necessarily becomes worship."[208]

In the experience of transcendence, "a person comes into the presence of the absolute mystery which we call 'God.'"[209] Indeed, transcendental experience is an experience of that absolute being which we call God, although in an unthematic or anonymous way. It is an "experience in which he whom we call 'God' encounters man in silence."[210] However, "a person knows explicitly what is meant by 'God' only insofar as he allows his transcendence beyond everything objectively identifiable to enter into his consciousness, accepts it, and objectifies in reflection what is already present in his transcendentality."[211] Nonetheless, when a person names this holy mystery as "God," such a person should not think that he or she has control over the mystery. "The concept 'God' is not a grasp of God by which a person masters the mystery, but it is letting oneself be grasped by the mystery which is present and yet ever distant. This mystery remains a mystery even though it reveals itself to man."[212]

Supernatural Existential

Transcendental experience can be interpreted theologically as the event of God's self-communication to human beings in history. For Rahner, the center of the Christian understanding of human existence is that a human person is the event of the self-communication of God.[213] This thesis entails

207. Ibid., 60.
208. Ibid., 65–66.
209. Ibid., 44.
210. Ibid., 21.
211. Ibid., 44.
212. Ibid., 54.
213. Ibid., 116.

an integration of both the doctrine of grace and the doctrine of the final vision of God. Grace and the vision of God are two aspects of a single event, namely, God's self-communication to human beings. In this event, "what is communicated is God in his own being [i.e., grace], and in this way it is a communication for the sake of knowing and possessing God in immediate vision and love."[214]

According to Rahner, the event of God's self-communication to human beings has two different modes: first, the mode of an offer or a call to human freedom, and second, the mode of a free response to this offer.[215] In the first of mode of God's self-communication, what God offers to human beings is God's self, God's own reality, God's own being. In other words, what God gives is his own Spirit. In God's self-communication to human beings, "the giver in his own being is the gift."[216] To say that God's self-communication is a gift means that it is an act of God's freedom. God's self-communication is gratuitous, and therefore, it is not due to the merits of human beings.[217] The event of God's self-communication entails the fact that God is not only a distant presence; God is also present in the mode of closeness to human beings. In this nearness, however, God does not become a categorical being, that is to say, a being among other beings in the world. As God communicates God's self to human beings, God does not cease to be an infinite being, and man does not cease to be a finite being.[218] As Rahner asserts, "Immediacy of God . . . cannot depend on the fact that what is not God absolutely disappears when God draws near. As God he does not have to find a place by having something else which is not him make room. For at least the presence of God as the transcendental ground and horizon of everything which exists . . . takes place precisely in and through the presence of the finite existent." Thus, "There is a genuine mediation of immediacy with regard to God."[219]

In God's self-communication to human beings, God makes God's self a constitutive principle of human beings.[220] In this sense, Rahner uses the term "supernatural existential" to express the constitutive presence of God in human beings. God's self-communication—in grace and in the immediate vision of God—is characterized as "supernatural." However,

214. Ibid., 117–18.
215. Ibid., 118.
216. Ibid., 120.
217. Ibid., 123.
218. Ibid., 118–20.
219. Ibid., 83.
220. Ibid., 120–21.

"the doctrine that grace and fulfilment in the immediate vision of God are supernatural does not mean that the supernatural 'elevation' of a spiritual creature is added extrinsically and accidentally to the essence and the structure of a spiritual subject." Rather, from the very beginning of his or her existence, the spiritual creature is constituted "as the possible addressee of such a divine self-communication."[221] Therefore, what is most intrinsic to all human beings is God's self-communication, at least in the mode of an offer. What is most intrinsic to a human person is God, and hence the supernatural. Human subjects are themselves through that which they are not, and that which they are not is God. In other words, that which human subjects are is given to them by God's self-communication to them.[222] God's self-communication to human beings "is present in *every* person at least in the mode of an offer."[223] Therefore, the term "supernatural existential" expresses the fact that every human person is always a "graced" human being.

The second mode of God's self-communication to human beings is that of a response to God's offer. This second mode means "that the acceptance of God's self-communication must be based upon God's offer itself, and hence that the acceptance of grace is once again an event of grace itself."[224] In other words, "God's self-communication is given not only as gift, but also as the necessary condition which makes possible an acceptance of the gift."[225]

In freedom, human beings can also reject God's offer, and this rejection is also a human response that is sustained by God's self-communication to human beings. God's self-communication is "the condition of possibility for a 'no' to itself . . . Consequently, there is in the act in which freedom says 'no' an absolute contradiction by the fact that God is affirmed and denied at the same time."[226] In the human act of rejecting God's offer, there is an absolute contradiction because human beings are using the freedom that they have received from God—in this way, God is affirmed—to reject the source of their freedom—in this way, God is denied. Therefore, in the act of rejecting God's offer, human beings are destroying themselves, for they are rejecting precisely the source of their being. This is why, according to Rahner, "this 'no' must never be understood as an existential-ontological parallel possibility of freedom alongside of the possibility of a 'yes' to God." To illustrate this

221. Ibid., 123.
222. Ibid., 124.
223. Ibid., 127.
224. Ibid., 118.
225. Ibid., 128.
226. Ibid., 99.

reality of self-destruction in the human act of rejecting God, Rahner uses the image of a miscarriage: "This 'no' is one of freedom's possibilities, but this possibility of freedom is always something abortive, something which miscarries."[227] In fact, every "no" derives the life that it has from a "yes," but in such a way that does not bring life, but death. To say that the human rejection to God's offer is sustained by God's self-communication does not mean that God is responsible for such a rejection. Rahner is very careful to point out that this interpretation of the reality of sin "does not explain the possibility of a radical, subjective, resolute and definitive 'no' to God. We shall have to allow this possibility to exist as the 'mystery of evil.'"[228] Thus, Rahner does not offer an explanation of the origin of sin and evil. It seems that, for Rahner, the only legitimate answer to the question of the origin of sin and evil is apophatic, that is, we do not know, it is a mystery.

Therefore, God is the source and the end of transcendental experience. In fact, the transcendental movement of the human spirit in knowledge, freedom, and love towards absolute mystery is borne by God's self-communication to human beings.[229] If we accept that God's self-communication to human beings is the source and the end of transcendental experience, then we can infer from this statement three theological points.

Firstly, God's self-communication occurs in the daily "secular" lives of human beings. As we said above, transcendental experience permeates the everyday life of human persons. Therefore, God's self-communication, as the source and the end of transcendental experience, occurs precisely in the "secular" life of people. Hence, the event of God's self-communication to human beings is not limited to the explicitly called "religious" realm. As Rahner says,

> The experience which we are appealing to here is not primarily and ultimately the experience which a person has when he decides explicitly . . . upon some *religious* activity, for example, prayer, a cultic act, or a reflexive and theoretical occupation with religious themes. It is rather the experience which is given to every person prior to such reflexive religious activity and decisions, and indeed perhaps in a form and in a conceptuality which seemingly are not religious at all. If God's self-communication is an ultimate and radicalizing modification of that very transcendentality of ours by which we are subjects, and if we are such subjects of unlimited transcendentality in the most

227. Ibid., 102.
228. Ibid.
229. Ibid., 129.

ordinary affairs of our everyday existence, in our secular dealings with any and every individual reality, then this means in principle that the original experience of God even in his self-communication can be so universal . . . and so "unreligious" that it takes places wherever we are living out our existence.[230]

Secondly, God's self-communication to human beings is mediated in and through the encounter of the human person with himself or herself, with other people, and with the world. As we said above, transcendental freedom is actualized and mediated in and through the interaction with the human world. Therefore, God's self-communication, as the source and the end of transcendental experience, occurs in the encounter of the human person with himself or herself, with other people, and with the world. Therefore, in the human response that is sustained by God's self-communication, a "yes" or "no" to oneself, to others, or to the reality of the world is what mediates a "yes" or "no" to God. As Rahner says, "man can deny himself in such a way that he really and truly says 'no' to God himself."[231] Likewise, "since in every act of freedom which is concerned on the categorical level with a quite definite object, a quite definite person, there is always present, as the condition of possibility for such an act, transcendence . . . towards God, there can and must be present in every such act an *unthematic 'yes' or 'no'* to this God."[232] Hence, for Rahner, there is radical unity between love of God and love of neighbor, for "the categorised explicit love of neighbour is the primary act of the love of God."[233]

Finally, God's self-communication to human beings takes place in the history of the world. As we said above, transcendental freedom is mediated in and through the history of humanity. Therefore, God's self-communication, as the source and the end of transcendental experience, occurs in the history of humankind. As Rahner asserts, "the divinized transcendentality of man . . . has itself a history in man, an individual and a collective history. This transcendentality takes place, as borne, empowered and fulfilled by the

---

230. Ibid., 132.
231. Ibid., 101.
232. Ibid., 98.
233. Rahner, "Reflections on the Unity," 247. Von Balthasar harshly criticized Rahner's notion of the unity between love of God and love of neighbor. See Balthasar, *Moment of Christian Witness*, 100–130. I agree with Marmion who says: "It seems that one of the reasons for [von] Balthasar's difficulty with Rahner's thesis is that he ([von] Balthasar) confuses the terms unity and identity. Although Rahner sometimes used the term 'identity,' his underlying concern was to emphasise a *perichoresis* or mutual conditioning of the two elements: love of neighbour and love of God" (Marmion, "Rahner and his Critics," 196 n. 6). See Kilby, "Balthasar and Karl Rahner," 257–62.

divinizing self-communication of God, this transcendentality *takes place* [in history]; it does not simply exist. It is for this reason that we said that man is the *event* of the . . . self-communication of God."²³⁴

Therefore, the supernatural existential has a history; "this existential itself has a history individually and collectively, and this is at once the single history of both salvation and revelation."²³⁵ It is a history of *salvation* because "God's offer of himself . . . is by definition man's salvation. For it is the fulfilment of man's transcendence in which he transcends towards the absolute God."²³⁶ It is a history of *revelation* because "the transcendental knowledge, which is present always and everywhere in the actualization of the human spirit in knowledge and freedom, but present unthematically," can "be characterized as God's self-revelation."²³⁷ This "single history of revelation and salvation is borne by God's freedom and man's freedom together."²³⁸ According to Rahner, "there is never a salvific act of God on man which is not also and always a salvific act of man. There is no revelation which could take place in any other way except in the faith of the person hearing the revelation. To this extent it is clear that the history of salvation and revelation is always the already existing synthesis of God's historical activity and man's at the same time."²³⁹ To be sure, for Rahner, the relationship between God and human beings in history is not that of a "synergistic cooperation," as if they were two equal agents working together. Since God is not a being among other beings in the world, the collaboration between God and human beings cannot be that of equal partners. Rather, "God is the ground of man's act of freedom, and he burdens man with the grace and the responsibility for his own accountable acts."²⁴⁰

Thus, the history of salvation and revelation is coextensive with the history of the human race.²⁴¹ In other words, the history of salvation and revelation takes place "in the whole history of man, in what he does and what he suffers in individual life; in what we call simply the history of culture, of society, of the state, of art, of religion, and of the external, technical and economic mastery of nature."²⁴² Therefore, the history of salvation takes

---

234. Rahner, *Foundations of Christian Faith*, 138.
235. Ibid., 141.
236. Ibid., 143.
237. Ibid., 149.
238. Ibid., 138.
239. Ibid., 142.
240. Ibid.
241. Ibid., 144.
242. Ibid., 153.

place not only "where this history is actualized in an explicitly religious way in word and in cult and in religious societies"; it also "encompasses the apparently merely profane history of mankind and of the individual person."[243] To say that the history of salvation is coexistent with the history of humankind does not mean that they are identical, "for in this single history there is also ... rejection of God, and hence the opposite of salvation."[244] Therefore, "the history of God's offer of himself, offered by God in freedom and accepted or rejected by man in freedom, is the history of salvation or its opposite."[245]

Rahner's Theological Aesthetics

Brent Little asserts that, in the past, theologians thought that Rahner lacked a theological aesthetics.[246] However, in the last few years, some theologians have reconsidered this assumption.[247] In fact, a theological aesthetics is implicitly and explicitly present in Rahner's theology. In this section, I will explain some essential points of Rahner's theological aesthetics. Here it is important to remember that theological aesthetics is a reflection on God and his saving relationship with the world from the perspective of aesthetics. In this sense, a theological aesthetics includes a theology of perception, of art, and of beauty. Rahner deals with the first two dimensions of theological aesthetics, that is, perception and art, and not with the third dimension, that is, beauty (at least not explicitly).[248]

Rahner shows great appreciation of the arts. He is neither an artist nor a literary writer, and he does not consider himself an expert in aesthetics and in art. "I understand little about these things," he humbly declares.[249] However, in spite of the fact that he is not a professional artist, a poet, an aesthetician, an art critic, or an art historian, Rahner is able to make remarkable statements about aesthetics and art. As Gesa Elsbeth Thiessen asserts, far from having little to say about aesthetics, Rahner's views of the arts are "astute and relevant," for "he addressed issues that continue to be central

243. Ibid., 144.
244. Ibid., 142.
245. Ibid., 143.
246. Little, "Anthropology and Art," 939.
247. See, for instance, Little, "Anthropology and Art"; Thiessen, "Karl Rahner"; Voiss, "Rahner, von Balthasar"; Fritz, *Karl Rahner's Theological Aesthetics*.
248. One may say that there is an *implicit* theology of beauty in Rahner's thought. Such an assertion is based on an interpretation that *we* can make of his theology. Rahner himself does not generally talk about beauty. Thus, a theology of beauty is not something that he explicitly formulated.
249. Rahner, "Theology of the Religious Meaning," 149.

to this day."[250] His capacity to make insightful remarks about aesthetics is in great measure due to his sensibility and appreciation of the arts. Especially, Rahner shows an empathy with literary forms of art.[251] I will consider some of his ideas about verbal arts as long as they can be applied to non-verbal arts, since my study focuses on painting.[252]

For Rahner, "arts and theology are mutually related."[253] Thus, there is a mutual correlation between theology and aesthetics, which is really a two-directional relationship, and not simply one-directional. On the one hand, aesthetics can be related to theology. In fact, Rahner does not approach aesthetics as an artist or as an aesthetician, but as a theologian. By doing so, he is making a twofold statement. First, he acknowledges the existence of a distinct discipline called aesthetics (in which he is not an expert, as he himself declares). Second, he thinks that aesthetics is not a complete independent discipline; rather, aesthetics has a relationship with theology (in which he is definitely an expert). Therefore, it is possible to consider the world of aesthetics not as pure aesthetics, but as a *theological* aesthetics.

On the other hand, for Rahner, theology can be related to aesthetics.[254] Theology should consider art as long as art is an expression of human self-understanding as a transcendental being. "The most perfect kind of theology," Rahner claims, "would be the one that appropriates these arts as integral part of itself." Thus, for instance, "when listening to a Bach oratorio," Rahner wonders, "why would we not have the impression that, not only through its text but also through its music, we are in a very special way brought into a relationship with divine revelation about humanity? Why would we not believe that this too is theology?"[255] If a Bach oratorio is not theology itself, at least it is or should be a source of theology. In fact, Rahner ventures to say that there is and should be a "poetic theology" as a legitimate mode of theology. A poetic theology is not about writing theology in a beautiful way; rather it is about a theology that takes into account the experience of poetry as a theological source.[256] In this sense, Thiessen says, for Rahner,

---

250. Thiessen, "Karl Rahner," 226.

251. Ibid., 230; Little, "Anthropology and Art," 947.

252. As Little says, "Rahner's reflection on the literary arts can be applied to other art forms if we understand 'word' as 'expression.' Every art form is an act of communication, an expression between the creator and the audience" (Little, "Anthropology and Art," 947).

253. Rahner, "Art against the Horizon," 163.

254. Rahner, *Foundations of Christian Faith*, 8.

255. Rahner, "Art against the Horizon," 163.

256. Ibid., 164.

art can be a *locus theologicus*.²⁵⁷ However, in order to consider art as source of theology, we need to have the praxis or the experience of art, either by "creating" art as an artist or by "experiencing" art as a recipient. As Rahner says, viewing artistic images can be a religious act; however, "this moment can be rendered intelligible only by performing it, not by talking about it."²⁵⁸ In other words, art can be a source of theology only if we "perform" art, that is, only if we have the praxis or the experience of art.

Rahner's theological aesthetics is based on his theological anthropology.²⁵⁹ This is why it was necessary to explain his theological anthropology in the first place. For Rahner, aesthetics is about transcendental experience, at two interrelated levels. First, a work of art is a mediation of transcendental experience at the sensory level.²⁶⁰ A work of art is a "peak experience" of a sense domain,²⁶¹ for instance seeing or hearing. Hence, Rahner asks, "when something exceptionally intense is seen or heard, is it not possible for the whole person, with all one's powers, to have a very powerful religious experience?"²⁶² We should not be surprised about the possibility of having a religious experience through the senses, Rahner says, for "Christian anthropology has always clearly insisted that sense knowledge and spiritual knowledge constitute a unity, that all spiritual knowledge, however sublime it may be, is initiated and filled with content by sense experience."²⁶³

Second, art is a mediation of transcendental experience inasmuch as it is an expression of human self-understanding.²⁶⁴ "Whatever is expressed in art is a product of that human transcendentality by which, as spiritual and free beings, we strive for the totality of all reality."²⁶⁵ According to Rahner, the arts are "ways in which people express themselves."²⁶⁶ Talking about literature, for instance, Rahner says that books present the human world "of joy and death, love and solitude, work and merry meetings, of heroes and of disaster, of nature and history."²⁶⁷ However, as a work of art shows the reality of the human world, it expresses the transcendental dimension of human

---

257. Thiessen, "Karl Rahner," 227.
258. Rahner, "Theology of the Religious Meaning," 156.
259. Thiessen, "Karl Rahner," 226; Little, "Anthropology and Art," 939.
260. See Rahner, "Theology of the Religious Meaning," 158.
261. Ibid., 157.
262. Rahner, "Art against the Horizon," 166.
263. Rahner, "Theology of the Religious Meaning," 150.
264. Rahner, *Foundations of Christian Faith*, 8.
265. Rahner, "Art against the Horizon," 165.
266. Ibid., 162.
267. Karl Rahner, "On the Theology of Books," 115.

existence. Through their works of art, artists present a "situation in which persons concretely realize their transcendental being in a new way."[268] For instance, even when a poet "speaks of the flowers and of the love of two human hearts," he or she is really expressing a "longing for an unsurpassable fulfilment, for perfect love."[269]

The transcendental experience in art is always historical. According to Rahner, "human transcendence in art is expressed in a certain historical way. Genuine art is the result of a determined historical event of human transcendentality. That is why art can and must always be historical. There exists a real history of art."[270] That the transcendental experience in art is always historical includes two aspects. First, not only the artist is a historical being, but also he or she belongs to a social context that is historical as well. Second, through his or her art, an artist expresses his or her interpretation of our humanity and of our world, which are essentially historical. As such, the work of an artist manifests a historical situation. Therefore, artists "announce what is eternal in a unique manner, in which their historical peculiarity and their longing for eternity are combined in a unity that constitutes the essence of the work of art."[271]

Art is a mediation and an expression of transcendental experience, and as such art is a mediation of God's self-communication to human beings. In other words, God's self-communication is the source and the end of the transcendental experience that human beings have in and through art. As Rahner says, "art, real art, is always more than just that. If ever art is pursued exclusively for the sake of the aesthetic, it ceases to be art . . . But that something more which belongs to it and from which it lives cannot come to art from itself. The openness to infinity which constitutes art does not itself give the infinite, it does not bring and contain *the* infinite." The openness to infinity that constitutes art comes from God. Therefore, as long as a "poet is driven forward by the transcendence of the spirit," he or she "has already been overpowered secretly and quite unknown to himself by the longing which the grace of the Holy Spirit has implanted in the human heart."[272] Likewise, "the self-expression contained in a Rembrandt painting or in a Bruckner symphony is so strongly inspired and borne by divine revelation,

---

268. Rahner, "Art against the Horizon," 166.
269. Karl Rahner, "Priest and Poet," 316–17.
270. Rahner, "Art against the Horizon," 166.
271. Ibid.
272. Rahner, "Priest and Poet," 316.

by grace, and by the self-communication of God that it tells us . . . what persons really are in the sight of God."[273]

Art is a mediation of God's self-communication to human beings from *the perspective of the artist*, inasmuch as he or she is "inspired" by God. What does it mean that a work of art is inspired by God? Rahner gives the example of having a "good idea." Let us say that I have a "good idea," and I consider it as an "inspiration of God." Is it correct to consider a good idea as a divine inspiration? On the one hand, it is possible to say that this "good idea" is the result of several worldly factors that are not God—for instance, physiological, psychological, historical, and sociological factors. To this extent, we can say that this "good idea" is not the result of any "intervention of God." However, as Rahner says, "the moment I experience myself as a transcendental subject in my orientation to God . . . , this 'good idea' receives objectively a definite and positive significance. Hence I can and must say: [this good idea] is willed by God in this positive significance as a moment of the one world established in freedom by its ground as the world of my subjective relationship to God, and in this sense is an 'inspiration' of God."[274] Therefore, insofar as something is integrated into one's relationship to God as the objectification and mediation of that relationship, it is in fact an inspiration of God.[275] In this sense, a work of art is inspired by God as long as we consider it as an expression and a mediation of transcendental experience.

Art is a mediation of God's self-communication to human beings from *the perspective of the recipient*. The recipient of a work of art can perceive the mystery of God through art as long as art is an expression of human transcendence. Among the different kinds of perception, Rahner pays special attention to the sense of seeing. "Sight is a power that cannot be replaced by other sources of experience within human sense faculties, . . . sight belongs to the sensory foundation of religious knowledge."[276] In this sense, Rahner says, "I may understand Dürer's hare as the most concrete aspect of a well-determined insignificant human experience, but when I look at it with the eyes of an artist, I am beholding, if I may say so, the infinity and incomprehensibility of God."[277] Indeed, a work of art can help its recipients to "see" the transcendental dimension of human existence, which is a dimension that can be missed in daily life. As Rahner says, "what is genuine and holy,

---

273. Rahner, "Art against the Horizon," 163.
274. Rahner, *Foundations of Christian Faith*, 88–89.
275. Ibid., 89.
276. Rahner, "Theology of the Religious Meaning," 154.
277. Rahner, "Art against the Horizon," 166.

eternal and valid, whether of man or of God, can only be found in everyday life when our eyes and our hearts have been opened to it in hours that lie outside everyday life."[278] Art can be that sort of experience that opens our eyes and our hearts.

Therefore, the religious character of art consists in its capacity to mediate and to express the experience of transcendence, that is, in its capacity to mediate God's self-communication to human beings. As Rahner says, "if religious images may exist, it must be possible for them to have such a mediating function with regard to the absolute God."[279] In this sense, Rahner makes the following observation,

> I may say, for instance, that the paintings of Impressionism are not religious because basically they try only to reproduce the color impressions of one's immediate surroundings. If this is their only purpose and result, we will probably have to say that they are not religious art. And we must, without hesitation, say that there may exist art that is not religious. It does not have to be anti-religious. But it moves in a dimension of humanity where the relationship to God is not yet present.
>
> But it is quite another question when I put the painting of an Impressionist of the early twentieth century in a wider context, a more human one, which would also bring up the question of its religiosity.[280]

Therefore, the religious character of Christian art does not consist in the explicit representation of religious themes, such as Jesus, Mary, or a saint. As Rahner asserts, "a religious painting is not simply identical with one that represents an explicitly religious object."[281] Therefore, on the one hand, a work of art that represents a "profane" theme can be a religious painting inasmuch as it expresses the transcendental dimension of human existence. For instance, "it is quite possible that a Rembrandt painting, which is not intended as religious, moves people so deeply, bringing up the question of life's ultimate meaning, that it is, strictly speaking, a religious painting."[282] This idea of Rahner is based on his theological anthropology. As he explains,

> an image that does not have a specifically religious theme can be a religious image . . . [This idea] should not surprise the theologian too much. A naive theology will spontaneously think or

278. Rahner, "On the Theology of Books," 124.
279. Rahner, "Theology of the Religious Meaning," 157.
280. Rahner, "Art against the Horizon," 167.
281. Ibid., 167.
282. Ibid.; see Rahner, "On the Theology of Books," 116–17.

> silently presuppose that only explicitly religious acts (of prayer, of expressed love of God, of explicit observation of a moral norm *as* a command of God) will bring about a salutary relation to God. But, theologically speaking, that is false . . . The totality of a free subject's way of life is always a yes or a no to God . . . Hence the statement that viewing an image that has no explicitly religious object may be the experience of a freely accepted transcendence toward God, may be a religious act, and that, in this sense, the image may have a religious significance, is not as surprising for the theologian as it may seem at first.[283]

The possibility of a work of art being religious even when it represents a worldly theme is based on the analogy of being. "Analogy makes it possible to understand a given reality as a secret revelation of a higher, different, more comprehensive reality." For instance, Rahner says, "*analogia entis* enables poets to understand a certain human experience as mysteriously pointing to God. They can present human love in its mysteriousness as an analogous reference to God's love."[284]

On the other hand, a work of art that represents an explicitly religious theme may fail to be truly a religious painting if it does not express the transcendental dimension of human existence. Rahner says,

> When I paint the crib with Jesus, Mary, and Joseph, using aureoles to show what is being represented, I have, objectively speaking, a religious picture. It may, in fact, not be very religious, because it is unable to evoke in those who see it a genuine and deep religious reaction. There exists what we call religious *Kitsch*. We might perhaps say that basically the pictures in the nineteenth century of the Holy Family were painted with the best intentions by pious people, but nevertheless, they were not truly religious paintings, because they do not affect us deeply enough to elicit religious feelings.[285]

In this sense, Rahner asserts, "there are paintings which, while not suitable for hanging in a church, because they do not have explicitly Christian themes . . . , are nevertheless much more 'Christian' in their human substance (given its concrete expression, perhaps, simply in still-life objects or a human face) than some painting lacking in human substance but supposed to represent St. Joseph."[286] This assertion does not mean that the represen-

---

283. Rahner, "Theology of the Religious Meaning," 159.
284. Rahner, "Art against the Horizon," 164–65.
285. Ibid., 167.
286. Rahner, "On the Theology of Books," 121–22.

tation of explicitly religious themes in art is unnecessary or irrelevant for Christian faith. As Rahner explains, "religious images represent events of salvation history that may be grasped by the senses . . . Such images provide the experience of visible historical events . . . One irreplaceable way of getting to know a person is to see and not just to hear that person; a portrait cannot be totally replaced by a biography. The same is true of salvation-historical events. They must also be seen, and seen in an image, if we are not actually present to see them."[287] In this way, the artistic representation of religious themes can help Christians "to keep in mind their faith in a special salvation history."[288] However, as Rahner says, this legitimate use of images in popular piety does not manifest "the proper nature of images and of seeing as a properly religious phenomenon."[289] Religious images are more than simple illustrations of biblical passages.[290] Religious works of art are those that mediate and express the transcendental dimension of human existence.

The Social and Historical Dimensions in Rahner's Theology and His View of Liberation Theology

Rahner's theology has been criticized for paying little attention to the historical and social dimensions of humanity, of Christian faith, and of theology.[291] Johann Baptist Metz, a former student of Rahner, is well known for being both a follower and a critic of his teacher. Metz criticizes Rahner on two points. First, Rahner does not give enough importance to the social dimension of Christian faith. In his transcendental theology of the subject, the Christian message becomes "privatized": "The categories most prominent in this theology are the categories of the intimate, the private, the apolitical sphere."[292] Second, the historical dimension of the subject in Rahner's theology is too abstract. "The concept of experience elaborated in the transcendental theology of the subject does not have historical experience's structure. To be specific, those social contradictions and antagonisms that are the stuff of painfully lived historical experience . . . disappear with transcendental theology's concept of experience, in the abstractness of a

287. Rahner, "Theology of the Religious Meaning," 157.
288. Ibid., 159.
289. Ibid., 157.
290. Ibid., 155.
291. See O'Donovan, "Orthopraxis and Theological Method," 48; Marmion, "Rahner and His Critics," 198; Martinez, *Confronting the Mystery of God*, 51–52.
292. Metz, *Theology of the World*, 198. See Metz, *Faith in History and Society*, 48–50, 58–59.

preconceived 'transcendental experience.'"[293] As Leo O'Donovan says, for Metz and other critics,[294] "Rahner's anthropology represses the conflict and negativity of life... Where in such a theology, it is asked, are the horrors of the Holocaust or of Hiroshima, of the Third World's poverty?"[295] If Rahner overlooks the historical and social dimensions of the human subject, and if his theology is insensitive to social problems, then his theology is "ineffectual in the realms of policy or social change," his critics claim.[296] Are these critiques correct? In the following paragraphs I will explore the social and historical dimensions of the subject in Rahner's theology in order to evaluate if these critiques are acceptable.

Regarding the *social* dimension, Rahner clearly says that the transcendental experience of the subject takes place in his or her interaction with other human subjects and in society.[297] In Rahner's understanding, love of neighbor and the social dimension of the subject are intrinsically related. "Love of neighbor cannot merely mean a private relationship to another individual, but also means something social and political, and implies responsibility for social and political structures."[298] God's self-communication to human beings—called the kingdom of God—takes place precisely in and through this intrinsic relationship between love of neighbor and the responsibility for socio-political structures. "Such love, ... wherever it truly exists and remains and *thus* really supports the social efforts between men ... constitutes a completely new society of men ... ; it allows the eternal kingdom of God to begin in secret."[299] Therefore, without love, any socio-political action loses its transcendental dimension.[300] According to Rahner, the notion of the unity between love of God and love of neighbor has the potential for the development of a socio-political theology. However, he recognizes that "one cannot construct a full-pledged political theology from this idea."[301]

Rahner pays attention to the social dimension of sin as well. If transcendental experience takes place in the interaction with other human beings at the interpersonal and the social levels, then the human rejection of their openness to infinity also has both an interpersonal and social dimensions.

---

293. Metz, *Faith in History and Society*, 74.
294. See Sobrino, "Karl Rahner and Liberation Theology," 65.
295. O'Donovan, "Orthopraxis and Theological Method," 54.
296. Ibid., 48.
297. See Rahner, *Foundations of Christian Faith*, 41, 51–52.
298. Ibid., 323.
299. Rahner, "Reflections on the Unity," 231.
300. Ibid., 231–32.
301. Rahner, *Faith in a Wintry Season*, 61.

Human guilt, that is, human responsibility for doing evil, "has its darkening and depraving effect on all of man's collective and social dimensions."[302] The situation of every individual and of every society is conditioned or affected by guilt, i.e., by sin.[303] Rahner gives the following example: "When someone buys a banana, he does not reflect upon the fact that its price is tied to many presuppositions. To them belongs, under certain circumstances, the pitiful lot of banana pickers, which in turn is co-determined by social injustice, exploitation, or a centuries-old commercial policy. This person now participates in this situation of guilt to his own advantage."[304]

Furthermore, Rahner points out the social dimension of Jesus' ministry and of his death. For Jesus, God was the ultimate reality. "It is precisely for this reason that he was someone who saw himself in radical solidarity with social and religious outcasts, because his 'Father' loved them. He resolutely accepted the struggle which his attitude and activity provoked on the part of the religious and social establishment. But in his own eyes he was not directly a social critic in the sociological sense." Therefore, Jesus "faced his death and accepted it at least as the consequence of fidelity to his mission," and in this sense "as imposed on him by God." According to Rahner, "Jesus did not think that everyone then and everyone in every age could follow him *only* through an *explicit* social and critical involvement for the underprivileged and the outcasts. This negative statement does not deny that *everything* which we do and do not do has social relevance even when it is not intended as such . . . , and that consequently the whole theology of Jesus can also be read as 'political' theology."[305] If Jesus' ministry has a socio-political dimension, then "the Church has a task toward society that is political in the strictest sense of the word."[306]

Therefore, for Rahner, Christian faith and theology definitely have a socio-political component that is based on the fact that human beings, as transcendental subjects, have a socio-political dimension. He asserts. "It's obvious that all of Christianity has a social, not to say political dimension, whereby the social dimension of humanity refers not to a particular aspect of men and women but to the whole of their humanity. To this extent theology, which wants to help people understand who they are, cannot leave this dimension out of the picture. Thus theology is political and socially critical

---

302. Rahner, *Foundations of Christian Faith*, 173.
303. Ibid., 110.
304. Ibid., 110–11; see Rahner, *Faith in a Wintry Season*, 64.
305. Rahner, *Foundations of Christian Faith*, 248.
306. Rahner, *Karl Rahner in Dialogue*, 202.

Von Balthasar or Rahner? 109

... A theology that wants to reach people ... will enter into the concrete social and political situation of people."[307]

Regarding the *historical* dimension, Rahner clearly and insistently says that the transcendental experience of human beings takes place in the history of individuals and of societies.[308] According to O'Donovan, the common way to describe Rahner's theology simply as "transcendental" is a one-sided and mistaken approach to his theology because it overlooks the historical dimension of Rahner's method. Instead of using only the transcendental method, Rahner uses a twofold method whose moments—the transcendental and the historical—are dialectically related.[309] However, while pursuing this twofold method, Rahner undoubtedly concentrates his efforts on the transcendental moment.[310]

Therefore, the social and historical dimensions of the human subject, of Christianity, and of theology, are present in Rahner's theological thought.[311] However, to my mind, the problem in Rahner's theology springs from the lack of specificity of the human subject. Who is the subject of transcendental experience in Rahner's theology? Probably the answer is "man" in general, without any further specification. It is this lack of specificity that seems to justify the common view that Rahner's theology lacks historical and social sensibility. Metz himself praises his teacher because "Rahner's theology is in some measure the mystical biography of the ordinary, the average Christian person."[312] However, the context of this average person in Rahner's theology seems to be that of a modern culture, without any further specification.[313] In this sense, J. Matthew Ashley wonders, "what if the reality that contextualizes and threatens modern belief is not ... that of secularization and unbelief, but the horrifying worldwide prominence of inhuman suffering, the existence of crucified peoples?"[314]

Therefore, is it true that Rahner overlooks the historical and social dimensions of humanity, of Christian faith, and of theology, as his critics say? On one level, it is not true. We have shown that Rahner pays attention

307. Ibid., 135.
308. See Rahner, *Foundations of Christian Faith*, 40–41, 140–42.
309. O'Donovan, "Orthopraxis and Theological Method," 48–49.
310. Ibid., 51.
311. In his last years, Rahner became more aware of the social and historical dimensions of theological reality, and tried to incorporate those elements in his theology in a more explicit way. See O'Donovan, "Journey into Time." See also Schüssler Fiorenza, "Method in Theology," 69, 79.
312. Metz, *Passion for God*, 103.
313. Martinez, *Confronting the Mystery of God*, 24.
314. Ashley, introduction to Metz, *Passion for God*, 14.

to the social and historical aspects of theological reality. On another level, it is true, in the sense that, in his theology, the subject of transcendental experience lacks specificity. However, the potential for the development of a socio-political theology that considers the concrete reality of the transcendental subject is present in Rahner's theology. As O'Donovan rightly observes, Rahner's "anthropology is inclusive rather than exclusive, containing the seeds for the very developments about which his critics have rightly been exercised."[315] Thus, if Rahner's theology is to be relevant in the realm of socio-political change, it is necessary to develop a theology that is based on Rahner's method, but at the same time goes beyond Rahner.

Liberation theology is precisely a type of theology that adopts Rahner's method in its own original way, and at the same time goes beyond Rahner. As Linda Hogan says, mindful of the indebtedness of liberation theology to Rahner, "there is a temptation to stress the points of affinity and continuity" between the two. "However it would be wrong to underestimate the innovative impact of the theology of liberation."[316] Martinez suggests that Gutiérrez's *Teología de la Liberación* is, broadly speaking, "a creative working out of the significance of the central tenets of Rahnerian theology . . . for the reality of a Latin American continent . . . [However] Gutiérrez does not simply apply Rahner's theology to Latin America. In adopting a new perspective, he opens new avenues that both challenge and transform the theology of Rahner." According to Martinez, "Gutiérrez builds upon the Rahnerian findings and adopts Rahner's anthropological perspective. However, he both transcends and critiques Rahner in two directions. First, Gutiérrez does not accept the Rahnerian subject in general but looks for the concrete and historical subject in his own society. That subject is recognized as the poor." Second, "Gutiérrez takes up the Rahnerian theme of the unity of history in general and history of salvation and applies it to the task of liberating the poor in history."[317]

Rahner's opinion about liberation theology is ambivalent. On the one hand, Rahner is generally very supportive of liberation theology. Sobrino claims, "I do not think that Rahner had any detailed knowledge of [liberation theology], but he was certainly aware intuitively of the fundamental issues at stake and he supported it."[318] In fact, for instance, Rahner says, "I can only rejoice when a theology develops in Latin America which is built up on the experience of community, on the grassroots experience of

---

315. O'Donovan, "Orthopraxis and Theological Method," 54.
316. Hogan, "Rahner and the Theologies of Liberation," 167.
317. Martinez, *Confronting the Mystery of God*, 122.
318. Sobrino, "Karl Rahner and Liberation Theology," 55.

the Church, on the socio-political task of the Church."³¹⁹ Likewise, he says, "liberation theology has opened our eyes to structural injustices."³²⁰ Rahner declares that he is "ready to learn from Latin America and its theology."³²¹ He acknowledges that he is neither a political theologian nor a liberation theologian, but the reason is not because he has something against those theologies. "The real reason is that every person has only a limited amount of time, a limited capacity to work, a finite potential."³²² As Sobrino says, at the end of his life, "Rahner was moving towards what was best in liberation theology, and he would have made his own contribution towards it," but these themes "came too late for him."³²³

On the other hand, Rahner has reservations about liberation theology. His main critique is that humanity, Christian faith, and theology, should not be reduced to their horizontal, social, and political dimensions. After accepting that Christianity and theology have a socio-political dimension, Rahner says, "Christianity cannot of course let itself be reduced to a movement of social emancipation. Christianity rightly objects to that sort of thing, because individual persons cannot be reduced to their social roles and because human beings and their history are always transcending themselves into the absolute mystery that we call God . . . Because of all this we have to view the theology of liberation with some reservation."³²⁴ Therefore, Christianity "cannot be replaced by a socio-political humanism, however respectable that humanism might be."³²⁵ "I will have nothing to do with such a pseudohumanistic and horizontal theology," Rahner exclaims.³²⁶ Thus, for him, "a true Catholic theology of liberation can and must exist," but "not every theology of liberation . . . is necessarily a true Catholic theology of liberation."³²⁷

---

319. Rahner, *Karl Rahner in Dialogue*, 202.
320. Rahner, *Faith in a Wintry Season*, 64.
321. Rahner, *Karl Rahner in Dialogue*, 202.
322. Rahner, *Faith in a Wintry Season*, 30.
323. Sobrino, "Karl Rahner and Liberation Theology," 65.
324. Rahner, *Karl Rahner in Dialogue*, 135.
325. Ibid., 203.
326. Rahner, *Faith in a Wintry Season*, 51.
327. Rahner, *Karl Rahner in Dialogue*, 201.

Is Rahner's Theology Helpful for a Theological Aesthetics of Liberation?

In this section, I will explain the reasons why Rahner's theology is helpful for the development of a theological aesthetics of liberation.

Firstly, Rahner's understanding of transcendental experience is helpful for a theological aesthetics of liberation. According to Rahner, human beings have the experience of transcendence, which is an experience of openness to infinite possibility. Human beings have this experience in every act of knowledge and freedom. The transcendental experience of human beings takes place in and through concrete and historical reality, that is, in and through their interaction with other human subjects and with the world. Rahner's understanding of transcendental experience is useful for a theological aesthetics of liberation that considers the experience of liberation as a concrete expression of transcendental experience.

Secondly, Rahner's notion of the supernatural existential is helpful for a theological aesthetics of liberation. According to Rahner, God communicates God's self in the mode of God's offer, which in turn is the ground for the human response to God's offer. God communicates God's self to human beings in and through categorical and historical reality. In this sense, the history of revelation and salvation takes place not only when human beings interpret themselves in an explicitly religious way. The history of revelation and salvation takes place also in and through the "secular" history of human self-interpretation. Rahner's notion of the supernatural existential is helpful for a theological aesthetics of liberation that interprets the historical process of liberation of the poor as a concrete expression of the event of God's self-communication to human beings.

Thirdly, Rahner's theological aesthetics is helpful for a theological aesthetics of liberation. For Rahner, art is both an expression and a mediation of transcendental experience, and therefore, it is both an expression and a mediation of God's self-communication to human beings. Rahner's theology of art is useful for a theological aesthetics of liberation that understands art as an expression and a mediation of liberation. Furthermore, Rahner pays attention to the relationship between the object and the subject in an aesthetic experience. In this sense, Rahner is useful for a theological aesthetic of liberation that considers a work of art not as an isolated object, but in its relationship with the artist and the recipient.

Fourthly, Rahner's theology is useful for a theological aesthetics of liberation because he pays attention to the historical and social dimensions of theological reality. Regarding the historical dimension, the history of individuals and of societies is where the event of God's self-communication to human beings takes place. Regarding the social dimension, the subject of transcendental experience is not only the individual person, but also subjects that form social units. Furthermore, for Rahner, love of neighbor and socio-political responsibility are intrinsically related. Moreover, Rahner considers the social dimension of Jesus' ministry and death. Therefore, Rahner's theology is useful for a theological aesthetics of liberation that pays attention to the historical and socio-political dimensions of theological reality.

Finally, the problem with Rahner's theology comes from its lack of specificity vis-à-vis the subject of transcendental experience. If Rahner's theology is to be relevant in the realm of socio-political change, it is necessary to develop a theology that considers the concrete reality of the transcendental subject. In this sense, liberation theology is a theology that adopts Rahner's method in its own original way, and at the same time goes beyond Rahner inasmuch as, for liberation theology, the subject of transcendental experience is not man in general, but human beings who suffer from material poverty and social exclusion. In this sense, the theological aesthetics of liberation that I will develop in the following chapters is a theology that adopts Rahner's method, but at the same time goes beyond Rahner.

At the end of my analysis of von Balthasar's theology, I also claimed that my approach to a theological aesthetics of liberation will go beyond von Balthasar. However, "going beyond Balthasar" and "going beyond Rahner" do not have the same meaning here. Going beyond Balthasar means adopting a non-Balthasarian approach to theological aesthetics for his thought is unhelpful and inadequate for a theological aesthetics that understands God as the liberator of the poor. Going beyond Rahner, on the other hand, means that, while recognizing the limits of his theology, we build upon his theological findings in aesthetics, for his intuitions and ideas have the potential for the development of a theological aesthetics that supports the liberation of social outcasts.

Chapter 3

A Theological Aesthetics of Liberation, Part One

A Pneumatology of Liberation through Art

In this chapter and the next I will develop what might be called a "theological aesthetics of liberation," which makes a mutual and critical correlation between liberation theology and theological aesthetics. The way I understand a theological aesthetics of liberation is different from the way Roberto Goizueta understands it. To be sure, he has published some articles in which he uses the term "theological aesthetics of liberation."[1] His understanding of the term is related to what he calls "U.S. Latino theology," which is a theology from the perspective of the reality of the Latin American people in the United States of America. Explaining all the tenets and implications of such theology is beyond the limits of my research. What concerns us here is to know why Goizueta thinks that a U.S. Latino theology is a theological aesthetics of liberation.

Goizueta argues that a U.S. Latino theology is an "attempt to reconcile liberation theology with theological aesthetics."[2] (I should immediately acknowledge that such an attempt sounds similar to what I am attempting to do in this work. However, it will become apparent that Goizueta's approach is different from mine.) On the one hand, according to Goizueta, a central

---

1. The subtitle of Goizueta's *Christ Our Companion* is precisely *Towards a Theological Aesthetics of Liberation*. See Goizueta, *Christ Our Companion*, 116, 126, 146, 148, 156; Goizueta, "Theo-Drama as Liberative Praxis," 62.

2. Goizueta, *Christ Our Companion*, 148.

dimension for the theological aesthetics of von Balthasar is the priority of God's love, that is, the Johannine assertion that "God loved us first." However, von Balthasar's theological aesthetics runs the danger of supporting a conservative agenda that is inattentive to socio-political realities. Against this danger, a U.S. Latino theology makes the priority of God's love socio-historically concrete by taking into account the preferential option for the poor, which is a central aspect of liberation theology. On the other hand, liberation theology runs the danger of turning Christian faith into pure social activism that is inattentive to instrumentalist presuppositions. Against this danger, a U.S. Latino theology makes the preferential option for the poor theologically concrete by founding such an option on the ground of God's love.[3] "While the normative claims of a theological aesthetics (i.e., the gratuity of God's love) ground theologically the struggle for justice, this latter always historically mediates a Christian theological aesthetics . . . ; the gratuity of God's love can only be experienced in and through the struggle for justice—even if that justice receives its fullest meaning only in the form of gratuity."[4]

According to Goizueta, von Balthasar insists on taking Jesus' humanity seriously. The Swiss theologian asks, "Why do we take the sacraments (which are human realities) so seriously, while we have so little awareness of the human world of Christ—the human side of his love and his commandment of love, for instance?"[5] Nevertheless, von Balthasar does not outline the implications of taking Jesus' humanity seriously. For Goizueta, "What liberation theologians [and U.S. Latino theologians] would add [to von Balthasar's theology] is that, if we are to take Jesus' humanity as seriously as [von] Balthasar demands, the commandment of love can neither remain abstract nor be reduced to individual relationships but must be rooted in a preferential option for the poor, a solidarity with the poor."[6] Goizueta finds this christological insight in popular religion. Reflecting on the religious practices of the Latin American people in the United States, such as the celebration of Good Friday, Goizueta comes to the conclusion that Jesus is our companion in our suffering, and that we are called to accompany Jesus in his suffering.[7] This relationship of mutual accompaniment is a necessary condition of solidarity with the poor.[8] Therefore, "the lived

3. Ibid., x, 126, 148.
4. Ibid., 152.
5. Balthasar, *Prayer*, 172; quoted in Goizueta, *Christ Our Companion*, 107.
6. Goizueta, *Christ Our Companion*, 107.
7. See Goizueta, *Caminemos con Jesús*, 32–36, 67–69.
8. See ibid., 206–10.

faith of Latino/a Catholics brings to bear a social perspective missing—or at least underplayed—in [von] Balthasar's theological aesthetics, a lacuna that undermines the Swiss theologian's own attempt to take Jesus' humanity seriously . . . The specificity of his humanity prevents the symbol of Christ . . . from becoming decontextualized, spiritualized, and thus reduced to a mere abstraction incapable of generating resistance in the world and infinitely manipulable in the service of political power and economic gain."[9]

Accordingly, Goizueta thinks that a U.S. Latino theology is a theological aesthetics of liberation because it reconciles theological aesthetics with liberation theology. On the one hand, U.S. Latino theology is a theological aesthetics because it incorporates von Balthasar's theology, especially the idea of the priority of God's love. On the other hand, a U.S. Latino theology is along the lines of liberation theology because it includes some of its essential components such as the preferential option for the poor.

Although Goizueta's understanding of a theological aesthetics of liberation is valuable and legitimate, I suggest three critiques of his theology. First, his understanding of theological aesthetics is too limited to the von Balthasarian approach. This narrow view of theological aesthetics raises in turn two problems. First, Goizueta ignores other legitimate ways of doing theological aesthetics that are also promising—and probably more appropriate—for the development of a theological aesthetics of liberation. And second, Goizueta overlooks some aspects in von Balthasar's theology that puts him very much at odds with liberation theology, for instance, the beautification or glorification of suffering in itself, and the almost total lack of social concern for the poor.

My second critique of Goizueta's theology is that his appreciation of the religious practices of the Latin American people in the United States is generally uncritical. He seldom formulates critical remarks about their religiosity. He almost seems to ignore that popular religion is also susceptible to manipulation.[10] There is no doubt that popular religion can strengthen

---

9. Goizueta, *Christ Our Companion*, 127.

10. Goizueta admits that popular religion is "susceptible to distortion," for example in the devotion to Mary; but as soon as he admits such a danger, Goizueta steps back and defends popular religion by saying that beneath the superficial appearance of distortion, there is more fundamentally a relationship of interdependence between the faithful and Mary. See Goizueta, *Caminemos con Jesús*, 118. Likewise, Goizueta observes that, in many bloody images of Jesus that are venerated in popular religion, "this Jesus seems somehow gruesome, exaggerated, medieval, even psychologically unhealthy in his suffering." However, Goizueta is prompt to defend popular religion: "If this Jesus bleeds, it is not to sanctify suffering but to sanctify the flesh; and to sanctify the flesh is to see in it a sacrament, or symbol, of the God of Jesus Christ" (ibid., 69).

cultural identity, and therefore, it can be a source of cultural resistance.[11] However, popular religion can also lead to different kinds of spiritualism that are socio-politically apathetic. Therefore, the connection between beauty and justice via popular religion is not as straightforward as Goizueta seems to suggest.

My final critique of Goizueta's theology is that both a theology and a praxis of accompaniment is not sufficient for the liberation of the poor. Indeed, the idea that Jesus is our companion in our suffering, and that we are called to accompany Jesus in his agony, is consoling. It can be an invitation to be with the poor in their suffering, and to allow the poor to be with us. This mutual accompaniment is necessary for the liberation of the poor, but is not enough. Those who engage in a praxis of accompaniment run the danger of remaining there at the level of being with one another, and of never taking the step of a praxis of liberation, which includes, for instance, a praxis of protest and of getting involved in politics in order to fight against social injustice.[12] We will study Edward Schillebeeckx's theology in the next chapter, but it is opportune to quote him here: "People began to put the emphasis on a God who shares in suffering, a God who endures suffering along with the poor and oppressed. That may be true, and I too shall lay stress on it, but it is not enough: it does not make clear *to what extent*, *how* and above all *whether* God is still a redeeming and liberating God. A God who only shares our suffering leaves the last and definitive word to evil and suffering."[13]

Therefore, in spite of the fact that I also intend to establish a "reconciliation"—using Goizueta's word, although I prefer the term "correlation"—between theological aesthetics and liberation theology, as Goizueta claims to do, my approach to a theological aesthetics of liberation differs from his in two main areas. First, my notion of theological aesthetics is not restricted to the von Balthasarian understanding of the term. Second, the *locus theologicus* of my theological reflection is not the experience of popular religiosity, but the experience of art.

---

11. See ibid., 102.

12. A praxis of accompaniment sometimes finds theological support in von Balthasar's idea of Jesus descending into hell to be in solidarity with the dead. However, Rahner is very critical of von Balthasar on this point. Rahner says, "To use somewhat primitive terms, there is no point in my getting out of my muck and filth and despair if—to put it crudely—God is just as mucky" (Rahner, *Karl Rahner im Gespräch* II, 245; quoted in Vorgrimler, *Understanding Karl Rahner*, 125). Cf. Rahner, *Karl Rahner in Dialogue*, 127.

13. Schillebeeckx, *Church*, 85.

My next step will be to develop my understanding of a theological aesthetics of liberation. In this chapter I will correlate a pneumatology of liberation—that we studied in chapter 1—with a theology of art—following the model of Rahner's theological aesthetics that we studied in chapter 2. In the next chapter I will correlate a Christology of liberation—that we also studied in chapter 1—with a theology of art. Both chapters should be seen together as part of one hermeneutical circle. However, we will move from pneumatology to Christology. The reason for starting with pneumatology—instead of Christology—is twofold. First, the Holy Spirit has been often forgotten or not sufficiently highlighted in theological aesthetics. For instance, according to Sherry, in von Balthasar's theological aesthetics, "The Holy Spirit seems to have almost dropped out of the picture."[14] In fact, "von Balthasar's *Glory of the Lord* is centred round the idea that God's glory is manifested in the self-emptying of the Son, and [he] discusses the role of the Holy Spirit only as subsidiary theme."[15] Likewise, de Gruchy opines that the role of the Holy Spirit in von Balthasar's theology is not as explicit as one might expect. For instance, von Balthasar fails to draw attention to the presence and the work of the Holy Spirit in creation and in artistic creativity.[16] Second, the work of the Holy Spirit is of great importance for a theological aesthetics that is truly concerned about the liberating action of God in history, for it is precisely through the power of his Spirit that God is working in the world today. Therefore, for the kind of theological aesthetics of liberation that I intend to develop here, the move from pneumatology to Christology seems more appropriate. This progression actually follows the lines of Rahner's theology. As O'Donovan says, "If pneumatology, Christology, and theology are inseparable, they are nevertheless also necessarily distinguishable, and Rahner came to speak of a 'universal pneumatology' that might precede Christology in the full development of a historical theology. The classical approach has, of course, discussed Christ before the Spirit, but from the perspective of a world-historical consciousness it is promising to consider the world's search for communion with God initiated through the Spirit and coming only gradually to acknowledge the historical ground of its hope in the figure of Jesus."[17]

Therefore, this chapter will establish a connection between a pneumatology of liberation and a theology of art. This will be a theology "from below," in the sense that it will start from the experience of art in order to

---

14. Sherry, *Spirit and Beauty*, 75.
15. Ibid., 87.
16. Gruchy, *Christianity, Art and Transformation*, 127.
17. O'Donovan, "Journey into Time," 629–30.

A Theological Aesthetics of Liberation, Part One 119

reflect, at a second stage, on the theological dimension of such an experience. Thus, this theology follows the methods of Rahner and of liberation theology. It follows the transcendental method of Rahner inasmuch as it starts from what Rahner calls the transcendental experience in and through art. However, as we know, for liberation theology, the experience of liberation is a concrete form of transcendental experience. Therefore, this theology follows the method of liberation theology because it starts from the experience of liberation in and through art. Accordingly, we will explore two double questions. First, is art liberating, and how is it liberating? The study of this question will be taken up in the first part of this chapter. Based on this analysis of the liberating power of art, we will ask secondly and theologically, is God involved in the liberating experience of art, and if so, how is God involved? This second question will occupy the second part of this chapter. To explore this material, I will draw upon the ideas of various theologians. The result of this exploration might be called a *pneumatology of liberation through art*, insofar as it understands the Spirit of God as liberator through the experience of art.

Before we move to the first section, it is important to recall that, following Tracy's threefold classification of theological disciplines, I previously suggested that the theological aesthetics of liberation that I intend to develop here falls under the category of practical theology. According to Tracy, "praxis" and "transformation" are two concepts that should be present in any practical theology that deserves such a name.[18] Therefore, at the end of the chapter, we should see if "praxis" and "transformation" are essential concepts that follow from this theological aesthetics of liberation, if indeed it is to be called "practical theology."

ART AND TRANSFORMATION

In this section I explore two questions, namely, "What is art?" and "What is the connection between art and liberation?" To answer these two questions, I explain seven interrelated aspects of art. Firstly, I consider art as part of a broader phenomenon called aesthetics, and the danger of aestheticism. Secondly, I indicate the scope of the realm of art, and four elements involved in an artistic phenomenon. Thirdly, I present an understanding of art as both praxis and poiesis. Fourthly, I analyze the capacity of art to present a world. Fifthly, I describe the power of art to disclose truth. Sixthly, I study some aspects of the relationship between the artist and the work of art, including

---

18. See Tracy, *Analogical Imagination*, 54–59.

imagination. Finally, I explicate some dimensions of the relationship between the recipient and the work of art, including transformation.

Art, Aesthetics, and Aestheticism

To define art it is probably appropriate to begin with a broader subject than art itself, namely, aesthetics. Here we should distinguish between aesthetics as an intellectual discipline, and aesthetics as a phenomenon that aesthetics (as an intellectual discipline) studies. Alexander Baumgarten (1714–1762) is probably the first philosopher who uses the term "aesthetics"[19] to name an intellectual discipline. For Baumgarten, the goal of aesthetics is to study the role of perception in the process of knowledge. However, later on, aesthetics becomes a philosophy of art and beauty.[20] This notion of aesthetics—namely, "philosophical reflection on the nature of art and beauty and of the response to both"[21]—is the understanding that remains current until today. In this general understanding of aesthetics, we can see the distinction made above: aesthetics as an intellectual discipline and aesthetics as a phenomenon that includes different aspects, such as art, beauty, and perception.[22]

Brown offers a broad definition of aesthetics that is helpful for our present study: "Aesthetics should perhaps be nothing less than basic theoretical reflection regarding all aesthetic phenomena, including their modes of significant interrelation with, and mediation of, what is not inherently aesthetic: abstract ideas, useful objects, moral convictions, class conflicts, religious doctrines, and so forth."[23] In this definition, Brown is making a critique of two concepts of aesthetics, namely, a purist interpretation of

---

19. The word "aesthetics" comes from the Greek $\alpha\iota\sigma\theta\eta\alpha\iota\varsigma$, meaning "perception by the senses."

20. For an explanation of the development of aesthetics as a philosophical discipline, see Viladesau, *Theological Aesthetics*, 6–11; Gruchy, *Christianity, Art and Transformation*, 55–61; Farley, *Faith and Beauty*, x n. 2.

21. Brown, *Religious Aesthetics*, 21.

22. Farley makes a distinction between "aesthetic" and "aesthetics": "'Aesthetic' refers to an aspect of human experience evoked by an immediate relation to what is beautiful . . . 'Aesthetics' refers to a branch of philosophy or art criticism whose task is to understand the unity and features of works of art and the experience of art" (Farley, *Faith and Beauty*, 117). The problem with Farley's distinction is that he reduces the "aesthetic" to an experience of beauty (as we will see later, the aesthetic is not only the experience of beauty), and that he reduces "aesthetics" to a philosophy of art (as we will see later, "aesthetics" is not only the study of the artistic phenomenon). But still, Farley is right to distinguish aesthetics as an intellectual discipline from aesthetics—or the aesthetic—as experienceable phenomena.

23. Brown, *Religious Aesthetics*, 22.

A Theological Aesthetics of Liberation, Part One 121

aesthetics, and a reduction of aesthetics to a philosophy of art.[24] We will analyze these two concepts in the following paragraphs.

First, Brown is against a purist interpretation of aesthetics. By "purist" he means those theories that consider an aesthetic event "as something essentially self-contained rather than as interactive. At their most extreme, they assume or claim that whatever is aesthetic is by definition or by nature autonomous and unalloyed: neither religious, cognitive, moral, practical, nor political."[25] Against this purist idea of aesthetics, Brown argues that aesthetics does not refer to "some ideal, uniform, and completely autonomous realm or entity."[26] The area of aesthetics is rather "elastic." There is "flexibility and permeability" in the boundaries that separate what is aesthetic from what is not aesthetic.[27] "The very distinction between aesthetic and non-aesthetic is relative; it marks a continuum." At one pole of the continuum are "qualities of form, process, sense, and imagination that we can notice and appreciate almost entirely in and for themselves, apart from any logical, cognitive, semantic, practical, ethical, or religious considerations. Such qualities and experiences can be regarded as aesthetic 'pure and simple.'" We find such qualities, for instance, in the beauty of a snowflake's geometry. At the other pole of the continuum are "expressions and objects that are valued almost exclusively for logical, utilitarian, moral, religious, or cognitive reasons and that therefore are minimally aesthetic." In between these two poles are "most of the things we think of as being meaningful or moving artistically and aesthetically."[28] The more we focus on the "aesthetic qualities" of an object or an event, the more we are in the "aesthetic milieu."[29] On the contrary, the more we focus on the non-aesthetic features of an object, the more we move away from the aesthetic realm. According to Brown, aesthetic objects that include non-aesthetic elements are not impure, dependent, or deficient, as a purist aesthetician would judge. Rather, these aesthetics objects are "integral," for "they integrate simpler kinds of aesthetic

---

24. Ibid., 5.

25. Ibid., 6. See Brown, *Good Taste, Bad Taste*, 79–86.

26. Brown, *Religious Aesthetics*, 11–12.

27. Ibid., 11, 23.

28. Ibid., 11–12. Brown gives the example of the *Oresteia*: "Were this trilogy somehow deprived of all moral, political, psychological, or religious seriousness, it would retain little of the aesthetic grandeur and power we now ascribe to it . . . [However,] we know that the *Oresteia* is significantly aesthetic, because any attempt to translate it into sheerly moral, political, or religious discourse diminishes its import significantly" (ibid., 12).

29. Ibid., 54. For Brown, "aesthetic qualities" have something to do with form; these qualities are perceived in a sensorial way, they are "felt," and they evoke a response. See ibid., 22, 54, 66.

and non-aesthetic perceptions into a more complex gestalt."[30] However, when aesthetic objects integrate what is non-aesthetic—be it historical, social, political, or religious—the non-aesthetic material is transformed into something new.[31]

Therefore, for Brown, aesthetics refers to a distinctive realm, which is not self-contained, but rather related to non-aesthetic fields. This notion of aesthetics is appropriate for the purpose of our study, since we are trying to find some connections between aesthetics, liberation, and theology. Within a purist understanding of aesthetics, these connections would be forbidden, nonsensical, or impossible to find. Brown rightly states, "the true, the good, the beautiful; thought, action, passion; theory, praxis, creativity: if we confine the aesthetic to but one of these venerable categories, it is sure to remain pure. At the same time it is sure to be of limited relevance to religion and theology and, one might add, to the self and the human community."[32]

Second, Brown is against a reduction of aesthetics to a philosophy of art. He states, "the artistic and the aesthetic are not coextensive or entirely correlative."[33] In fact, "not everything aesthetic is at all artistic."[34] For instance, a natural sunset is an aesthetic event that is not produced by a human person. Indeed, the aesthetic phenomenon extends "to two kinds of entities. First, there are objects that are made, displayed, or presented with the primary purpose of evoking aesthetic response. Second, there are those objects that one at least temporarily considers specifically with respect to their capacity to evoke such a response, even though such a capacity is unintentional, incidental, or of secondary interest."[35] Since aesthetics includes not only objects and events that are intentionally aesthetic—such as a work of art—but also objects and events that are unintentionally aesthetic—such as a sunset—we can assert that the area of aesthetics is broader than the field of art. Thus, it is a mistake to reduce aesthetics to a philosophy of art.

30. Ibid., 78.

31. Ibid., 75–76.

32. Ibid., 77. We found this limitation of aesthetics to the realm of beauty in von Balthasar's theological trilogy, who associates the beautiful with theological aesthetics, the good with theological dramatics, and the true with theological logical theory. Thus, aesthetics has to do with beauty, but not with goodness and truth. Likewise, we find this reduction of aesthetics to the realm of beauty in Goizueta, who says, "If Tridentine Western theology stressed the fact that God is known in the form of the True (Doctrine), and liberation theology that God is known in the form of the Good (Justice), U.S. Hispanic theology stresses the fact that God is known in the form of the Beautiful" (Goizueta, *Caminemos con Jesús*, 106).

33. Brown, *Religious Aesthetics*, 14.

34. Ibid., 11.

35. Ibid., 55.

While recognizing that aesthetics has a broader reach than art, Brown prefers to focus on artistic phenomena in his study: "Our treatment of aesthetica deals more with art than with other aesthetic phenomena. This is because the different levels of the aesthetic, and the different uses and transformations of the aesthetic in religion, can best be observed through a study of the meaningful making—poiesis—that occurs in art, and through examining what we ourselves make of art in aesthetic experience (aesthesis)."[36] By "different levels of the aesthetic," Brown means "aesthetic objects (aesthetica), aesthetic experience (aesthesis), and aesthetic making (poiesis)."[37] These three levels can be found in an artistic phenomenon, whereas in other aesthetic phenomena, such as aesthetic events in nature, the level of aesthetic making is practically absent. Hence, while I acknowledge that aesthetics is not only about art, I will also focus my study on the artistic phenomenon because the dimension of aesthetic making is important for a theological aesthetics of liberation. Besides, although it is true that aesthetics should not be reduced to a philosophy of art, Brown declares, "aesthetics without art would be like astronomy without stars—not impossible, but altogether less interesting."[38]

As a consequence of the critique of a purist interpretation of aesthetics, our understanding of art here—as a specific area of aesthetics—is opposed to a purist notion of art that understands the artistic phenomenon as an autonomous and self-contained sphere separated from any moral, social, political, and religious reality. Indeed, according to Brown, a purist understanding of aesthetics becomes aestheticism, "which is the intense appreciation and high appraisal of only those elements and kinds of art that have little or nothing directly to do with religious and moral values. Thus an aesthete can be so devoted to 'art for art's sake' that he or she simply cannot apperceive the moral and spiritual intensity of [artistic] works."[39] Contrary to a purist notion of art, here we understand art as a field with its own specificity, but in relationship with non-artistic fields, such as social, political,

36. Ibid., 14.
37. Ibid., 6.
38. Ibid., 22.
39. Ibid., 152. According to Begbie, Immanuel Kant's aesthetic ideas created or bolstered a purist understanding of both aesthetics and art. "Kant's aesthetics all too easily generates a divorce of art from action. His concept of 'disinterestedness' bears this out." Likewise, "Kant's aesthetics quickly spawned the idea of 'art for art's sake'—the view that art is answerable only to itself and must never be judged according to the degree of correspondence it has to phenomena beyond itself, such as a moral order, the artist's intentions, the circumstances of its production, and so on. Considerations of social and psychological context are strictly barred from consideration" (Begbie, *Voicing Creation's Praise*, 192, 194).

and religious realities. As Begbie says, "we cannot wrap art up in a cocoon and protect it from judgements which move beyond the purely aesthetic. If a work of art is capable of disturbing and unsettling us, illuminating our daily lives, changing our perception of the world, provoking us into a different course of action, then moral appraisal [social, political, and religious appraisals, as well] cannot be discounted."[40]

The notion of art in relationship with social, political, and religious realities does not mean that art should lose its specificity in its relationship with those realities. As Begbie claims, art can illuminate reality without converting into something other than art.[41] In fact, the danger of becoming something other than art—for instance, the danger of becoming mere political propaganda—is always present in art. As de Gruchy warns us, "the way in which fascist and communist ideologies sought to manipulate art should make us wary of control by those in positions of power." In fact, if art is to fulfill its proper social function, then the idea of the autonomy, disinterestedness, and uselessness of art has some validity and meaning, that is, it "prevents art from being ideologically abused."[42] Therefore, we can identify two dangers in the field of art. On the one hand, art can be understood as something totally isolated from non-artistic realities, such as social, political, and religious issues. On the other hand, art can be totally absorbed and manipulated by non-artistic realities to the point that it loses its distinctiveness. A challenge for a kind of art that wants to be socially significant is to hold the tension between these two poles. As Gerardus van der Leeuw says,

> Art cannot get along without life ... The motto l'art pour l'art is valid whenever art must protect itself from subservience to any tyranny which forces its way in from outside. But one cannot say that art must have no "meaning," that a concrete goal in the context of life must remain denied it. On the contrary, art has always been greatest when it has placed itself at the service of a great idea, a great conviction, a great, suprapersonal emotion, assuming that this service is not a slavery but a community of life, an interpenetration of artistic form and the content of life.[43]

For the kind of theological aesthetics of liberation that we are developing here, art embodies this tension of being authentically art, but in relation with non-artistic fields, such as social, political, and religious realities.

---

40. Begbie, *Voicing Creation's Praise*, 219.
41. Ibid., 216.
42. Gruchy, *Christianity, Art and Transformation*, 58; see ibid., 197–98.
43. Leeuw, *Sacred and Profane Beauty*, 275.

The Scope and Four Elements of Art

What is art? When we use the word "art," what kind of art are we speaking about? As we try to answer this question, we face the difficulty that Edward Farley expresses as follows:

> We confront a certain ambiguity in the term, "the arts." In the texts of Western history, art (*techné, ars*) has had a variety of meanings: skilled activity, (for example, the art of living), anything requiring teaching and learning, a select group of highly valued activities (music, poetry), the seven "liberal arts" of the Middle Ages. According to Paul O. Kristeller, the "modern system of the arts" (painting, sculpture, architecture, music and poetry) arose in the eighteenth century. With this nucleus, plus certain satellite arts of dance, theatre and engraving came the notion of "high arts," and thus the hierarchy of *the* arts in contrast to crafts, folk arts and technology. Kristeller, Ortega y Gasset and others have also traced the decline of the concept of "high arts" in the twentieth century in which trends within the old nucleus group, plus the emergence of new arts, blurred the boundary between "high arts" and the arts of popular culture. The point here is that the very concept of *the* arts is historically variably and culturally determined . . . [Today] we face a new problem—the status of the "arts" of a consumer society and its mass culture. Power, hierarchy, elitism and patronage have always had a function in the arts of both the East and West, but marketing and consumer societies of the postmodern West seem to have produced a new phenomenon. Aggressively marketed music, poster art, movies, television and certain kind of novel are neither "high arts" nor "folk arts" in the sense of individually produced and locally oriented, craft-like works.[44]

Sherry points out that "theological aesthetics tends to draw its examples from the fine arts, especially music, painting, sculpture, and literature . . . One notices that some arts get short shrift from writers on theological aesthetics, for example architecture . . . The cinema, too, is relatively neglected, and cookery almost wholly so."[45] In fact, those who work on the area of theological aesthetics have the danger of falling into the trap of an aesthetic elitism. "What is truly elitist," Brown suggests, "is to believe that popular arts are not concerned with questions of quality, or that they are strictly for the 'masses,' or that they must always be mere kitsch. It is also elitist to think

---

44. Farley, *Faith and Beauty*, 111.
45. Sherry, *Spirit and Beauty*, 25–26.

that 'elite' and formal arts are always cheapened whenever they become popular and accessible."[46] Aesthetic elitism contains a sort of "intolerance." Brown says, "intolerance is readily found within communities of taste associated with the so-called elite arts. A large number of connoisseurs and professionals within all these arts assume that . . . much of what transpires at a folk level, and all of what transpires at the level of popular and mass culture, is either abominable or completely trivial."[47]

Against an elitist and "intolerant" notion of art, some authors prefer not to draw a rigid separation between high arts and other kinds of art. For instance, in his study, Farley declares that his "inclination is not to permit the old nucleus of high arts to set the question of arts in the life of faith."[48] Similarly, de Gruchy claims that "when we speak of 'the arts' in English we usually mean 'fine arts,' that is 'works of art' which meet certain aesthetic criteria and in doing so can be distinguished from craft and 'popular art.' But the boundaries between 'fine' and 'popular art,' or between 'art' and 'craft,' are fluid."[49] I maintain the same position here. As I talk about art in this chapter, I will try to keep a general approach that may refer to high arts, popular arts, and crafts.

Yet so far we have not answered the question "what is art?" I endorse Brown who broadly defines art as "any and all of the creative skills, informed practices, and primary products manifest in the making of publicly recognizable aesthetica."[50] In other words, a work of art is "anything that is at least partially artificial in origin, that reflects creativity, skill, or know-how, and that in large measure is, or could be, something appreciated by a public attentive to aesthetic factors such as form and style, and responsive to aesthetic effects such as those we regard as intrinsically interesting, expressive, or beautiful."[51]

Therefore, an artistic phenomenon involves several elements. In Brown's definition of art, we can identify three interrelated elements: the artistic object or event (the "primary products" in Brown's definition), the artist (who has "creative skills" and "informed practices"), and the recipient (i.e., the "public" who "recognizes," "appreciates," and "responds" to the aesthetic qualities of an artistic object or event). As García-Rivera says, "the aesthetic experience consists of the intrinsic triad of artist, work of art, and

---

46. Brown, *Good Taste, Bad Taste*, 158.
47. Brown, *Religious Aesthetics*, 153–54.
48. Farley, *Faith and Beauty*, 111.
49. Gruchy, *Christianity, Art and Transformation*, 3.
50. Brown, *Religious Aesthetics*, 86.
51. Ibid., 88.

audience."[52] Besides these three elements, Tracy indicates a fourth element, that is, the world that a work of art presents. He writes, there are "four elements basic to the total situation of any work of art: the artist who creates the work . . . ; the work itself . . . ; the world the work creates or reveals . . . ; and the audience the work affects."[53] In the present study, we will pay attention to these four elements of art.

Therefore, the phenomenon of art includes not only the artistic "object" itself (for instance, a painting or a piano sonata), but also the human "subjects" involved in the experience of art, namely, the artist and the recipient. Thus, art includes the relationships between the artist and the work of art (in the process of producing an artistic object), between the recipient and the work of art (in the process of experiencing an artistic object), and between the artist and the recipient through the mediation of a work of art. By this dynamic and relational definition of art, I distance myself from a static definition of art that focuses only on the artistic object. Viladesau rightly claims, "the theological-aesthetic appreciation of a work of art involves a complex hermeneutical *interaction* among the artist, the work, and the viewer of hearer . . . These elements may be present to varying degrees and may *interact* in different ways."[54] The word "interaction" seems appropriate here, for art is indeed an inter-action, that is, an "action" between the artist, the work of art, and the recipient. "What kind of action is it?" is the question that we will explore in the following section.

Art, Praxis, and Poiesis

In this section, I argue that art is action. If we return to Brown's definition of art as "any and all of the creative skills, informed *practices*, and primary products manifest in the making of publicly recognizable aesthetica,"[55] we

---

52. García-Rivera, *Community of the Beautiful*, 164. In his study, Wolterstorff mentions another element that is present in some artistic phenomena, namely, the performer. Regarding some works of art, he writes, there are "three kinds of practices: the practice of making such works, the practice of performing or presenting such works, and the practice of public engagement with such works" (Wolterstorff, *Art Rethought*, 314). We find this element of the performer or interpreter, for instance, in music and theatre. The musician or singer interprets a song created by a composer. Or a stage actor performs a piece written by a playwright. I will not analyze this element of the performer as the present study focuses mainly on painting, which is a type of art that generally does not include a performer.

53. Tracy, *Analogical Imagination*, 113.

54. Viladesau, *Theological Aesthetics*, 147 (emphasis mine).

55. Brown, *Religious Aesthetics*, 86 (emphasis mine).

find that for Brown as well art is a kind of action or practice. However, the question remains, what kind of action is art? As we try to respond this question, we have to answer the question, whose action is art? Is it the action of the artist or the action of the recipient? Anticipating the answer, I suggest that art is the action of both, the artist and the recipient. The actions of the artist and the recipient are different, but they are interrelated. To explain why this is so, I will present two different theories on the issue of art as action, one given by Roberto Goizueta and the other by Nicholas Wolterstorff.

Goizueta argues for an aesthetic notion of praxis, as distinguished from and opposed to an instrumental notion of praxis. To explain and support this differentiation, Goizueta refers to Aristotle's distinction between praxis and poiesis. According to Goizueta, Aristotle defines praxis on the one hand as "*all human activity whose end is internal rather than external to itself*, i.e., all human activity which is *an end in itself*." On the other hand, Aristotle describe poiesis as a "human action whose end is *external* to itself." Human production is an example of poiesis: "When we produce, or make something, the activity of producing or making has no intrinsic value or end. The end of production is not the action itself, but the object (product) which results from the action, *after* the action is already completed. Whereas praxis is its own reward, the reward of poiesis is in its own results, what is left over *after* the activity of production is completed."[56]

To illustrate the difference between praxis and poiesis, Goizueta refers to the metaphor of playing and making a musical instrument. On the one hand, playing a musical instrument is an example of praxis. When someone plays an instrument, the enjoyment is in the activity itself. The goal of playing a musical instrument is achieved in the act of performing. On the other hand, making a musical instrument is a kind of poiesis. The enjoyment of someone who makes an instrument does not come from the activity itself—i.e., the physical work involved in making the musical instrument—but from the result of such work—i.e., the musical instrument. The person who makes an instrument "enjoys" only once he or she has finished the act of producing it. Therefore, the goal of making a musical instrument is not the activity itself, but the final product. Likewise, the difference between praxis and poiesis is analogous to that between "making a home" and "making a house." "The value of the former resides in the activity itself. The end of home life is nothing other than the family's enjoyment of that life itself . . . The value of constructing a house, however, resides in the *product* of the activity. The end of the process of making a house is not the activity of

---

56. Goizueta, *Caminemos con Jesús*, 82–83.

construction itself, but the house that is left over *after* we have *finished* the activity."⁵⁷

If poiesis is valuable as long as it is useful for something, the essence of praxis is in its uselessness.⁵⁸ In this sense, Goizueta agrees with Aristotle, who says, "life is action [praxis] and not production [poiesis]."⁵⁹ Goizueta claims that life is "an absolute value in itself—regardless of its productivity, usefulness, or practicality."⁶⁰ Therefore, "While poiesis, or production, is a necessary aspect of human life, it does not *define* human action . . . What *defines* human action as such is praxis."⁶¹

However, according to Goizueta, most Western people today do not understand "praxis" in the way that Aristotle understood it. The notion of praxis or human action that has mostly functioned in Western society since Modernity is that of poiesis. That is to say, today praxis or human action is "the action of an *autonomous* subject *upon* his or her external environment . . . Human action, or praxis, is thereby reduced to *technique*, or 'practicality': the value of human action, or life, is predicated upon its practicality, or usefulness . . . Human action is thus reduced to the autonomous subject's physical, technical manipulation of the external world." Other human beings are also part of the external world upon which the modern subject acts. Therefore, "Other subjects, or persons, are themselves but passive, inert objects to be acted *upon* . . . Thus, a person's interaction with another person is not substantially different from his or her 'interaction' with a computer, a hammer, a pencil, or an automobile."⁶²

This modern notion of praxis or human action, Goizueta suggests, is present in Karl Marx, who "was himself a product of a modern, post-Enlightenment, Western society."⁶³ Goizueta's critique of Marx is ambivalent. On the one hand, Goizueta claims that Marx identifies praxis or human action with production.⁶⁴ For Marx, "what defines human action as human is precisely its productive capacity, the human ability to transform environment. Whether what one is transforming is raw wood, in order to make a house, or social structures, in order to make a 'just society,' or one's very 'self,' in order to make a 'better person,' what defines human life and action

57. Ibid., 83.
58. Ibid., 85.
59. Aristotle, *Politics* 1.4.1254; quoted in Goizueta, *Caminemos con Jesús*, 84.
60. Goizueta, *Caminemos con Jesús*, 84.
61. Ibid., 105.
62. Ibid., 80.
63. Ibid., 85.
64. Ibid., 82.

is its usefulness in achieving the desired result."[65] On the other hand, Goizueta claims that there is a contradiction and ambiguity in Marx's notion of human action. Sometimes Marx defines life as production—as was described above—but other times he seems to define human life as intrinsically valuable. Hence, for Marx, "is praxis intrinsically valuable, or is it valuable only insofar as it is 'useful'? Is human action a value in and of itself, or is it valuable only insofar as it contributes to or produces some valuable *result*?"[66]

According to Goizueta, "liberation theologians have inherited the ambiguity latent in Marx's notion of praxis."[67] Their characterization of praxis or human action as transformative and liberating shows the influence of Marx on their thought. Thus, with regard to liberation theology, Goizueta asks, "Is liberation the *result* of praxis, that is, the 'product' of our struggle to transform society? Or, is liberation a *concomitant*, or *by*product, of praxis— i.e., the change that takes place in us *as* we engage in that struggle? Do we become liberated only *after* and *as a result* of our social action, or do we become liberated *in the course* of our action? Is praxis, or human action its own end and, thus valuable in and of itself, or is praxis valuable only insofar as it leads to a liberated society?"[68] For Goizueta, this notion of human action as productive, useful, and transformative, is an *instrumental* notion of praxis that reduces human life to an instrument for an external goal, i.e., a goal that is not life itself. Goizueta finds the risk of this instrumental notion of praxis in Marx,[69] and therefore in liberation theology as well: "Instrumental notions of social transformation tend implicitly to regard 'the poor,' 'social structures,' and 'society' as abstract categories and objects which can be manipulated—by the social reformer, bureaucrat, or revolutionary—to achieve the desired result of 'liberation.' . . . Human life then is no longer its own end; now it becomes but a means to another end, e.g., the achievement of a more just society."[70]

To avoid the danger of an instrumental notion of praxis, Goizueta suggests a different or alternative notion of praxis, that is, an aesthetic understanding of human action.[71] Whereas an instrumental notion of praxis is similar, equivalent, or analogous to Aristotle's understanding of poiesis, an

65. Ibid., 84.
66. Ibid., 85.
67. Ibid., 86.
68. Ibid., 86–87.
69. See ibid., 86.
70. Ibid., 106–7.
71. Ibid., 89.

A Theological Aesthetics of Liberation, Part One 131

aesthetic notion of praxis is similar, equivalent, or analogous to Aristotle's understanding of praxis. In other words, an instrumental notion of praxis understands human action as an instrument for a goal that is not the praxis itself, whereas an aesthetic notion of praxis comprehends human action as an end in itself.

For Goizueta, celebration and play are paradigms of an aesthetic understanding of human action. When we play or celebrate, we are immersed in the action itself, and the action is an end in itself.[72] Goizueta discovers this aesthetic dimension of praxis in popular religion, especially in the liturgical celebrations of the Latin American people in the United States. "Popular Catholicism is the liturgical celebration of life as an end in itself, life as *praxis*."[73] In liturgical celebrations, such as the procession on Palm Sunday or the way of the cross on Good Friday, the goal of the action is the activity itself.[74] In this sense, "the symbols and the rituals of popular religion are prime examples of the intrinsic value of beauty."[75] According to Goizueta, "when we are in the presence of beauty, we lose our control and are swept up into the experience."[76] Thus, popular religion has an aesthetic character inasmuch as, through its symbols and rituals, it draws us into the liturgical celebration.

Furthermore, an aesthetic notion of praxis includes the dimension of human interaction. For Goizueta, "the aesthetic celebration of life reminds us that the ultimate goal of all human action is nothing other than the active participation in relationships and the enjoyment of those relationships."[77] In this sense, "human intersubjective action is 'beautiful' and, as such, is its own end."[78] Therefore, an aesthetic notion of praxis includes those areas in which the human interactions of the poor mostly occur, such as their domestic lives and their daily struggle to survive. These ordinary actions and interactions in the lives of the poor are the "seedbed" of political action:

> The daily struggle to keep food on the table, to keep the children clothed, to educate them and provide for their safety, to help one's spouse deal with discrimination at work, to put up with that indignity in order to bring home a paycheck, to keep one's patience while one's ill brother or sister is shuttled from

72. Ibid., 94.
73. Ibid., 105.
74. Ibid., 103.
75. Ibid., 102.
76. Ibid., 108.
77. Ibid., 130.
78. Ibid., 131.

one hospital emergency room to another because he or she has no medical insurance—all these common experiences, common forms of praxis, among the poor, are themselves forms of ethical-political praxis. It is here, in these everyday ("private") relationships, that, by continuing to struggle in the face of such dehumanizing conditions, the poor affirm daily the intrinsic value of their lives. It is *that* affirmation that is empowering, liberating, and, thus, the most fundamental form of ("public") resistance to oppression. The seedbed of all ethical-political action is the basic affirmation: I am a person . . . or, more accurately, We are persons . . . We are a people![79]

Thus, Latin American liberation theology highlights the "socio-political dimension of praxis," whereas U.S. Latino theology emphasizes the "racial-cultural dimension of praxis." For Goizueta, "this difference reflects, to some extent, the different socio-historical locations: the overwhelming *economic* poverty experienced by the people of Latin America, and the equally overwhelming sense of *cultural* alienation experienced by Latinos and Latinas in the United States."[80]

However, Goizueta does not simply point out the difference between Latin America liberation theology and U.S. Latino theology. He criticizes Latin American liberation theology for neglecting those aspects of the lives of the poor that are important for U.S. Latino theology, such as popular religion and domestic life. "Whenever the social transformative character of human praxis is considered foundational for theology [as happens in liberation theology], popular religion will tend to be viewed with suspicion, as a form of praxis that, because often explicitly apolitical, cannot contribute to liberation and may, in fact, function as an obstacle to its realization."[81] Likewise, "while liberation theologians have not explicitly subordinated the family to society, implicit in the emphasis on praxis as social transformation is a relative depreciation of praxis as domestic life."[82] However, in his experience of Latino communities in the United States, Goizueta has learnt that it is precisely in those areas "depreciated" and "viewed with suspicion" by Latin American liberation theologians that the praxis of liberation occurs: "In these communities, I have witnessed a type of empowerment and liberation taking place which, at least initially and explicitly, seems to have relatively little connection to any social or political struggles. Indeed, in many cases,

---

79. Ibid., 130.
80. Ibid., 102.
81. Ibid., 101.
82. Ibid., 116.

empowerment and liberation are not explicit goals at all. Seemingly, the only explicit goals are day-to-day survival and, especially, the affirmation of relationships as essential to that survival . . . Central to the struggle for survival and relationships, moreover, is the community's life of faith, which also, at least on the surface, seems little related to social transformation."[83] In other words, it is based on his experience with Latino communities in the United States that Goizueta asserts, "paradoxically, only when human action is not directly used (as poiesis) for ethical-political ends, but is instead affirmed as an end in itself, can praxis, in fact, be empowering and liberating . . . Paradoxically, only by remaining 'apolitical,' that is, only by remaining 'useless,' can aesthetic celebration have ethical-political and economic consequences."[84]

I suggest that Goizueta's aesthetic notion of praxis, as distinct from and opposed to an instrumental notion of praxis, is not totally correct. In my opinion, his aesthetic notion of human action betrays aestheticism, i.e., what we called a "purist" interpretation of aesthetics. Instead of accepting that aesthetics has a socio-political dimension, or that aesthetics has a relationship with social and political realities, Goizueta asserts the "paradox" that praxis has socio-political consequences as long as it remains *purely* aesthetic.

In his thorough analysis of the concept of "praxis," Daniel Pilario also finds this element of "purism" in Goizueta's discourse on praxis. According to Pilario, "the difficulty with Goizueta's paradigm is found in the rigid boundaries he has established between praxis and poiesis . . . Such an interpretation of Aristotle is, at best, debatable or, at worst, unfounded."[85] According to Pilario, the boundaries between praxis and poiesis are not rigid, but rather "fuzzy and blurred."[86] As we already know, for Aristotle, the difference between poiesis and praxis is that, "While making has an end other than itself, good action is itself its end."[87] According to Pilario, Aristotle's example of the flute or harp player and the house-builder (that we mentioned above) "serves Aristotle to forward an assertion central to his ethical theory: that some human actions, like the ethical virtues, political practices . . . can be called *praxis* because, like flute-playing, they are aimed at no other ulterior motives . . . One does not act generously to be praised nor does one

---

83. Ibid., 88.
84. Ibid., 129–30.
85. Pilario, *Back to the Rough Grounds*, 503.
86. Ibid., 15.
87. Aristotle, *Nicomachean Ethics*, 1.1, 1094a1–5; 2.4, 1105a8–b17; 6.4, 1140a1; 6.5, 1140b5–7; 10.6, 1176a36–b7; quoted in Pilario, *Back to the Rough Grounds*, 12.

engage in political exercise to amass fortunes."⁸⁸ However, Pilario continues, "Even as Aristotle affirms that *praxeis* are ends in themselves, he also states, in his discourse on choice and deliberation in *NE* 3.3, that they are done 'for the sake of things other than themselves.' [For instance] he praises political action as great and noble, that is, as *praxis*; yet it is also aimed at other things like power, honor, or happiness of the city—ends which are outside of and different from political *praxis* itself."⁸⁹ Therefore, Aristotle's distinction between praxis and poiesis is not as definitive as Goizueta suggests, but rather has some "incoherence." Thus, "the border once established between the uncontaminated world of disinterested moral praxis and the 'interested-laden' sphere of poietic production is, in fact, not clear-cut but appears to be ambiguous."⁹⁰

For Pilario, a rigid distinction between praxis and poiesis as proposed by Goizueta "cannot realistically account for the complexity, fuzziness and tensions present in all human historical practices . . . Any practice is in fact dual-faced; it is both praxis and poiesis . . . , an end-in-itself and for another purpose."⁹¹ In this sense, Goizueta's interpretation of praxis betrays some kind of "elitism." Pilario observes, "Honoring the poor's vibrant celebrations and warm interpersonal relations as 'authentic praxis' and, at the same time, rejecting as 'instrumentalist' their daily struggle to produce, to earn, to fight for better working conditions, to transform society, amounts to confining them to their miserable conditions . . . For human actions do not merely exist as 'ends-in-themselves'; they are always done for a cause, for a reason or for some 'interest,' one of which is human well-being."⁹²

Therefore, Goizueta's aesthetic notion of praxis is not helpful for the theological aesthetics of liberation that we are developing here. We have to find a different way of understanding art as praxis. This is why now we look at Nicholas Wolterstorff's theory of art. In his book *Art in Action*, Wolterstorff criticizes what we have called a "purist" notion of art. For him, "we all live in the fading glow of that movement which told us to treat the work of art *as* a work of art—to regard it for its own sake and not for the sake of some ulterior end . . . Art, we have been told, is useless."⁹³ Concomitant to this idea of art for art's sake is the assumption that art is mainly for contemplation.

---

88. Pilario, *Back to the Rough Grounds*, 13.
89. Ibid., 13–14.
90. Ibid., 15.
91. Ibid., 505.
92. Ibid., 503.
93. Wolterstorff, *Art in Action*, 3.

> The person who recommends that we focus all our attention on the work itself is not really recommending that we abstract the work entirely from the context of action. Rather he is recommending that we give preferential status to one action—that of *focussing* on the work. He is not recommending that we put the work of art to *no* use. He is recommending that we give preference to the use of serving as object of *contemplation*. That explains why the autonomist movement has provided us not only with analyses of works of art but also with theories of contemplation—disinterested contemplation, aesthetic contemplation, and the like.[94]

According to Wolterstorff, the assumption that art is mainly for contemplation is the result of what he calls the "institution of high art."[95] For Wolterstorff, the "separation of art from life is endemic to our institution of high art." In fact, "to engage in perceptual contemplation one must focus one's attention on the work of art, immerse oneself in it; and that requires disregarding for a time all else that beckons for one's attention. To the one who contemplates, life is a distraction."[96] Therefore, although "our concept of the fine arts is parasitic on the concept of disinterested contemplation,"[97] in reality contemplation of works of high arts has an interest. People contemplate works of art with the purpose of "finding *aesthetic satisfaction* in the contemplating."[98]

> The concept of aesthetic satisfaction first began to receive articulate formulation in eighteenth-century Europe. No doubt before that time people derived aesthetic satisfaction from contemplating works of art and other objects, and no doubt they sometimes contemplated for the purpose of achieving aesthetic satisfaction . . . But in earlier centuries people lacked the conceptual equipment necessary to make clear to themselves that the purpose and function of their contemplation was aesthetic satisfaction. The construction of that equipment seems to have begun in eighteenth-century Europe . . . It was shortly thereafter, at the beginning of the nineteenth century, that our museums began to arise. That was no coincidence. It is only when people are widely interested in practicing contemplation of works of art

---

94. Ibid., 3.

95. Ibid., 11. Wolterstorff also explains the "institution of high art" as the "grand narrative of art." See Wolterstorff, *Art Rethought*, 5–82.

96. Wolterstorff, *Art in Action*, 27.

97. Ibid., 37.

98. Ibid., 33.

for the sake of aesthetic satisfaction that the museum with its horde of works from all times and places, most of them ripped from their original intended uses, becomes a possibility.[99]

The idea that art is exclusively for contemplation is closely related to an elitist notion of art. In many societies, the cultural elite appreciates those works of art that are considered to be exclusively for contemplation, i.e., those kinds of art that are classified as "high art" or "fine arts."[100]

Wolterstorff is against the idea of the institution of high art. We should "repent ourselves of our elitism," Wolterstorff says, "dropping the assumption, so deeply ingrained in us by our institution of high art, that perceptual contemplation . . . is per se the noblest use to which a work of art can be put."[101] We have been bewitched by the institution of high art, but "we must break the spell."[102] The idea that art is exclusively for contemplation is "not universal but idiosyncratic."[103] The assumption that all works of art are made by artists only and primarily to provide aesthetic satisfaction to their recipients is false.[104] "The universality of art corresponds only to a diversity and flux of purposes, not to some pervasive and unique purpose."[105] In fact, there is no such a thing as *the* purpose of art. Rather—and this is one of the main theses of Wolterstoff's book—"works of art are instruments and objects of action—and then, of an enormous diversity of actions."[106] For instance, "works of art are instruments by which we perform such diverse actions as praising our great men and expressing our grief, evoking emotion and communicating knowledge . . . Works of art are accompaniments for such actions as hoeing cotton and rocking infants. Works of art are background for such actions as eating meals and walking through airports."[107]

---

99. Ibid., 33.
100. See ibid., 22, 38.
101. Ibid., 198.
102. Ibid., 11, 24.
103. Ibid., 11.
104. Ibid., 10. Wolterstorff accepts that probably "there is no society totally devoid of satisfaction in contemplation. I think it even unlikely that there is any society in which the intent to produce something satisfying as an object of disinterested contemplation is completely missing." However, the problem lies in the assumption that aesthetic satisfaction is the *primary* intended public use of art. For Wolterstorff, disinterested contemplation is just one among other intended public uses of art (ibid., 38–39).
105. Ibid., 8.
106. Ibid., x.
107. Ibid., 4.

Indeed, Wolterstorff understands "the arts as social practices."[108] A work of art can function, for instance, as a memorial, as a social protest, and as a religious object.[109]

Therefore, Wolterstorff's understanding of art, with which I agree, is appropriate for the theological aesthetics of liberation that we are developing here. Thus, going back to our original question, what kind of praxis is art? now we can answer with Wolterstorff: "works of art are objects on which we perform actions. They are things to which we do things. By using works of art as *objects* of action we generate other actions, for which those works are then the *instruments*."[110] In other words, art is an action in itself, but it can function as an instrument for other actions as well. Using Aristotle's categories, we can respond that art is a human action that is both praxis and poiesis. Art is both the skilled action of an artist—for instance, the action of painting and singing—and the product of the action—for example, a painting and a song. The end of art is in the activity itself, but it can also have a goal that is external to the activity. The purpose of art can be the finding of aesthetic satisfaction in the act of contemplating an artistic object, but it can also have a goal that is external to the artistic event itself, for instance, the liberation of social outcasts.

Art as World-Presentation

We said above that four elements are involved in an artistic phenomenon: the work of art, the world that an artistic work presents, the artist, and the recipient. In this section I will focus on the second element, i.e., the concept of world-presentation in art. However, in talking about art as world-presentation, I am implicitly speaking about the other elements as well, for it is the artist who presents to the recipient a world in and through the work of art. However, for the sake of clarity, we will discuss the elements of the artist and of the recipient in the following sections.

---

108. Wolterstorff, *Art Rethought*, 83.

109. See ibid., 123–254. Instead of a purist understanding of aesthetics, which "tends to think of an experience or object as either aesthetic or non-aesthetic," Brown suggests a "multi-layered" model of perception, in which something is "perceived as" or "seen as" in, through, or in relationship with another perception. For instance, music can be heard *as* truly divine (Brown, *Religious Aesthetics*, 26–27, 31–34). This multi-layered model of perception, I suggest, is present when Wolterstorff comprehends art *as* social practices.

110. Wolterstorff, *Art in Action*, 14.

Some works of art have the capacity of presenting a world. The term that Wolterstorff uses to describe this power of art is "world-projection."[111] An initial way to understand this idea of world-presentation or world-projection is through the notion of fiction. We associate fiction especially with "literary, dramatic, and cinematic arts. But fiction in the arts extends well beyond these. We regularly find fiction in painting and sculpture as well." The word "fiction" seems appropriate, since the world of a work of art is distinct from our real or actual world. Yet, "world-projection is not confined to fictional world-projection."[112] For instance, when a work of art presents historical events, it is not totally a fiction—for it is presenting events that happened in history—but still it presents those events in a new and different way—different from the way a historian or a journalist, for instance, would present historical facts. As Brown says, some works of art incorporate "what is not artistic or aesthetic—be it historical, moral, or religious. This material is then transformed in the aesthetic milieu. It is not annihilated but made new."[113] In this sense, de Gruchy claims, works of art "do not simply mirror reality: they construct reality."[114]

World-presentation in art can be used for different purposes.[115] I will analyze three of these functions: art can illuminate different aspects of our reality, art can project a world as a possibility, and art can work as a dangerous memory. Therefore, firstly, some works of art can present a world that illuminates something about our reality. This function of art, which Wolterstorff calls "illumination," is linked to the fact that art can show something about our actual world.[116] For instance, art can show different dimensions of our interior world, that is, "the world of our most intimate feelings and emotions,"[117] and art can present dimensions of our external world, for instance, social realities. Art can illuminate what is positive, beautiful, and good in our world, and art can also show what is negative, ugly, and evil in our world. Regarding the latter, for instance, art can reveal the emptiness and despair that many people experience today.[118] It can show what is unjust or senseless in our world.[119] As long as art presents what is negative,

---

111. Ibid., 122.
112. Ibid., 124.
113. Brown, *Religious Aesthetics*, 75.
114. Gruchy, *Christianity, Art and Transformation*, 237.
115. See Wolterstorff, *Art in Action*, 144–50.
116. Ibid., 146–47.
117. Austin, *Explorations in Art*, 13.
118. Ibid., 166.
119. Brown, *Religious Aesthetics*, 111.

ugly, and evil in our world, art can work as a protest against those realities. In this sense, de Gruchy remarks, "many so-called anti-social works of art are a form of protest against the ills, the meaninglessness, and the blind hypocrisies of society."[120]

Secondly, some works of art can present a world as a possibility. Art can disclose, using Tracy's expression, "possibilities of authentic life," or "new possibilities for existence."[121] As Wolterstorff says, a work of art can project "a possible, though nonactual state of affairs. The artist presents to us a way things could be, but aren't."[122] In this sense, Begbie asserts, art can be "a protest against things as we find them [in our current world] in the name of some intuition of what they are meant to be or could be."[123] Thus, Brown states, "art has powers that are experienced by the whole self as visionary, revelatory, or prophetic."[124] Indeed, art can be revelatory when it shows dimensions of our current reality that we do not see or we do not want to see. Art can be visionary inasmuch as it presents a world that can be an alternative or a future possibility. Art can be prophetic insofar as it functions as a protest against the current state of affairs.

Finally, some works of art can present a world as a "dangerous memory," using Metz's expression.[125] Certainly, as de Gruchy says, art can help us "to remember what was best in the past."[126] However, art can allow us to recall what was worst too. This power of art that enables us to remember the suffering and the horrors that have happened in human history involves a protest that says, "it should never have happened." Remembering the suffering of the past is not about reopening historical wounds. Rather, it is a warning that it should never happen again. It is a way to prevent similar atrocities in the present and in the future.

120. Gruchy, *Christianity, Art and Transformation*, 197.

121. Tracy, *Blessed Rage for Order*, 207–8.

122. Wolterstorff, *Art in Action*, 131.

123. Begbie, *Voicing Creation's Praise*, 214. George Steiner points out the critical role of art in its power to present a world as a possibility. "All serious art, music and literature is a critical act . . . Be it realistic, fantastic, Utopian or satiric, the construct of the artist is a counter-statement to the world. Aesthetic means . . . interactions between the constraints of the observed and the boundless possibilities of the imagined. Such formed intensity of sight and of speculative ordering is, always, a critique. It says that things might be (have been, shall be) otherwise" (Steiner, *Real Presences*, 11).

124. Brown, *Religious Aesthetics*, 108. See Dillenberger, *Theology of Artistic Sensibilities*, 244.

125. For an explanation of the concept "dangerous memory" in Metz's political theology, see Metz, *Faith in History and Society*, 74–75, 105–13. See also Rodenborn, *Hope in Action*, 252–59.

126. Gruchy, *Christianity, Art and Transformation*, 200.

Art as Disclosure of Truth

Another function of art is that it can present truth. This role of art is included or related to the roles of art studied in the previous section, for when we claimed that some works of art can show both what is positive and what is negative in the world, we were saying that some artistic works can present a truth about our world. However, in this section I want to highlight the notion of truth, or to be more precise, the relationship between art and truth. To understand this role of art I introduce here Tracy's notion of the "classic."

Before I say what a classic is, it is important to make three preliminary remarks. First, when Tracy talks about classics, he is not speaking only about works of art. A classic can be a text, an image, an event, a person, or a symbol.[127] Yet, the experience of art is paradigmatic for the understanding of what a classic is. Second, the notion of a classic should not be limited by "the elitist criteria of the classicist." In fact, "candidates for classical status" can be found also "in jazz and the spirituals, in films, popular music, and 'popular' (not 'low') culture."[128] Third, the term "classic" should not be confused with the idea of "the latest cultural fad or celebrity," which is how some people understand the word "classic" today. For Tracy, the understanding of classic as the "latest sensation" is a "debasement of the very notion 'classic' into a synonym for its opposite."[129]

Tracy suggests that the classics are texts, events, images, rituals, symbols, and persons in which "we recognize nothing less than the disclosure of a reality we cannot but name truth." The experience of a classic, Tracy continues, is "a realized experience of that which is essential."[130] In other words, "If, even once, a person has experienced a text, a gesture, an image, an event, a person with the force of the recognition: 'This is important! This does make and will demand a difference!' then one has experienced a candidate for classic status."[131] In this sense, some works of art are classics because "in the actual experience of art . . . we recognize the truth of the work's disclosure of a world of reality."[132]

To be sure, when Tracy talks about art as a disclosure of truth, he is not speaking about an abstract truth. For Tracy, art is an encounter with

---

127. Tracy, *Analogical Imagination*, 102, 116.
128. Ibid., 108.
129. Ibid., 108–9.
130. Ibid., 108. Tracy's concept of "classic" is inspired by Hans-Georg Gadamer, who insists that "the actual experience of the work of art can be called a realized experience of an event of truth" (ibid., 111).
131. Ibid., 115–16.
132. Ibid., 110.

something "we can call truth about ourselves" or about our reality.[133] In this sense, Tracy agrees with Paul Tillich, who thinks that works of art are "cultural expressions" that interpret our "situation." However, Tracy says that unlike the "situation" in Tillich's time, the reality of our world today poses no one dominant question. The sense of meaninglessness and absurdity was probably an important—perhaps the most important—aspect of the situation in Tillich's time, an aspect that raised the fundamental question of the meaning of existence. However, today the question about the meaning of life is just a question—although still an important one—among other fundamental questions.[134] For instance, a characteristic of our contemporary situation, which is shown in some works of art, is the "presence of the negative." According to Tracy, "We may find frightening the profound realism in the later Michelangelo or the breaking of all forms to see reality in Cezanne and van Gogh. Yet we cannot deny that their firmer disclosure of the truth of the fascinating and frightening complexity of actual lived existence resonates more deeply to our actual experience of life than does the untroubled world disclosed in art resonant with the beauty and created goodness of finitude as in Raphael or Renoir."[135]

According to Brown, Tillich's claim about the capacity of art to reveal "something of the depth of our world and of ourselves, something of the mystery of being,"[136] applies not to all, but certainly to some artworks.[137] In this sense, regarding the notion of art as disclosure of truth, Brown says, "not everything artistic or aesthetic has *directly* to do with anything we think of as true or even meaningful. Part of the realm of the aesthetic . . . is the sheerly delightful within perception . . . , which can freely exist beyond even truth-as-event or meaning-as-meaningfulness."[138] For instance, a colorful painting of Monet might not have anything to do with the issue of truth and meaning, at least not directly. However, it is important to recall what Rahner says about the religious dimension of an Impressionist painting: "I may say, for instance, that the paintings of Impressionism are not religious because basically they try only to reproduce the color impressions of one's immediate surroundings . . . But it is quite another question when I put the painting of an Impressionist of the early twentieth century in a wider context, a more human one, which would also bring up the question of its

---

133. Ibid., 111.
134. Ibid., 340–41.
135. Ibid., 166.
136. Tillich, *On Art and Architecture*, 247.
137. Brown, *Religious Aesthetics*, 91.
138. Ibid., 11 (emphasis mine).

religiosity."[139] In this sense, on the one hand, I agree with Brown, who says that not everything artistic has *directly* to do with truth. On the other hand, not only some works of art have directly something to do with truth, but also perhaps all works of art can *indirectly* or *potentially* have something to do with the dimension of truth.

Works of art that are classics, that show a truth about our reality, are good works of art. When Tracy claims that "candidates for classical status" can be found in "'popular' (not 'low') culture,"[140] he means that the opposite of classic is not popular culture, but "low" culture. Likewise, de Gruchy asserts, "the distinction is not between 'fine art' and 'popular art,' but between good art of all kinds and . . . art which is mediocre and banal."[141] Good art, understood here as a classic, is that which endures through time because it takes our humanity seriously. Tracy says, the memory of classics—that is, of good works of art—"haunts us. Their actual effects in our lives endure and await ever new appropriations, constantly new interpretations. Their existence may be trusted to time."[142] Likewise, Sherry claims,

> How then are we to assess [what is good] art and literature? One obvious answer is that they must have stood the test of time, i.e., be continuously convincing, not ephemeral or eccentric, and so be in some sense classical . . . Since the arts and literature of redemption are usually concerned with deep and difficult issues of good and evil, it would seem to be a matter of our deciding what is most profound and cogent: what these works say and show . . . should disclose sometimes a compelling truth about the world, which fosters our understanding of human life.
>
> . . . The questions arise of who [i.e., what artist] has seen and portrayed life more fully, profoundly, and convincingly, and of who has expressed our deepest needs and discerned possibilities of meeting them. No doubt personal experience will affect each reader's judgement, but certain faults will render a work of art or literature suspect to many people, and make it unlikely to survive "the test of time": I am thinking especially of shallowness, vulgarity, triviality, cynicism, and sentimentality. Moreover, although "the uses of adversity" is a perennial theme in art and literature, any seeming belittling of human suffering is suspect to people today: life is hard enough, and art and literature

---

139. Rahner, "Art against the Horizon," 167. Cf. Wolterstorff, *Art in Action*, 86.
140. Tracy, *Analogical Imagination*, 108.
141. Gruchy, *Christianity, Art and Transformation*, 76.
142. Tracy, *Analogical Imagination*, 108–9.

should do justice to this fact. Superficiality is as bad here as it is in the theodicies of some philosophers or theologians.[143]

The opposite of good art, some authors say, is called "kitsch." According to de Gruchy, mediocrity and banality are two characteristics of kitsch.[144] Likewise, Pattison claims, "triviality, cynicism and the wanton or careless exercise of the creative gift . . . are not the principles of art but of kitsch."[145] Milan Kundera, in his novel *The Unbearable Lightness of Being*, defines kitsch as the "absolute denial of shit."[146] Indeed, de Gruchy says, "kitsch obfuscates reality, ignoring the ugly as the necessary counterpoint to the beautiful."[147] Likewise, Richard Harries observes, "in art kitsch takes the form of the pretty, the sentimental . . . It excludes all that is truly disturbing and harrowing. In morality, kitsch takes the form of totalitarianism."[148] For instance, de Gruchy says, the "totalitarian art of Nazism and Soviet Russia was invariably kitsch."[149] And Harries adds, "But not only communists. Whenever politicians rush to kiss children in front of the cameras the same tendency is at work."[150] Therefore, kitsch is a type of art that does not show the truth of our reality, especially its ugliness. Furthermore, kitsch is a kind of art that is not able to keep its specificity while being political. It is a kind of art that can be ideologically abused. In this sense, we should be wary when we see art that supports socio-political structures of injustice. As Harries says, one of the strengths of Kundera's notion of kitsch is that "he keeps alive the sense of protest against the world as it exists at the moment."[151]

---

143. Sherry, *Images of Redemption*, 186. Regarding the "test of time" for a work of art, Steiner avers, "no stupid literature, art or music lasts" (Steiner, *Real Presences*, 11).

144. Gruchy, *Christianity, Art and Transformation*, 76.

145. Pattison, *Art, Modernity and Faith*, 154.

146. Kundera, *The Unbearable Lightness of Being*, 242.

147. Gruchy, *Christianity, Art and Transformation*, 76.

148. Harries, *Art and the Beauty of God*, 58.

149. Gruchy, *Christianity, Art and Transformation*, 76.

150. Harries, *Art and the Beauty of God*, 58–59.

151. Ibid., 59. Kitsch is also used for religious purposes, especially in popular religion. I agree with de Gruchy when he says: "Theology must certainly take popular piety and its images into account, sensitive to the role they play, and the challenge which they present to elitist religion and art . . . But where such art reinforces prejudice, encourage jingoism and prevents Christians from maturing in their faith . . . responding to the needs of society, theological and aesthetic criticism is necessary. The fact that theology must be sensitive to 'popular religion' does not excuse it from critically evaluating kitsch and taking a stand against vulgarity in all its forms, especially when coated with religiosity" (Gruchy, *Christianity, Art and Transformation*, 77). Cf. Brown, *Good Taste, Bad Taste*, 128–47, 156–59.

Art, Artist, and Imagination

In the previous two sections, I analyzed the work of art as world-presentation and as disclosure of truth. In this section, I will develop some aspects of the relationship between the work of art and the artist. However, when I explained those roles of art in the previous two sections, I was already describing something about the artist, for it is the artist who can present a world and can show a truth through his or her artistic work. Artists can do this because they have the capacity to see the world with different eyes. As Austin claims, "artists possess this gift of true vision and also possess the ability to communicate their seeing."[152] Artists are "seers." They see "the ordinary everyday truths to which most of us are blind," and through their works of art they "reveal to us a dimension of reality."[153]

An artist can perform all these actions in and through art because he or she has at least two interrelated gifts. First, an artist has an artistic skill. We should remember that, for Brown, art includes "skills," "informed practices," and "know-how."[154] For instance, an artist knows how to combine colors and how to use different materials. However, artists are good in their art not only because they have the "gift," but also because they have cultivated their art, that is, maybe they have received a training in their art, and especially they have had the discipline of practicing their art.

Second, an artist has creative imagination. Creativity is the capacity of seeing and making something new or different. Creativity is related to imagination. An artist is able to create because he or she has the capacity to imagine something new or something different. The term that Wolterstorff uses to talk about imagination is "envisagement." For him, the creativity of the artist consists in his ability to envisage states of affairs that we have never come across in actuality. "It is the capacity for envisagement, not the capacity for imitating the actual, which lies at the basis of our . . . projection of worlds."[155] These two gifts, namely, artistic skill and creative imagination, are interrelated in every good artist. A person may know how to combine colors or how to use different materials, but if he does not have creative imagination, he will not be a good artist. And vice versa, a person may be very creative or imaginative, but if she does not know how to use colors or materials, then she will not be a good artist.

---

152. Austin, *Explorations in Art*, 138.
153. Ibid., 165–66.
154. Brown, *Religious Aesthetics*, 86, 88.
155. Wolterstorff, *Art in Action*, 132.

Imagination has been known in the philosophical tradition as a "place-between" or a "mediator" between the senses and the intellect.[156] According to García-Rivera, the description of imagination as a mediator between the sensible and the intellect bears a resemblance to aesthetic theory vis-à-vis the objective and the subjective dimensions of aesthetics. "As 'imitator' of sensual reality crafting an image for the abstractive intellect to 'appreciate,' this view of the imagination resembles the objective pole of aesthetics. As inventive 'expressor' of images from within the human spirit, the imagination resembles the subjective pole of aesthetics."[157] Garrett Green offers an overview of the concept "imagination" that is helpful for our present study. He writes:

> Common to the various uses of *imagination* . . . is an image or picture representing some object that is not directly accessible to the imagining subject. Kant offers a surprisingly simple definition: "*Imagination* is the faculty of representing in intuition an object that is *not itself present*." Imagination re-presents what is absent; it makes present through images what is inaccessible to direct experience. As a point of departure for a conceptual grammar of *imagination* in ordinary usage, Kant's straightforward definition is useful, as long as his emphasis on representation is not taken too literally. The point is that imagination makes accessible what would otherwise be unavailable to us; whether *representation* is the best way to express this function is open to question.[158]

According to Green, "objects of imagination may be either real or illusory." On the "illusory" side, imagination can be used to produce what is known as fantasy. A characteristic of this illusory or "fantastic" use of imagination is that it departs from the real world. On the "real" side, imagination has to do with real objects that are not directly and physically accessible to us in time and space.[159] Regarding *time*, Green says, "The clearest case of *temporal* absence is past reality, and it has long been recognized . . . that memory requires an act of imagination. Not quite so obvious but surely undeniable is the role of imagination in recalling the social or collective past in history . . . Much more obvious is the role of imagination in the case of future reality,

---

156. According to Garrett Green, in Kant's "*Critique of Pure Reason* imagination plays the important role of mediating between the sensible given and the concepts of the understanding. Later, in the *Critique of Judgment* . . . he puts greater emphasis on the role of the imagination in aesthetics and the arts" (Garrett, *Imagining God*, 13).

157. García-Rivera, *Community of the Beautiful*, 23–24.

158. Green, *Imagining God*, 62.

159. Ibid., 63–64.

which can be presented by means of extrapolations from past experience, anticipations of new developments, and hypothesis about future states of affairs. This anticipatory use of the realistic imagination merges at some point into fantasy."[160] Regarding *space*, Green says, the realistic use of imagination comes into play in situations where a real object is not accessible because of its spatial relationship to the observer. Spatial imagination is used, for instance, when we imagine the table that is in the next room.[161] "Common to the various uses of imagination are selective and integrating images that serve to present—whether as illusion or reality—something that would otherwise remain inaccessible."[162] Besides these realistic and fanciful uses of imagination, Sherry also talks about the use of our imagination in our moral and social life. For instance, we can use our imagination "to interpret the outward signs of others' lives and behaviour, and to put ourselves in their place. Imagination, too, may give people a new moral vision, by helping them to see things from an unfamiliar point of view."[163] All these uses of imagination—realistic, illusory, or moral—play a role in art.

Artists can contribute to the process of transformation of the world precisely by using their artistic imagination. According to Thiessen, "imagination has to do with possibility," that is, imagination functions "in the perception of what may, could, and will be—in short, in picturing the possible."[164] Likewise, Wolterstorff says, "we human beings have the marvellous capacity of envisaging states of affairs which for all we know are merely possible, and even states of affairs which are impossible."[165] Indeed, we human beings have the capacity of imagining a different world—a world more human and more just—even if it seems impossible to be built in real life. In this sense, Boff asserts, "Creative imagination enables us to break away from things that are taken for granted, to abandon accepted presuppositions and begin to think in unorthodox ways. It enables us to set off on a different direction. Fantasy enables us to unmask the limitations of reality. The latter is the concrete embodiment of one possibility . . . But all the other infinite possibilities are not thereby squelched. With them human beings can dream about and even construct what has not yet been experienced in reality before."[166] In fact, as William Dych says, "The capacity to imagine and envi-

160. Ibid., 64.
161. Ibid.
162. Ibid., 65.
163. Sherry, *Spirit and Beauty*, 113.
164. Thiessen, *Theology and Modern Irish Art*, 262, 267.
165. Wolterstorff, *Art in Action*, 74.
166. Boff, *Liberating Grace*, 96.

sion the human . . . is the first and necessary step towards its realization." Our world becomes a human world by the design of those who have the imagination to see it as a human world. In this sense, the role of imagination is central not only in the life of the individual, but also in the life of a whole society in its movement towards humanization.[167] In this sense,

> Perhaps it is the artist who must point the way [towards humanization] by giving expression to truly human images of the real. For by helping us to see the human face of things and to hear the human sound of things, by showing us the human touch and the human soul of things in words and sounds, in colors and shapes, in movement, rhythm and gesture, they are helping us to realize what the possibilities of the human are, a realization which includes both the moment of "seeing" in the work of art, and the "making real" beyond art in life itself.[168]

According to Boff, "Imagination is a form of liberty."[169] Likewise, Thiessen points out, "The imagination enables a person to free her/himself from their own confines."[170] In fact, a characteristic of artistic imagination is freedom. Artists give free rein to their imagination to create their artistic works. Artists can contribute to the process of social transformation as long as they have the freedom to create their works of art, and as long as their works of art are expressions of freedom. For many people, art can be a space of personal freedom in a world where liberty is sometimes threatened or lacking. As Boff says, "common people somehow manage to retain their freedom even though they are oppressed socially and politically . . . They remain free in their popular culture . . . , their music, their cuisine . . . They have not stopped being hospitable, gracious, and jovial in their music, their festivals, and their get-togethers. [It is] the people's way of finding the strength they need to go on living and survive their burdens."[171]

According to de Gruchy, "all art is located within a particular cultural matrix. Unless we have an understanding of its milieu, it is difficult to appreciate its significance."[172] Likewise, for Pattison, art is always local; it does not stand outside history.[173] However, works of art are expressions of a culture because their creators are part of specific cultures. In other words, art is

---

167. Dych, "Theology and Imagination," 123–24.
168. Ibid., 124.
169. Boff, *Jesus Christ Liberator*, 90.
170. Thiessen, *Theology and Modern Irish Art*, 265.
171. Boff, *Liberating Grace*, 86.
172. Gruchy, *Christianity, Art and Transformation*, 191.
173. Pattison, *Art, Modernity and Faith*, xiii, 9.

the expression of a culture because the artist, as Tracy claims, "is a particular self with a particular history in a particular culture. The artist, too, is a finite, social, historical self."[174] For this reason, in order to better understand a work of art, it is helpful to hear what the artist says about his or her own work. As Pattison suggests, "although artists are by no means invariably the best commentators on their own work, conversations with artists are a vital part of any theological engagement with art."[175]

Begbie also thinks that, in works of art, "style, structure and content are all grounded in historical particularity." Hence, "when interpreting art works, the refusal to date or historicise them lest such location distort some putative purity of aesthetic apprehension appears singularly misguided." However, Begbie continues, "that a work of art can direct our attention to states of affairs beyond itself (and beyond the consciousness of the artist), and that it can reflect (with varying degrees of potency) values which transcend cultural preference . . . seems *de facto* undeniable." Therefore, "considerations of context do not, of course, provide an exhaustive explanation of an art work, and the dangers of over-estimating authorial context (and intent) are well known."[176] Likewise, Austin claims, "an artwork is much more than a mere expression of the artist's inner feelings and unrecognised emotions."[177] For this reason, Tracy says, "in the actual experience of art we do not experience the artist behind the work of art. Rather we recognize the truth of the work's disclosure of a world of reality."[178] Therefore, on the one hand, to appreciate more a work of art, it helps to know about the intentions of the artist and about his or her cultural and historical contexts. On the other hand, the meaning of a work of art does not end there. Using Tracy's expression, a work of art has an "excess of meaning"[179] that goes beyond the particularity of the artist.

According to Begbie, one of the reasons why the meaning of a work of art goes beyond the particularity of the artist is that "art works possess a measure of independence from their artists."[180] However, we should be

---

174. Tracy, *Analogical Imagination*, 124.

175. Pattison, *Art, Modernity and Faith*, xii.

176. Begbie, *Voicing Creation's Praise*, 216–17. Likewise, Wolterstorff suggests, art can express the "artist's world-and-life view, his or her *Weltanschauung*." However, "to focus just on this relation of work to consciousness of artist is to overlook all the rest of the rich embeddedness of art in the life of mankind" (Wolterstorff, *Art in Action*, 89–90).

177. Austin, *Explorations in Art*, 13.

178. Tracy, *Analogical Imagination*, 110.

179. Ibid., 150 n. 103.

180. Begbie, *Voicing Creation's Praise*, 217.

careful here. The idea that a work of art "has a life of its own independent of the artist," as Austin also claims,[181] does not mean that art is separated from its creators and its recipients. The idea of art as an independent entity can lead us into the traps of a "purist" interpretation of art. Rather, taking a relational approach, we ought to say that art goes beyond the particularity of the artist because it includes the reality of the recipient as well. As Viladesau remarks, "the existential situation of the viewer or hearer [of an artistic work] may permit a new interpretation or appreciation of the work's revelatory power."[182] This is how we can understand van der Leeuw's assertion, "works of art do possess their own life; they perhaps mean something very different to him who receives them than to him who created them."[183] Thus, for instance, Austin says, "Michelangelo's great uncompleted series of slaves or prisoners . . . speak for and to all those of us striving to escape from any one of a million prisons whether or not this was Michelangelo's intention."[184] In other words, the phenomenon that we call art includes not only the relationship between the artist and the work of art, but also the relationship between the recipient and the work of art.

As such, art can be a mediation in the relationship between the artist and the recipient. Begbie asserts, art is "inherently dialogical." It is a "medium of personal exchange" between an artist and those who appreciate his or her work.[185] In other words, art is a mode of inter-action between the artist and the receiver. Thus, on the one hand, through his or her works of art, an artist presents a world to all those potential recipients of his or her work. As Wolterstorff points out, an artist, through his or her art, "is projecting a world *for us*, presenting *to us* a world *for our consideration*."[186] Likewise, Austin asserts, an artist, through his or her art, "can and does often confront *us* with truths" about ourselves and about our world.[187] However, art is a two-way relationship between the artist and the receiver. Not only the artist has something to say to the recipients through his or her works of art, but also the recipients have something to say to the artist about his or her work. Indeed, many artists are interested in how their viewers, listeners, or readers re-act to their art. The artist is often open to see and to hear what the recipients make of his or her works of art, even or especially when they

---

181. Austin, *Explorations in Art*, 13.
182. Viladesau, *Theological Aesthetics*, 147.
183. Leeuw, *Sacred and Profane Beauty*, 277.
184. Austin, *Explorations in Art*, 13.
185. Begbie, *Voicing Creation's Praise*, 220.
186. Wolterstorff, *Art in Action*, 123 (emphasis mine).
187. Austin, *Explorations in Art*, 13 (emphasis mine).

find something new in his or her art, something that was not intended by the artist. This relationship between the artist and the recipient is so real that, when it happens, we can say something like what Austin claims about one of his favorite artists: "Forever, Paul Cézanne and I will be brothers."[188] Through the experience of art, sometimes we feel interconnected with the artist, that is, we experience a kind of friendship, even if we have never met the artist in real life.

Art, Recipient, and Transformation

Art affects the whole being of the recipient. The expression "whole being" implies an integral notion of the human being. Contrary to a dualist understanding of the human person, here we understand the human being as a whole. Although the human person has different faculties that can be distinguished—for instance, sensing, feeling, imagining, thinking, and willing—they are nevertheless interrelated, for the human being is a single unit. Therefore, some works of art can affect the whole being of their recipients. Tillich states, "the artist brings to *our senses* and through them to *our whole being* something of the depth of our world and of ourselves."[189] Likewise, Brown says, art "engages '*body, mind,* and *heart,*' and through these something that might be called the integral '*soul.*'"[190] Body, mind, and heart are, figuratively speaking, "distinguishable but inseparable 'parts' or functions of the self," whereas the soul is "the self as a whole."[191] Thus, "some art allows one not only to think more, but also to feel more, and . . . in both of these ways it manages to mean more, possibly even letting one be and become more."[192] Similarly, Austin claims, "art engages both our emotions and our intellect. It makes demands of us intellectually, morally, emotionally and, I am certain, spiritually."[193]

Art affects our body. Through colors, sounds, smells, textures, and movements, which are arranged in a particular way or style, art has the power to touch our senses, and through the senses it moves our whole being. Art affects our emotions too. Through its power of presenting a world, art makes us feel joy, sadness, peace, love, and anger. Wolterstorff claims, "it is true that our apprehension of projected worlds [through works of art]

---

188. Ibid., 134.
189. Tillich, *On Art and Architecture*, 247 (emphasis mine).
190. Brown, *Religious Aesthetics*, 100.
191. Ibid., 103.
192. Ibid., 92.
193. Austin, *Explorations in Art*, 15.

does, over and over, evoke emotions in us, and that often this contributes crucially to what we find gripping and compelling about them."[194] Art affects our imagination as well. Through its power of presenting a world, art helps us to imagine worlds that we would have never envisaged by other means. As Tracy states, "human beings need story, symbol, image, myth, and fiction to disclose to their imaginations some genuinely new possibilities for existence."[195]

Art affects our minds too. Austin says, "art can widen our perceptions of ourselves and of others and of our responsibilities and duties." It enables us "to have a wider perception of the possibilities that the world offers and therefore can enhance our awareness of truth, value and freedom."[196] Through its power of presenting a world, art allows us "to see more deeply into ourselves and therefore more deeply into our relationship with the universe of people and things."[197] Therefore, "art gives us life by enabling us to see and therefore to know."[198] For this reason, Begbie asserts, "the autonomy of art will best be safeguarded . . . not by wrenching it apart from knowledge, nor by equating it with conceptual and moral knowledge, but by [seeing] it as a distinctive, particular, but quite genuine means of knowing the world."[199] In fact, "Art has potential to help us grow in our grasp and understanding of the world we inhabit . . . The experience of art is a mode of knowing the world, certainly different from conceptual and moral knowledge, but by no means inferior to them."[200]

Art affects our will, and thus our actions. Begbie claims, "a work of art, even if fictional, may lead us to change our attitude to the states of affairs with which it deals and which inform our day to day lives."[201] According to Austin, art can confront us with truths about ourselves and about our world—for instance, the sufferings and the horrors of humanity—to which we prefer to be blind. By doing so, we are jolted out of our comfort. "To see this world for what it is in its essential integrity is to be set free from complacency."[202] Likewise, Wolterstorff argues that some art aims to alter people's convictions, "by showing them how things are, illuminating them,

---

194. Wolterstorff, *Art in Action*, 148.
195. Tracy, *Blessed Rage for Order*, 207.
196. Austin, *Explorations in Art*, 13.
197. Ibid., 140.
198. Ibid., 166.
199. Begbie, *Voicing Creation's Praise*, 217.
200. Ibid., 257.
201. Ibid., 252.
202. Austin, *Explorations in Art*, 166.

so as thereby to awaken them from their somnolence, or release them from their self-indulgent ideologies, or energize them into action."[203]

Therefore, art affects us wholly, and by doing so, art transforms us. As Tracy says, in the actual experience of art, "we recognize the truth of the work's disclosure of a world of reality transforming, if only for a moment, ourselves: our lives, our sense for possibilities and actuality, our destiny."[204] In experiencing art, "I am transformed by its truth when I return to the everyday, to the whole of what I ordinarily call reality."[205] Likewise, de Gruchy claims, "good art, whatever its form, helps us both individually and corporately to perceive reality in a new way, and by so doing, it opens up possibilities of transformation."[206] In this way, as Brown asserts, "art is widely engaged in the transformation of life and world."[207]

The experience of being affected and transformed by art requires the active participation of the recipient. Tracy describes this experience as one of being "caught up." In the experience of art, "we find ourselves 'caught up' in its world," which means that we are not in control of the artistic event.[208] However, in order to be affected and transformed by the experience of art, we need to be open to such an experience. Tracy uses the analogy of the "game" to explain this requirement. "In playing, I lose myself in the play. I do not passively lose myself. In fact, I actively [allow] myself fully to enter the game."[209] Similarly, in the experience of art, "we can control, manipulate, deny the truth of art," but then we are refusing to play the game.[210] But if we choose to be open to the experience of art, we run the risk of being "caught up" by it, that is, being "shocked, surprised, challenged," and ultimately transformed by the experience of art.[211] Art can transform us as long as we allow art to change us, and we let art transform us as long as we actively participate in the experience of art.

In this sense, Begbie says, the meaning of a work of art "could only be grasped in performance, by a personal, imaginative fusion of frame and story . . . Whatever meaning is disclosed in a piece of art is given in and

---

203. Wolterstorff, *Art in Action*, 146.

204. Tracy, *Analogical Imagination*, 110.

205. Ibid., 112.

206. Gruchy, *Christianity, Art and Transformation*, 253.

207. Brown, *Religious Aesthetics*, 111; see Brown, *Good Taste, Bad Taste*, 86, 96.

208. Tracy, *Analogical Imagination*, 110–11.

209. Ibid., 113. Tracy's analogy of the "game" is inspired by Gadamer who chooses "the phenomenon of the 'game' to understand the experience of art" (ibid., 113).

210. Ibid., 114.

211. Ibid., 110.

with the work itself, not as an ingredient to be distilled out, but as a total impact which claims our attention and involvement."[212] In other words, the only way to perceive the truth of a work of art is by participating in the work of art itself. Nobody else can see, hear, or read the work of art for me. Other people can tell me about their own experience of a particular work of art. However, their information does not substitute my personal experience. The only way in which I can know the truth that is disclosed in a work of art is by a personal involvement with the work of art itself. It is in the encounter between me—with everything that I am—and the work of art that the experience of art occurs. For this reason, the word "recipient" is not an accurate word to describe the person who sees, listens, or reads a work of art, for it suggests a mere passive attitude in the experience of art. Even "words like 'viewer,' 'listener' and 'reader' imply far too passive a role," Austin asserts. They suggest no participation in the process of art. In the experience of art "something happens and I am an essential contributor to this happening. Without me this happening would not have happened in the way that it has happened."[213]

For the recipient, the experience of a work of art is an experience of freedom. In fact, the recipient is free to open himself or herself to the experience of art. The recipient is free to allow the work of art to affect him or her. Indeed, art has the power to transform human beings only in freedom. Works of art are interesting, attractive, and appealing to those who appreciate them. However, authentic works of art only appeal, move, and inspire. They do not control their recipients. They do not try to manipulate the mind, feeling, imagination, and will of their recipients. As Brown says, "even the highest art cannot coerce a fitting response; it can only invite."[214] Indeed, a difference between good art and kitsch, I suggest, is that the latter is a type of art that exploits the feelings and emotions of its recipients, while authentic art sets its recipients free.

ART AND THE HOLY SPIRIT

Based on the analysis of the phenomenon of art developed in the previous sections, now I will make a theological interpretation of the artistic phenomenon. In other words, now I will develop what might be called a "theology of art." A goal of this kind of theology, Begbie says, is "to enquire

---

212. Begbie, *Voicing Creation's Praise*, 248–49.
213. Austin, *Explorations in Art*, 133–34.
214. Brown, "Is Good Art Good for Religion?," 162.

as to how the arts might relate to the character and purposes of God for his world."[215] This is the question that I will try to answer in this section.

Following Rahner, first of all we should say that the experience of art can be both a mediation and an expression of transcendental experience. The experience of transcendence generally takes the form of human longing. That is, the yearning for more, at the level of knowledge, freedom, love, or justice, is a manifestation of human transcendence. Some authors point out that art can express this human longing,[216] and as such, the experience of art can be a mediation and an expression of transcendence. Theologically speaking, we Christians affirm that such longing is fulfilled in God. Only in God will we find the fullness of life. Therefore, looking at the relationship between God and humanity, on the human side, we say that we are attracted or oriented towards God. On the divine side, we claim that God is the absolute mystery who is calling us and attracting us to participate in his divine life. Therefore, the experience of transcendence in art is another mediation through which God attracts us to God's self.

The concept of God that is present here is that of "immanent transcendence," using Brown's expression, which understands God as "the extraordinary and miraculous reality ever present and immanent in us and in all other things, which intimately share in the very life of God."[217] This understanding of the relationship between God and humanity, that is, of a God who is actively present in us, "cherishes aesthetica that can open us to new possibilities for cooperating with God to create a future in which we can truly though limitedly share, thanks to that One in whom we live and move and have our being."[218]

We can understand this cooperating with God in the area of aesthetics from the perspective of the Holy Spirit in relationship with artistic inspiration. The concept of inspiration is commonly used in aesthetics. For instance, Sherry says, "an inspired work of art" is the description of an artistic piece that shows excellence.[219] Likewise, inspiration is the word that we use to describe the event when an image, a song, or a poem "comes suddenly and unexpectedly" to an artist.[220] Finally, by extension, inspiration occurs in

---

215. Begbie, *Voicing Creation's Praise*, xix.

216. See Sherry, *Spirit and Beauty*, 149–50; Harries, *Art and the Beauty of God*, 91–99.

217. Brown, *Religious Aesthetics*, 128.

218. Ibid., 131.

219. Sherry, *Spirit and Beauty*, 105.

220. Ibid., 114.

A Theological Aesthetics of Liberation, Part One

the viewer, hearer, or reader of an artistic work, "for after all it is common to speak of people being inspired by a work of art."[221]

Sherry notes that "the term 'inspiration' means literally 'blowing upon' or 'breathing into.'" Therefore, inspiration is related to the concept of "spirit," which, as we studied in chapter 1, originally means "wind" or "breath" in Greek, Latin, and Hebrew. Thus, if "the Bible often envisages the spirit of God as a power which 'blows through' or permeates people, giving or heightening certain capacities . . . , then it would seem that inspiration was originally seen as an empowering of this kind."[222] Therefore, Sherry claims, artistic inspiration can be also the work of the Holy Spirit. In the process of creating works of art, "inspiration is the way in which God through His spirit lets us share in His creativity." However, in the creation of art, "the Holy Spirit may be seen as a kind of prompter, energizing us and opening us up to new potentialities within us. Such a role does not exclude the influence of economic and social factors, nor the internal connections with whatever artistic, intellectual, and religious traditions we happen to belong to; nor does it exclude the use of our normal mental processes."[223] In this respect, Begbie suggests that artistic inspiration should not be regarded as a completely passive affair. Rather inspiration requires responsiveness from the artist.[224]

> The artist is not simply a tool in the hands of some irresistible force, nor is he one who effortlessly receives divinely authenticated visions from above and then simply lets them flow out through paint or stone or whatever . . . Rather, it is better to speak about the Spirit initiating, enabling and sustaining a process of interaction, spurring the artist into a profound engagement with his subject, artistic medium, fellow artists, society, or whatever. This, we hardly need say, is an immensely costly business . . . Even artists who have been most conscious of being "inspired" know only too well that they cannot escape hard struggle, the sweat of physical and mental exertion. Inspiration does not do away with the need for strenuous, painstaking and often frustrating efforts.[225]

---

221. Ibid., 109.
222. Ibid., 103–4. For biblical passages that play with the words "spirit" and "inspiration," see ibid., 108.
223. Ibid., 120.
224. Begbie, *Voicing Creation's Praise*, 226–27.
225. Ibid., 227.

Therefore, the work of the Spirit through inspiration does not inhibit artistic freedom, but actualizes it, for "the Spirit is the one who draws alongside us, making us not less human but more human, not less free but more free. His work in us is to open us up to things as they really are, yet without disrupting our nature as limited, finite and contingent creatures."[226]

We can understand the active presence of the Holy Spirit in art through the notion of grace. Sherry says, art and literature can be "channels of grace."[227] Indeed, Boff finds the work of divine grace in the realm of artistic creativity, which is "one of the areas of human experience where gratuitousness shows up more clearly . . . The brush of a painter or the fingers of a violinist create a whole new universe of colors or sounds in a matter of moments. This creativity seems to well up like a fountain."[228] In fact, theologically speaking, creative imagination and artistic skills can be described as graces, for they are generally experienced as something "given" to artists, that is, as gratuitous gifts from God.[229] In this sense, it is appropriate to say that art and artists are charisms. We said in chapter 1 that charisms are graces or gifts from the Holy Spirit which are meant to be used for the building of the community. In particular, personal talents are considered to be charisms for the construction of a better world. In this sense, artistic talents are certainly charisms from the Holy Spirit. As Robert Faricy says, every charism is "for service, for building up the community, for the common good (1 Corinthians 12:7). Charisms of art, also, are for serving."[230]

Therefore, the Spirit of God works in and through art as a secondary cause. However, in a theological understanding of the artistic phenomenon, we should not limit ourselves to the concept of efficient cause. A theological view of art involves the notion of final cause as well. A theological account of art should consider its purpose. The purpose of the work of the Holy Spirit in and through art is salvation.[231] Indeed, art can be an instrument of salvation. Wolterstorff says, art is "a crucial component in the shalom for which men and women were made . . . Art can serve as instrument in our struggle to overcome the fallenness of our existence, while also . . . anticipating the shalom which awaits us."[232] Theologically speaking, it is not art that saves us. Rather, it is God who saves us through the experience of art.

226. Ibid., 228.
227. Sherry, *Images of Redemption*, 10.
228. Boff, *Liberating Grace*, 95.
229. See Sherry, *Spirit and Beauty*, 161.
230. Faricy, "Art as a Charism," 98.
231. See Sherry, *Spirit and Beauty*, 119.
232. Wolterstorff, *Art in Action*, 84.

A Theological Aesthetics of Liberation, Part One   157

As Austin asserts, "perhaps it would be extravagant to claim that a work of art can be redemptive, but it cannot be denied that it may be a means of redemption."[233] Likewise, Sherry says, "although art and literature cannot themselves redeem people, they may nevertheless be channels of grace . . . , and therefore have a redemptive function."[234]

How can art be an instrument of salvation? Here we have to remember what we said in the previous chapters about salvation, that is, salvation is a process that takes place now in history, and which will reach its fulfillment in the eschatological future. Therefore, art can be an instrument of God's saving action in at least two ways. First, art can show the eschatological future that is promised to us by God. Thiessen suggests, "This sense of the possible, of the future, of the other, of transformation is what unites the creative imagination with and makes it an instrument in eschatological concerns. Without vision, without acts of the imagination, hope for transformation, both in the present and in the ultimate future . . . is unthinkable. Transformed beings, glimpses of the kingdom of God realised through justice, peace, liberation and the integrity of creation, as well as eternity's ultimate transcendence and fulfilment need to be envisioned, imagined."[235] This power of imagination is present in art. Pattison suggests, "art anticipates . . . the messianic kingdom itself, the return of the world to that created fulness in which we may declare, with God, that it is all 'very good.'"[236] In the experience of art, Sherry says, sometimes we glimpse "*this* world, transfigured." This experience both expresses and provokes "a yearning for something more which would fulfil what has been given already."[237] Indeed, art can be a "medium for conveying eschatological ideas." For instance, for Sherry, Gluck's "Dance of the Blessed Spirits" conveys "a yearning for an everlasting peace, for a kingdom beyond suffering and disharmony."[238] This longing for a kingdom of peace, which is hinted at in the experience of art, can be a source of hope and of courage in the process of creating a better world, which is part of the process of God's saving action in history through the work of men and women.

Second, art can be an instrument of salvation inasmuch as it has the power to transform the world through the work of men and women who have been affected and transformed by the experience of art. As we said above, art has the capacity to present a world. With such a power, art can

233. Austin, *Explorations in Art*, 47.
234. Sherry, *Images of Redemption*, 10.
235. Thiessen, *Theology and Modern Irish Art*, 267–68.
236. Pattison, *Art, Modernity and Faith*, 153.
237. Sherry, *Spirit and Beauty*, 147–48.
238. Ibid., 155.

illuminate a dimension of our reality. For instance, it can make us see what is ugly and horrendous in our world. In this sense, art can be an instrument of what Metz calls a "mysticism of open eyes," which is "a mysticism that especially makes visible all invisible and inconvenient suffering."[239] Not only can art reveal the situation of our current world. It can also present events of the past, especially it can allow us to remember the atrocities of human history. As such, art can function as a dangerous memory. By showing us the reality of the world and by reminding us our history of inhumanity, art can provoke both indignation in us and a protest against the status quo. This indignation and this protest can be part of the process of creating a better world, which, as I said above, can be a manifestation of God's saving action in history through the work of men and women.

Therefore, art can be used by human beings as a positive response to God's call for salvation. However, art can be used also for the opposite of salvation. In fact, Wolterstorff says, "art is not isolated from the radical fallenness of our nature." Art can be an instrument of sin. It can be an accomplice in the crimes of humanity.[240] Art can be "racist, . . . sexist, colonialist, elitist, nationalist, fascist—you name it." It can function as "an instrument of oppression and exploitation."[241] Indeed, as de Gruchy claims, "images have the power to do good, they can also do a great deal of harm."[242] However, it is not art itself that can be sinful. Rather, human beings can use art in a sinful way.

The use of art as an instrument of salvation is certainly God's call to artists who consider themselves Christians. As Wolterstorff says, the church is "the community of those who have taken up the call of God to work on His behalf in His cause of renewing human existence." Thus, "It is in the context of this community that the Christian artist is also now called to do his work. He is called as artist to share in his people's task of being witness to God's work of renewal, its task of serving all men everywhere by working to bring about righteousness and peace."[243] In fact, it is regrettable when Christian artists fail to collaborate in the Kingdom of God. This shortcoming happens, Begbie asserts, when, for instance, "much so-called 'Christian' art has degenerated into an inoffensive and superficial Kitsch which turns a blind eye to the pain of the world."[244] However, Wolterstorff says, "the

---

239. Metz, *Passion for God*, 163.
240. Wolterstorff, *Art in Action*, 84.
241. Wolterstorff, "Beyond Beauty and the Aesthetic," 130.
242. Gruchy, *Christianity, Art and Transformation*, 50.
243. Wolterstorff, *Art in Action*, 197–98.
244. Begbie, *Voicing Creation's Praise*, 213.

Christian knows indeed that God has never confined His mode of working to the church."[245] In fact, as Brown notes, "the art that has the greatest religious significance is not necessarily the art of institutional religion." The Spirit of God can be found also in the prophetic, visionary, and revelatory artistic expressions outside the community of Christian faith.[246] Thus, as Begbie claims, "the Holy Spirit can be operative and effective in artists who have no Christian allegiance."[247] In fact,

> to the extent to which Christianity calls for the moral and religious transformation of society, it calls in part for arts that will in some fashion help the continual reformation and transformation of the Christian's own necessarily limited vision of society and world, along with the world's vision of itself. Not all such arts will be Christian . . . Some of the human and social transformations advocated by Christians—transformations such as those entailed in the promotion of peace, responsible freedom, mutual respect, and justice—are ones that many non-Christians likewise hope for and work toward. In these areas, surely, not all arts and aesthetica valued by Christians need to be specifically Christian themselves. What they must be is genuinely transformative.[248]

GOD, ART, AND LIBERATION

At the beginning of this chapter I said that, in order to establish a connection between a pneumatology of liberation and a theology of art, we would explore two double questions. First, is art liberating, and how is it liberating? Second, is God involved in the experience of liberating art, and how is God involved? Here I will summarize the results of this exploration.

In the first section, I presented seven different dimensions of art. Firstly, I examined the relationship between art and aesthetics. Art is part of a broader phenomenon called aesthetics. Our notion of aesthetics rejects a purist understanding of the term, one which considers aesthetics as an isolated realm, separated from any social, political, and religious realities. On the contrary, here we understand aesthetics as a distinctive area, which nevertheless is in relation with social and political fields. Consequently, art,

---

245. Wolterstorff, *Art in Action*, 197.
246. Brown, *Religious Aesthetics*, 111.
247. Begbie, *Voicing Creation's Praise*, 226.
248. Brown, *Religious Aesthetics*, 131.

as a specific area of aesthetics, is also in relation with social and political realities.

Secondly, regarding the scope of art, we rejected the elitist stance that values only those artistic expressions labelled as "high." The line that divides fine arts from other kinds of art is blurred and flexible. Besides, for several cultural, social, and economic reasons, the poor generally do not have access to the fine arts. However, they do practice and enjoy other kinds of art, especially popular arts and crafts. If we consider these kinds of art as irrelevant for a theological reflection, then we are missing an important dimension of the liberation of the poor in their experience of art. Therefore, our understanding of art here is inclusive. It involves fine arts, popular arts, and crafts.

Thirdly, I argued that art is action. There is no such a thing as *the* purpose of art. The idea that art is only for aesthetic contemplation is mistaken. Rather, art has a plurality of purposes. We describe art as an action that is both praxis and poiesis. The end of art is in the activity itself, but it can also have a goal that is external to the activity itself. The purpose of art can be, for example, the joy of creating and contemplating an artistic object, but it can also have an aim that is external to the artistic event itself, for instance, the goal of liberating social outcasts.

Fourthly, I explained the power of art to present a world. The action of presenting a world in and through art has different purposes. Art can illuminate different aspects of our reality. For example, it can show the reality of the poor. Art can present a world as a possibility, as something that could be or should be. For instance, art can present as a real possibility a world where justice and peace reign. Art can present a world as a dangerous memory, reminding us of all the atrocities committed against humanity in our history.

Fifthly, I explicated the power of art to disclose a truth about our world. In fact, art has the power to show truths to which people want to turn a blind eye. A work of art that discloses truth can be called a "classic." For example, Picasso's *Guernica* can be considered a classic work or art, for it discloses a truth of our human condition, specifically the negativity of war. In fact, contrary to kitsch, which neglects the ugliness of our reality, good art takes our humanity seriously.

Sixthly, I suggested that artists can contribute to the transformation of the world through their art. Through their works, artists can show us all the maladies of our human reality. However, artists do not only have the capacity to show the reality of the world as it is. They also have the capacity to imagine a different world as a possibility. Artists can contribute to the process of liberation precisely by using their creative imagination and by presenting an alternative world through their work. The vision of a just society in and through their works of art can awaken a sense of hope, that is, a sense that a different world is possible.

Finally, I argued that art has the power to transform us wholly. Art affects the entire being of the recipient. Art affects our senses, emotions, imaginations, minds, wills, and actions. It is by doing so that art has the power to transform us wholly, and we are transformed to change the world into a better place, that is, a place where everyone may have a worthy life. Through the experience of art, those who are social outcasts—and all those who struggle with them in the process of liberation—can have an experience of personal transformation that enables them to change the world.

Then, I developed a theological interpretation of this process of liberation in and through art. First of all, the experience of art can be seen as an expression and a mediation of what we call transcendental experience. From the perspective of social outcasts, transcendence is experienced in their longing for liberation. Art can express this yearning for justice. Theologically speaking, we Christians affirm that such longing is fulfilled in God, who wills to share his life with human beings. Indeed, God is actively present in our world liberating the poor from unjust suffering and death. In this sense, God works through the experience of liberation that occurs in and through art.

The liberating action of God in and through art can be seen from the perspective of the Holy Spirit, especially with regard to the concept of inspiration. It is the Holy Spirit who inspires the artist to create works of art that support the liberation of social outcasts. The work of the Spirit in the artist does not exclude, annihilate, or disrupt the freedom of the artist. Rather the Spirit actualizes, enhances—and counts with—the freedom of the artist. Therefore, theologically speaking, it is neither art nor the artist that liberates. Rather, it is God who liberates through the experience of art.

Christian artists can collaborate in the kingdom of God by creating art that takes our humanity seriously. However, the Holy Spirit can also be actively present in artists who do not belong to a Christian denomination. Indeed, the Spirit of God can be found in artists who are not Christians, and in works of art that are not explicitly religious, as long as they promote social justice. However, if art presents explicitly religious themes, then, as Viladesau asserts, "The question posed to theology in general by the theologies of liberation takes on a particular acuteness when applied to aesthetics: how can religious art—and especially the portrayal of the cross—be liberative, rather than being a source of a privatized spirituality of suffering and submission, as it has so frequently been in the past?"[249] The fact is that from

---

249. Viladesau, "Beauty of the Cross," 151.

the perspective of a theological aesthetics of liberation, if art with explicitly religious themes inspires and supports the liberation of social outcasts, then the Spirit of God is there.

Chapter 4

A Theological Aesthetics of Liberation, Part Two

A Christology of Contrast in Art

In this chapter I will develop the second part of our theological aesthetics of liberation. In the previous chapter, I correlated a pneumatology of liberation with a theology of liberating art. In this chapter, I will correlate a Christology of liberation with a theology of contrasting art. The previous chapter was a theological interpretation of art. This chapter moves in the other direction: it is an aesthetic interpretation of God in Jesus Christ. It reflects on the question: from the experience of art, what can we say about the God that is revealed in Jesus Christ? This aesthetic interpretation of Jesus Christ presumes what has been said in the previous chapter, i.e., that the Spirit is actively present in the experience of art. In other words, this aesthetic understanding of the person of Jesus Christ is inspired by the Holy Spirit who works in the experience of art.

Therefore, in the first section, I will explain what might be called an experience of contrast in art, and I will sketch some theological and christological ideas based on the artistic experience of contrast. In the second section, I will systematize and expand these theological insights with the help of Edward Schillebeeckx's theology. The results of this exploration, which are summarized in the third section, form what might be called a *Christology of contrast in art*. This Christology of contrast is a corrective to the christologies of Jon Sobrino and Hans Urs von Balthasar that we studied in previous chapters.

FROM THE EXPERIENCE OF CONTRAST IN ART TO THEOLOGY

This section explains what might be called the experience of contrast in art. To do so, firstly, I will indicate the existence of other aesthetic concepts besides beauty. Secondly, I will explore some aspects of the relationship between beauty and justice. And finally, I will explain the notion of contrast in art, and I will sketch some theological and christological insights that can be raised from the artistic experience of contrast.

Other Aesthetic Concepts Besides Beauty

Probably it was noticed that the concept of beauty did not play any major role in the theological aesthetics of liberation developed in the previous chapter. This did not happen by chance. I intentionally put the notion of beauty in parentheses in order to explore here the role of beauty in a theological aesthetics of liberation.

First of all, it is a mistake to associate aesthetics and art *only* with beauty. To understand this assertion, it is important to consider some approaches to the concept of beauty. Due to the limits of the present study, it is impossible to offer a full explanation of such a concept. I will explain only those aspects that are relevant for our analysis. Sherry notes, the word "beauty" "seems to create so many problems: what is beauty, why do we find it so difficult to define and to judge, why do people disagree so much about it, is it in things themselves or rather, as people say, 'in the eye of the beholder'?"[1] One of the reasons why beauty is difficult to define is that the word has been given different meanings throughout history. In his book *Faith and Beauty*, Farley gives an account of such variety, in what he calls the "Western story of beauty."[2]

According to Farley, the notion of beauty that existed from classical Hellenism to the Middle Ages is probably the first understanding of beauty in Western culture.[3] During those centuries, beauty is basically understood as something that is pleasurable. One of the best examples of this understanding is found in Thomas Aquinas, who provides the classical definition: "beautiful things are those which please when seen."[4] What are those qualities of beautiful things that are pleasing when these are seen or heard?

---

1. Sherry, *Spirit and Beauty*, 22.
2. Farley, *Faith and Beauty*, 118.
3. See ibid., 17–23.
4. Aquinas, *Summa Theologiae*, I 5.4 ad. 1. See Wolterstorff, *Art Rethought*, 306–7.

Aquinas suggests, "beauty includes three conditions: 'integrity' or 'perfection,' since those things which are impaired are by the very fact ugly; due 'proportion' or 'harmony'; and lastly, 'brightness' or 'clarity,' whence things are called beautiful which have a bright colour."[5] Therefore, as Brown says, "scholastic and classical thinkers reasonably contend that we are delighted by what we perceive to be the integrity and wholeness of the object, by the harmony of its parts, by a just proportion in the relation of parts to the whole, and often by a certain radiance or *claritas* emanating from the object."[6] To be sure, Aquinas "is not expressing a subjectivist view of beauty."[7] In other words, wholeness, harmony, and radiance are qualities of beautiful objects that make them pleasing when seen or heard. According to Wolterstorff, "Aquinas' account of beauty captured the understanding that had become traditional by his time and . . . remained traditional until well into the eighteenth century."[8]

In fact, it was in the eighteenth century that the understanding of beauty began to change. According to García-Rivera, "when Kant appeared on the scene relatively soon after Baumgarten's proposal, philosophical aesthetics decidedly shifted from an emphasis on the objectivity of Beauty to its subjective reception . . . as the beautiful."[9] As Brown says, "beauty strictly speaking is (for Kant) not a property of the object itself but of what the subject makes of the object in 'reflective judgement.'"[10] Kant introduces the idea of "disinterestedness" in relation to beauty, which means, "the beautiful is inherently isolated from moral, theoretical, and practical interests."[11] Hence, the beautiful "is valued for its own sake."[12] In other words, "Pleasure in the beautiful is disinterested and non-utilitarian. We appreciate and enjoy the beautiful simply because it is beautiful."[13]

According to de Gruchy, it was around that time that aesthetics came to be equated with the study of beauty.[14] Moreover, according to Wolterstorff, "it was in the eighteenth century that people began to identify the worth of a

---

5. Aquinas, *Summa Theologiae*, I 39.8 c. See Sherry, *Spirit and Beauty*, 29–30; Harries, *Art and the Beauty of God*, 19–22.

6. Brown, *Religious Aesthetics*, 66.

7. Wolterstorff, *Art Rethought*, 308.

8. Ibid., 306.

9. García-Rivera, *Community of the Beautiful*, 13.

10. Brown, *Religious Aesthetics*, 64.

11. Ibid., 25.

12. Ibid., 64.

13. Gruchy, *Christianity, Art and Transformation*, 58.

14. Ibid., 56.

work of the arts with beauty."[15] Therefore, it should not be a surprise that the understanding of the beautiful as something valued for its own sake led to the notion of art for art's sake, i.e., art as an end in itself. In this sense, the attention to art should be disinterested, or rather, the "disinterested" attention to art should have a single interest: the pursuit of aesthetic pleasure in the contemplation of the beautiful. In other words, "art serves no other purpose than to provide such enjoyment."[16]

This narrow identification of both aesthetics and art with the reality of beauty is still present today in some thinkers. It is definitely present in some theologians. For instance, as we said in chapter 2, we find this limited understanding of aesthetics as a theory of beauty in von Balthasar. Likewise, we find a limited understanding of art as an experience of beauty in van der Leeuw, who states, "The impression and expression of the beautiful we usually call art."[17]

However, the identification of aesthetics with the reality of beauty is far from obvious. Some phenomena are aesthetic, but not beautiful. For instance, Brown suggests, "the chants and roars of a crowd at a sports stadium can be aesthetically interesting and exciting without being judged beautiful."[18] In fact, the sounds produced by such a crowd are neither harmonious nor disinterested. The association of art with beauty is not evident either. On the one hand, not all beauty is artistic. For instance, a natural sunset can be beautiful, but it is not the product of human artistry. On the other hand, not all art is about beauty. For example, "beautiful" is an inadequate term to describe Picasso's *Guernica*.[19]

In fact, this concept of beauty is to some extent outdated. Traditional works in aesthetics more or less correlated art and beauty, Farley says, "thus allowing beauty to define the arts. It is fair to say [however] that virtually no contemporary theory of the arts (or perhaps even artist) would grant beauty such a powerful status."[20] Likewise, Sherry observes, "beauty is not as central a concept in much modern aesthetics as it was in ancient and medieval aesthetics."[21] In fact, current philosophical aesthetics deals with questions that are not generally related to beauty. "This depreciation is found not only

---

15. Wolterstorff, *Art Rethought*, 310.

16. Gruchy, *Christianity, Art and Transformation*, 58. See Wolterstorff, *Art Rethought*, 311.

17. Leeuw, *Sacred and Profane Beauty*, 6.

18. Brown, *Religious Aesthetics*, 21.

19. See ibid., 21.

20. Farley, *Faith and Beauty*, 111.

21. Sherry, *Spirit and Beauty*, 40.

amongst critics and philosophers, but also among many artists, who reject or disregard the traditional view that their role is to celebrate the beauty of creation."[22]

Sherry asserts, today "the term 'beautiful' seems inappropriate [for] many great works of art."[23] In fact, "the modern critical vocabulary extends very widely and includes concepts like 'graceful,' 'elegant,' 'profound,' 'moving,' 'joyous,' 'lively,' 'imaginative,' 'life-enhancing,' 'illuminating,' and 'sublime.' Of course, some of these terms were found in earlier times too."[24] In my judgement, these words still describe the aesthetic experience of "positive" aspects of reality, as the term "beautiful" does. Nevertheless, "the more striking characteristic of modern aesthetics," Sherry says, "is that it recognizes certain aesthetic qualities which were not previously acknowledged, at least not explicitly," qualities such as, "uncomfortable," "upsetting," "horrifying," "disturbing," and "grotesque."[25] These terms, I suggest, express an aesthetic experience of "negative" dimensions of reality, which are not beautiful, and cannot and should not be reconciled with beauty. These concepts that express an aesthetic experience of the negative are useful and fitting for the theological aesthetics of liberation that I am developing here, as we will see later.

Furthermore, current aesthetics questions and challenges not only the concept of beauty, but also the validity of other aesthetic ideas that are related to the beautiful, such as the notion of aesthetic pleasure.[26] For instance, "pleasure" or "delight" is not exactly the kind of experience that we have when we see Picasso's *Guernica*. For this reason, Sherry asserts, "we should look at other functions of art besides its ability to please us, for example its symbolic, representative, expressive, and emotionally moving capacities."[27] In fact, I suggest, "moving" is a word that describes well our experience with many works of art. However, I disapprove of the idea that the "beautiful" is the only characteristic that moves us in the experience of a work of art. For instance, the "grotesque" that is depicted in some works of art has the capacity to move us as well.

Thus, I disagree with García-Rivera who says, aesthetics is "the science which asks a more profound question: *what moves the human heart?* Put in

22. Ibid., 23.
23. Ibid., 24.
24. Ibid., 40.
25. Ibid., 40–41. For some remarkable essays on the theological significance of the grotesque, see Adams and Yates, *The Grotesque in Art and Literature*.
26. Sherry, *Spirit and Beauty*, 41.
27. Ibid., 25.

this way, aesthetics has existed since the first human heart was moved by the influence of the beautiful."[28] García-Rivera also says, "The beautiful has to do with what moves the heart and thus the grotesque and unattractive can also manifest beauty."[29] I disagree with García-Rivera on three points. First, aesthetics should not be limited to the appreciation of beauty. Second, beauty is not the only thing that has the power to move the human heart. Indeed, other aesthetic qualities besides the beautiful have the power to move those who engage with works of art. In fact, García-Rivera acknowledges that other characteristics such as the grotesque and the unattractive have the power to move people. However, the problem is that García-Rivera suggests that the grotesque and the unattractive are or can be manifestations of beauty. This is my third point of disagreement with García-Rivera. In my judgement, the grotesque and the unattractive cannot be manifestations of the beautiful because they are the opposite of beauty. These aesthetic categories that express negative dimensions of reality—such as the grotesque and the unattractive—have a dialectical relationship with the beautiful, and therefore they cannot be reconciled with the concept of beauty.

Like García-Rivera, Harries claims, "beautiful works of art often include that which is disturbing and ugly, dark and disruptive. They can express violence, evoke sorrow and depict the sordid."[30] According to Harries, beautiful works of art can include what is ugly because beauty and truth are related. In other words, some works of art are beautiful because they show a truth of our world.[31] In fact, as we studied in chapter 3, I agree that works of art can reveal a truth about our reality. However, I disagree with idea that it is beauty which allows art to show truths about our human lives. To my mind, we do not have to assign only to beauty the power of art to reveal truths. Some works of art have such a power simply because they are good works of art, and the excellence of some works of art relies on the fact that they take our humanity seriously.

Beauty and Justice

That one concept of beauty is outmoded does not mean that the term is obsolete.[32] Sherry remarks, "Despite the difficulties of analysis and availability of a wide range of others aesthetic terms, the word 'beautiful' is

28. García-Rivera, *Community of the Beautiful*, 9.
29. García-Rivera, *Wounded Innocence*, 5.
30. Harries, *Art and The Beauty of God*, 22.
31. See ibid., 47–54.
32. Sherry, *Spirit and Beauty*, 21.

still in common use. It is certainly not an abstruse or technical term. It is used mainly to give a verdict on something or someone, which can then be justified in term of more detailed aesthetic judgments."[33] In fact, he says, the concept of beauty is still used as "a catch-all for all forms of aesthetic excellence."[34] I agree with Sherry's assertion to some extent. In my judgement, beauty can be used as a "catch-all" concept for artworks that present positive dimensions of reality. For instance, we can assess a colorful, bright, and joyful painting of Monet as "beautiful." However, we cannot use the term "beautiful" to describe those artworks that present negative aspects of reality, for instance Picasso's *Guernica*. However, it is true that "beautiful" is still a common term to make an aesthetic appreciation. Therefore, the idea of eliminating it completely from aesthetic considerations is too radical, and presumably incorrect.

I agree with Sherry, who says, "The solution which I shall adopt is to continue to employ the concept of beauty, but to draw on other concepts as well."[35] Indeed, I will use the category of the beautiful, but in relationship with other aesthetic concepts. Sherry rightly asserts, "modern aesthetics tries to 'place' the concept of beauty logically by elucidating the relationship between it and other aesthetic concepts, showing that it is part of a network of such concepts. But this development is all to the good, since there is no reason why we should confine our treatment to a single concept."[36] Hence, we should not endorse García-Rivera's complaint: "art itself seems to be in a crisis. It, too, has forgotten its service to beauty."[37] We should not support García-Rivera's comment because neither has beauty disappeared completely from art, nor is the appreciation of other aesthetic qualities, besides beauty, a bad thing. On the contrary, the development of other aesthetic concepts is a good thing, not only because it shows the breadth of the world

---

33. Ibid., 28.

34. Ibid., 42.

35. Ibid., 24. However, for Sherry, beauty is not one concept among other aesthetic concepts. For him, beauty is still the most important aesthetic concept, but nevertheless this should not prevent us from considering other aesthetic qualities. The concept of beauty, he says, "is still a central one, perhaps *the* central one, in aesthetics . . . It is still used as a catch-all for all forms of aesthetic excellence. We can accept such usage, provided that we keep in mind . . . the vast range of other aesthetic terms" (ibid., 42). Similarly, Viladesau claims that there is "art whose reason for being is the quest for beauty . . . This is arguably its most significant form." However, "while acknowledging the central importance of the pursuit of the beautiful in art, let us . . . admit that 'art' is not necessarily a single thing and does not have a single goal" (Viladesau, *Theological Aesthetics*, 143–44).

36. Sherry, *Spirit and Beauty*, 164.

37. García-Rivera, *Wounded Innocence*, 5.

of aesthetics, but also because those other aesthetic concepts besides beauty are promising for the development of theology.

If we keep the concept of beauty in a theological aesthetics of liberation, it is worth asking if there is any relationship between beauty and justice. My answer to that question is that beauty *alone* or beauty *in itself* cannot create a just society. As de Gruchy says, "Beauty, however defined, cannot transform humanity or society by its own power."[38] Likewise, Wolterstorff says,

> attending to beauty does not, in fact, have the inherent power of energizing the beholder to struggle for justice . . . The evidence points unmistakably in the opposite direction. We have all known people who were intensely attentive to beauty but cared not a fig for justice; we have all heard about people who live in large elegant houses, work in elegant offices, have extensive art collections, but are horrible persons. Historians tell us that a good many of the Germans who supervised the concentration camps during the day attended concerts in the evening and expanded their art collections with paintings plundered from the occupied countries. And let us not forget that many of the artifacts whose beauty now mesmerizes us were created on the backs of indentured labor.[39]

True, beauty alone cannot create a just society. Nevertheless, like Gutiérrez, I suggest that beauty can collaborate in the process of building a better world. In its relationship with other dimensions of reality, beauty can help in the promotion of social justice. I propose three ways in which beauty can do this.

Firstly, a just world can be analogically seen as beautiful. Patrick McCormick says, "while beauty and justice are not identical, they are analogous."[40] The similarity between the two is that "beauty and justice are both concerned with the harmonious arrangement of the different parts or elements of a work or society, and the just or righteous community has a certain well-ordered beauty to it that creates peace and harmony, while the unjust society is characterized by the chaos of violence and iniquity."[41] In this sense, "injustice itself is always ugly and mars the world and all it touches with its ugliness." For instance, "we see the grotesque and dreadful

---

38. Gruchy, *Christianity, Art and Transformation*, 94.
39. Wolterstorff, *Art Rethought*, 200.
40. McCormick, *God's Beauty*, 4.
41. Ibid., 7.

conditions in which the world's poor and oppressed live and work."[42] McCormick describes,

> Streets and alleys in their barrios, ghettos, and slums are dark, filthy, and dangerous, littered with uncollected trash, car wrecks, and potholes. Houses and storefronts are boarded up and windows and street lamps shattered. Schools and grocery stores are fortified like prisons. These overcrowded, polluted, dangerous, and exhausted places are not beautiful . . .
>
> The view of the poor is also crowded with the unpleasant humiliation of being unable to provide for oneself and one's family, and with the ugly scorn of those who see them as miserable freeloaders and failures . . .
>
> And when they do find employment, it is the poor who are assigned the work that is dirty and ugly. It is the poor who are expected to pick up and empty our trash, pull our weeds, pluck our chickens, slaughter and butcher our meat, pick our strawberries, change and wash our dirty laundry, mop our floors, scrub our toilets . . . If there is dirty, messy, filthy job to be done, there is certainly a poor person—most likely an immigrant or woman of color—ready to do it.[43]

Therefore, for the theological aesthetics of liberation that we are developing here, life—especially life for the poor—is the criterion that distinguishes beauty from ugliness in its relationship with justice. Richard states,

> Fundamentally life means: work, land, food, health, housing, education, environment rest, and celebration (festival) . . . I am saying that life, especially the lives of the poor, must be taken as theology's rationale. I am not talking about the meaning of life or an economic or political program, but about *life* as a criterion for discerning what is *rational* and what is *irrational*; as the criterion for discerning *true* from *false*, *good* from *evil*, the *beautiful* from the *ugly*. What is rational, logical, true, good, and beautiful is that all, especially the poor, should have life. What is irrational, illogical, false, evil, and ugly is that the poor should not have life. Hunger, unemployment, malnutrition, illiteracy, and the destruction of nature is irrational, illogical, evil, and ugly.[44]

42. Ibid., 61–62.

43. Ibid., 71–72.

44. Richard, "Liberation Theology," 504. Here it is important to remember what we said in chapter 1 about the Holy Spirit: life, especially a worthy life for the poor, is the criterion to discern the presence of the Spirit of God in the world.

Secondly, the artistic experience of beauty has the potential to elicit a longing for justice, a yearning that in turn has the potential to be an affective and effective source of hope in the praxis of liberation. Sherry mentions that the artistic experience of beauty sometimes brings with it a "feeling of longing."[45] In the artistic experience of beauty, sometimes we have a glimpse of "*this* world, transfigured." This experience both expresses and provokes "a yearning for something more which would fulfil what has been given already."[46] Likewise, Brown observes, "The greater the art's beauty, the greater the sense of yearning that it evokes. Even in those rare moments when the aesthetic experience becomes graciously transformed into a glimpse of genuine beatitude . . . it soon fades, leaving behind something like a promise, an eschatological hope."[47] The experience of beauty in art can evoke the idea that things can be different, that the situation of injustice in our world can be overcome, that the notion of a better world—a beautiful world—is not a fanciful idea, but a real possibility. Therefore, the experience of beauty can awake both the longing for liberation and a sense of hope that nourishes the praxis of liberation. This is why Viladesau says, "The poor are always with us . . . ; and it is not always clear in the concrete whether the more 'beautiful work' of love . . . is in meeting their material needs or in nourishing the spirit's hunger. We do not live by bread alone; and *the inspiration of hope through artistic beauty* can also be a 'word from the mouth of God.'"[48]

Finally, the struggle for justice can be analogically considered as beautiful. Sherry points out, "Talk of the beauty of good deeds and of virtue was . . . a commonplace in the ancient world."[49] "This way of speaking," Sherry says, "has not entirely disappeared today."[50] For instance, when we say "she is a nice person" or "a lovely person," we are applying aesthetic qualities related to the concept of beauty to describe the good character of a person. To say that a charitable work is a beautiful and graceful deed is not a puzzling appreciation; rather it would make sense for most people.[51] However, when we make those sorts of comments, we are employing aesthetic concepts in an analogical way to describe moral virtues and good deeds. In the order

---

45. Sherry, *Spirit and Beauty*, 51.
46. Ibid., 147–48.
47. Brown, *Good Taste, Bad Taste*, 121.
48. Viladesau, *Theological Aesthetics*, 213 (emphasis mine).
49. Sherry mentions Plato, Aristotle, and Cicero as examples of thinkers who talk about the beauty of virtues and good deeds. See Sherry, *Spirit and Beauty*, 31–32.
50. Ibid., 31–32.
51. García-Rivera hints at the beauty of a charitable work when he asks, "How can critical thought illumine the beauty sensed in the 'ugly' work of art that was Mother Teresa's ministry to the poor of Calcutta?" (García-Rivera, *Community of the Beautiful*, 99).

of knowledge, Sherry says, we learn the concept of beauty—and other aesthetic concepts too—from our aesthetic experiences with nature and with works of art. It is that concept of beauty that we use in an analogical way to describe the excellence of good actions.[52] In this sense, we can assert, the praxis of liberation is beautiful. Likewise, de Gruchy notes, there is something beautiful about friendship.[53] In fact, friendship and solidarity with social outcasts are beautiful. Sharing one's life with them, struggling with them for justice, and giving one's life for them are beautiful acts.

Theology and Christology from the Experience of Contrast in Art

Now we move from aesthetics to *theological* aesthetics. Based on our reflections about beauty in the previous sections, what can we say about theology? We can assert that the same narrow understanding of aesthetics as a theory of beauty is present in theological aesthetics as well. Theological aesthetics is often reduced to a theology of beauty. The examples are abundant. In chapter 2, we detected this problem in von Balthasar's theology. Not surprisingly, the same reduction is found in those who follow or are influenced by his theology. For instance, we find this limited understanding of theological aesthetics in Roberto Goizueta and Alejandro García-Rivera.[54] Furthermore, a narrow understanding of art as an expression of beauty is present in theologies of art as well.[55] For instance, García-Rivera says, "We must learn to find beauty once again . . . But how is beauty once more to be found? It would do no good to simply say, 'Look and see, beauty is all around you.' For that is the problem. We have forgotten how to look and see. That is where a theology of art comes in."[56] Thus, for García-Rivera, a theology of art teaches us to see beauty again.

A common claim of those who narrowly understand theological aesthetics as a theology of beauty is that beauty is an attribute of God's being. In tandem with the idea of divine beauty, they assert that earthly beauty somehow participates in God's beauty.[57] Especially according to

---

52. Sherry, *Spirit and Beauty*, 35–36.

53. Gruchy, *Christianity, Art and Transformation*, 156.

54. See Goizueta, *Christ Our Companion*, 124; García-Rivera, *Community of the Beautiful*, 9.

55. For a typical example of a limited understanding of art as an expression of beauty, see Harries, *Art and the Beauty of God*.

56. García-Rivera, *Wounded Innocence*, 4.

57. For a typical example of a theology that maintains that beauty is a characteristic of God's being, and that earthly beauty participates somehow in God's beauty, see Harries, *Art and the Beauty of God*, 31–43.

neo-Platonic strains of Christian theology, "all light and all beauty in nature as well as in art share in some way . . . in the light and beauty of God. Thus, however dimly, they reflect God's glory."[58] This understanding is present in Augustine's famous cry: "Late have I loved you, beauty so old and so new."[59] In contemporary theology, we already said, von Balthasar champions the idea of God's beauty, and those who follow him do the same. For instance, García-Rivera claims, "God is beauty. And the beautiful is the medium par excellence by which we experience the love and knowledge of God."[60]

Those who think that beauty is an attribute of God often believe that Jesus Christ is the manifestation of divine beauty. Again, a typical example of this aesthetic notion of Christ is found in von Balthasar's theology. However, we find such understanding in other theologians such as van der Leeuw, who describes the Son of God as "the most beautiful."[61] So far I do not see any problem in talking about God's beauty and about Christ as the manifestation of divine beauty. The problems start when these theologians talk about the beauty of the cross. As Sherry says, these theologians have the "tendency to stress the paradoxical nature of the beauty of the Cross."[62] The paradox consists in that, although Jesus' death on the cross is ugly, it manifests the beauty or the glory of God. We found this paradoxical understanding of the cross in von Balthasar's theology, and we find it in those who are influenced by his theology. For instance, according to Goizueta, "the paradigmatic form of God's glory is that of a criminal hanging from a cross . . . The starting point for a Christian theological aesthetics [which Goizueta defines as a theology of beauty] is the One who 'had no form or beauty.'"[63] Thus, in Goizueta's understanding of the cross, the paradox is that the crucified One, who has no beauty, is the form of God's beauty. Likewise, García-Rivera claims, "theology can discern the beautiful in the agonized face of a crucified man."[64] This paradox is what García-Rivera implies when he says, "the grotesque and unattractive [of the cross] can also manifest beauty."[65] Thus, in García-Rivera's understanding of the cross, the paradox is that we

---

58. Brown, *Religious Aesthetics*, 126. For some biblical examples of the word "glory" as indicating God's beauty, see Sherry, *Spirit and Beauty*, 56–60.

59. Augustine, *Confessions*, X.xxvii.38; quoted in Brown, *Good Taste, Bad Taste*, 98.

60. García-Rivera, *Wounded Innocence*, 3.

61. Leeuw, *Sacred and Profane Beauty*, 340.

62. Sherry, *Spirit and Beauty*, 75.

63. Goizueta, *Christ Our Companion*, 122.

64. García-Rivera, *Wounded Innocence*, 5.

65. Ibid., 5.

find beauty in what is not beautiful, but rather grotesque and unattractive, namely, the crucified Jesus.

In my judgement, the reduction of theological aesthetics—and a theology of art—to a theology of beauty, and especially its focus on the beauty of the cross, is fraught with problems. To be sure, I am not saying that it is wrong to understand theological aesthetics as a theology of beauty. It is indeed a legitimate form of theological aesthetics. What I am saying is that it is a mistake to *reduce* the understanding of theological aesthetics to a theology of beauty, and this is due to two interrelated reasons. First, it is a mistake to reduce theological aesthetics to a theology of beauty because there are other aesthetics concepts besides beauty that can and should be considered in theology. Second, it is a mistake because a theological aesthetics that is reduced to a theology of beauty does not correlate to the contemporary situation of people today, especially the situation of those who suffer from poverty and social exclusion. A theological aesthetics that is reduced to a theology of beauty does not and cannot respond to the reality of those who are victims of social structures that perpetuate injustice, since as we said above, the connection between beauty and justice is not straightforward. The contemplation of beauty alone, either earthly or divine, either in a work of art or in prayer, does not inherently incite people to struggle for justice. For this reason, as Brown states, theological aesthetics should free itself from the "tyranny of the beautiful."[66] It is necessary to find other aesthetic concepts besides beauty that may contribute to the development of a theological aesthetics that cares for the liberation of social outcasts.[67] If we decide to keep using the concept of beauty in a theological aesthetics of liberation, then we should not consider beauty alone, but in relationship with other aesthetic concepts.

Furthermore, the notion of the beauty of the cross is a problematic concept, if not a mistaken one. I suggest at least three problems in such

---

66. Brown, *Religious Aesthetics*, 23.

67. Cf. García-Rivera, "On a New List of Aesthetic Categories," 169–83. The title of García-Rivera's article "On a New List of Aesthetic Categories" may sound promising for the development of a theological aesthetics of liberation that takes into account other aesthetic categories besides beauty. However, this is not the case. Commenting on Gutiérrez's study of the book of Job, García-Rivera suggests that an "Authentic talk of God in a suffering world . . . is to be found more in how well we speak of God" (ibid., 169). A theological aesthetics that speaks well of God requires a "sense of Beauty," which is not simply about "contemplation," but "requires a new list of aesthetic categories" (ibid., 171–74). This new list includes a "unitive revelatory experience" (ibid., 177) and a "dramatics" (ibid., 172). In my judgement, the "new list of aesthetic categories" that García-Rivera suggests is not so new, and it is all positively related and integrated into the concept of beauty.

an understanding of the cross. First, it generally focuses on the cross itself, without any further clarification or qualification. Those theologians who talk about the beauty of the cross tend to overlook the life of Jesus that led him to have conflicts with the authorities who condemned him to death.[68] Second, the concept of the beauty of the cross reconciles the beautiful with the ugly. Those theologians say that, "paradoxically," the beauty of God shines through the ugliness of the cross. And third, the concept of the beauty of the cross ultimately attributes Jesus' death to God. Those theologians generally claim in an implicit or explicit way that it is God's will for Jesus to die on the cross. Therefore, the notion of the beauty of the cross beautifies and glorifies unjust suffering. As a consequence, such a concept only serves to justify the unjust suffering of the poor, since the cross—as a prototype of unjust suffering—is beautiful and glorious. To say that the unjust suffering of the crucified is paradoxically beautiful, that it is the will of God, that it is the way by which God's glory shines in the world, all this is a form of theological aesthetics that serves to perpetuate the suffering of social outcasts. For this reason, it is necessary to find other aesthetic concepts besides beauty that may contribute to the development of a theology of the cross that stands against unjust suffering. If we continue using the concept of beauty in a theological aesthetics of liberation, then we should try to find beauty not in the cross itself, but in relationship with other dimensions of Jesus Christ.

The other aesthetic concepts, I propose, that we can use for the development of a theological aesthetics of liberation are those concepts that express negative dimensions of reality, concepts such as "horrifying," "shocking," "unsettling," etc.[69] These terms, as I already said, cannot and should not be reconciled with beauty, since they express precisely the opposite of beauty. Therefore, the relationship between these aesthetic concepts that express the negative, on the one hand, and the concept of beauty, on the other, is not analogical, but dialectical. In other words, the relationship of the aesthetic concepts that express the negative with the concept of beauty is

---

68. Trying to defend those theologians who talk about the beauty of the cross, Sherry says that he presumes that "these writers are appealing to Christ's moral . . . beauty" (Sherry, *Spirit and Beauty*, 75). Precisely, the problem is that those authors are not speaking of Christ's moral beauty. They are not talking about the beauty of the moral values that Jesus showed during his life, for instance, his compassion for the poor. When they talk about the beauty of the cross, they focus on the death of Jesus, isolated from his life.

69. Brown makes the following remark in passing: "when theology comes to grips with modern arts in particular, it must ponder the possible religious value of art that disrupts and distorts, and in ways that are far from beautiful" (Brown, *Good Taste, Bad Taste*, 59). However, Brown himself neither analyzes the theological values of non-beautiful art, nor suggests how to make such analysis.

that of contrast. In fact, the horrifying, the shocking, and the unsettling do not manifest beauty, since they are precisely manifestations of the absence of beauty. However, *by contrast*, the horrifying, the shocking, or the unsettling reminds us of what is not there, that is, beauty. Farley expresses this experience of contrast in art as follows:

> a work need not be beautiful to be an authentic work of art. What gives it artistic authenticity is something broader than beauty. The authentic work of art can bring into form (or nonform) what is disturbing, oppressive, frightening, ugly or meaningless . . . The photographer may capture on film a trash heap in an urban alley or the final moments of a starving child. But if the photographer works as an artist, she or he will so photograph these things that their "ugly" and pathetic content will constitute a self-transcending experience for the observer. Is that experience simply one of ugliness, entirely reducible to the photograph's shocking, disgusting contents? I suggest that . . . beauty ever hovers on the edge of the ugly because the ugly suggests what *contrasts* to it . . . The devastating battle may be horrifying but Picasso's *Guernica* is not mere ugliness: its very horror depends on the viewer's ability to *contrast* it to non-suffering and non-brutality.[70]

Therefore, the artistic experience of the negative entails, by contrast, an experience of the positive that is not there. In other words, the artistic experience of contrast not only shows the ugliness of reality, but also alludes to the beauty that is not there and should be there. In this way, the artistic experience of contrast is a "no" against the ugliness—of injustice, of violence, of poverty, etc.—in our world, and it is a "yes" to the beauty—of justice, of peace, of solidarity, etc.—that is not there in the world, but could and should exist in our world. Therefore, the artistic experience of contrast involves protest and hope. As de Gruchy says, even when art reflects despair, it expresses hope.[71]

In Christian terms, such hope is hope in a God who will liberate us and save us from unjust suffering and death. In fact, Sherry says, contemporary art and literature rarely engage with explicitly soteriological themes. However, "modern art and literature, and music too, have often shown an overwhelming concern with the great evils of the age, and with our desire to be free of them: with the horrors of modern war, genocide, racial strife and persecution, concentration camps, and the loneliness and alienation

---

70. Farley, *Faith and Beauty*, 111–12 (emphasis mine).
71. Gruchy, *Christianity, Art and Transformation*, 212.

of much urban life."[72] Why do they show such things? Because sometimes, the most effective way in which an artist can express the liberating effects of grace is by representing its seeming absence, i.e., "depicting a 'graceless' world in need of redemption."[73]

In this soteriological context, the contribution to Christology of an artistic experience of contrast is that the life-journey, death, and resurrection of Jesus Christ can be seen as an event of contrast. Based on the experience of art, Begbie hints at this understanding of Christ as an event of contrast as he says,

> God in his Son has declared a "No" against all evil . . . All cries of anger and indignation can only issue from some more ultimate conviction. Disorder is recognised as such only because of some prior conviction about what is orderly . . . All art to some extent exhibits a dialectic between negation and affirmation—a protest against things as we find them in the name of some intuition of what they are meant to be or could be . . .
>
> Put in theological terms, a "No" of protest in art may well echo God's rejection of all that corrupts his world, but it will never be sufficient on its own. The Christian confession is that God's "No" yields its true meaning only in the light of his "Yes," his unconditional love towards creation, a "Yes" which has found its supreme enactment in the resurrection of Christ from the dead.[74]

Therefore, Begbie is making an analogy between the experience of contrast in art and the Christ event. In the same way that there is a "no" and a "yes" in the artistic experience of contrast, there is a "no" and a "yes" in the Christ event. The "no" in the Christ event is the "no" of God against everything that is unjust in the world, including the unjust death of Jesus on the cross. This divine protest becomes clear in the light of the divine "yes," which is found in the resurrection of Christ as an affirmation of Jesus' life. The negativity of the cross is indeed recognized in its contrast with the positivity of Jesus' life.

Thus, the experience of contrast in art can contribute to a theology of the cross. Picasso's *Guernica* is a classic example of an artistic experience that helps us to understand the reality of the cross as an experience of contrast. Tillich describes such a work of art as "one of the most famous, if not the most famous painting of the twentieth century. It is the story of Guernica, a small Basque town in northern Spain which was bombed to

---

72. Sherry, *Images of Redemption*, 183.

73. Ibid., 169.

74. Begbie, *Voicing Creation's Praise*, 213–14.

rubble . . . [Guernica] conveys to us a world that is indeed in pieces. What is not in pieces, what is still whole, utters a cry of desperation as it is about to disintegrate through bombs, fire, and other forms of death."[75] *Guernica* expresses "immense horror,"[76] "extreme ugliness,"[77] the "negativity of man's predicament," and "meaninglessness."[78] However, *Guernica* also has a positive dimension inasmuch as it "encounters the reality of the world with protest and prophetic wrath against the destructive and demonic powers of the world."[79] Thus, according to Tillich, *Guernica* represents the symbol of the cross.[80]

In fact, I suggest, when we see Picasso's *Guernica*—and many other paintings that express negative dimensions of reality[81]—we have an understanding of the cross as an experience of contrast.[82] This understanding of the cross implies what follows. In opposition to those theologians who talk about the beauty of the cross, such as von Balthasar and his followers, who focus on the cross itself, reconcile the beauty of God with the ugliness of the cross, and attribute Jesus' death to God, we, based on the experience of contrast in art, understand that the cross in itself is not beautiful, that we should not reconcile the beauty of God with the ugliness of the cross, and that we should not attribute Jesus' death to God. In fact, the cross in itself is ugly. The beauty of God is not in the cross. Rather, the beauty of God is manifested in Jesus' life—i.e., in his friendship with the poor and in his

75. Tillich, *On Art and Architecture*, 179.
76. Ibid., 95.
77. Ibid., 110.
78. Ibid., 124.
79. Ibid., 179.
80. Ibid., 124. See Pattison, *Art, Modernity and Faith*, 112.

81. Francis Bacon is another artist that is often mentioned by theologians as someone who presents artistically negative dimensions of reality such as suffering, violence, and despair. See Begbie, *Voicing Creation's Praise*, 214; Austin, *Explorations in Art*, 165; Sherry, *Spirit and Beauty*, 42, 156. For a theological interpretation of Bacon's artwork, see Arya, *Francis Bacon*; Yates, "Francis Bacon."

82. I have a similar experience of contrast when I see the painting *La Hora Oscura* (The Dark Hour) of the Ecuadorian artist Eduardo Kingman. The painting shows a man who has been flogged in front of people who have clown-like faces or who are wearing masks that show a mocking smile. It seems that the artist intended to portray leaders of totalitarian regimes in those wry, smiling faces that are laughing at the flogged man who represents suffering humanity. This aesthetic experience of looking at the grotesque figures who are sardonically contemplating the suffering of humanity arouses in me a feeling of indignation. However, the similarity between the scourged man and the suffering of Jesus reminds me that this humiliation is not the final word in the story. In fact, the final word in the story of the humiliated person is liberation.

solidarity with social outcasts—a life that is reaffirmed by God in the resurrection of Jesus Christ.[83]

SCHILLEBEECKX'S THEOLOGY OF CONTRAST

Now we will develop in a systematic way our understanding of Jesus Christ as an event of contrast based on the theology of Edward Schillebeeckx. The Flemish theologian does not come to the notion of contrast from the experience of art as we did here. (Indeed, he has very few comments about aesthetics and art, which I will mention in due course.) Rather, he comes to such a notion from critical theory.

The critical theory of the Frankfurt School helps Schillebeeckx to articulate his own understanding of "critical negativity" or "negative dialectics."[84] He borrows especially two elements from critical theory. First, Schillebeeckx agrees with the negativity of critical theory. According to Aloysius Rego, negative dialectics, especially in Theodor Adorno's philosophy, is "nonidentity thinking. It explores the relationship between concept and object, pointing out the contradictions between the object's ideal existence

---

83. Cf. Stoker, "Beauty as a Theological Concept." In this article, Stoker's stance on the aesthetic value of the cross is ambiguous. On the one hand, he is very influenced by von Balthasar's theology of the cross. Agreeing with von Balthasar, Stoker says, "A theological concept of beauty cannot be developed without allowing for the ugliness of the Cross, suffering and injustice" (ibid., 163). In fact, "a combination of beauty and the Cross is possible" (ibid., 165). The meaning of the Cross can be understood as "God's identification with the ugliness of suffering and the injustice of humankind." Using W. B. Yeat's expression in the poem "Easter 1916," Stoker says, "Connecting the Cross with beauty is an instance of what is called 'terrible beauty.'" On the other hand, Stoker acknowledges that the beautiful and the ugly are opposites. For instance, Picasso's *Guernica* cannot be called beautiful. Furthermore, Stoker recognizes the experience of contrast in art. Some works of art in the Hungarian National Museum of Budapest show "the alienation in Hungarian society created by the political and economic situation. Through these works, the ugliness of alienation became an experience that referred to its opposite, to the beautiful, to a society of peace, justice and freedom." Therefore, Stoker says, "As a symbol of violent death, the Cross is ugly. In contrast, the Cross experienced in terms of Christ's surrender to the Father, represents an act which receives eternal value through God's victory over death" (ibid., 169–70). Therefore, at the end of the article, the reader is not sure if, for Stoker, the relationship between beauty and the cross is that of identification or that of contrast. In other words, it is not clear if in Stoker's mind the cross is a manifestation of terrible beauty (a term which somehow reconciles beauty and ugliness), or if the cross is ugly (as opposed to beauty).

84. Schillebeeckx, *Understanding of Faith*, 79. Schillebeeckx acknowledges that he has borrowed the term "critical negativity" from Theodor Adorno. See Schillebeeckx, *God*, 116 n. 8. For an account of the influence of critical theory on Schillebeeckx's theology, see Rodenborn, *Hope in Action*, 122–49.

(given by the concept) and its actual existence."[85] Critical theory rejects identity thinking because it has "totalitarian tendencies," and it "leads to domination."[86] For this reason, Schillebeeckx says, critical theory restricts itself to "making negative statements about a better society in the future; it cannot say anything positive about that future society." Critical theory "also rejects the classical marxist standpoint that the proletariat is the special class in society which is or will be responsible for the definition of the total meaning of history."[87] Second, Schillebeeckx agrees with Jürgen Habermas who gives "a position of central importance in his own critical theory to the relationship between 'theoretical reason' and 'practical reason.'"[88] However, Schillebeeckx agrees with critical theory only to some extent. Schillebeeckx does not accept critical theory insofar as it is a pure *"philosophie du non"* that has a "tendency to make negativity itself into a new fetish and to intensify 'no' until it becomes an absolute."[89] Contrary to this "system of the non-system,"[90] Schillebeeckx suggests that negative dialectics is "sustained by a positive sphere of meaning which will direct praxis."[91] Therefore, according to Schillebeeckx, "there is a convergence between the emancipative interest by which critical theory is guided, and the liberating power which proceeds from the gospel, although they are not identical . . . This implies that the theologian who meditates on the implications of the gospel will also have specifically Christian reasons for making critical theory, constitutively linked to a critical praxis, his own."[92] In this sense, it is possible to speak of a "critical theology."[93]

To some extent, Schillebeeckx's theology is a sort of liberation theology. He positively understands and appreciates the theology of liberation in Latin America.[94] Liberation theology, he says, while being contextual

85. Rego, *Suffering and Salvation*, 78.
86. Ibid., 79.
87. Schillebeeckx, *Understanding of Faith*, 104.
88. Ibid., 92.
89. Ibid., 112.
90. Schillebeeckx, *God*, 116 n. 8.
91. Schillebeeckx, *Understanding of Faith*, 112.
92. Ibid., 122.
93. Ibid., 131.
94. See Schillebeeckx, *Christ*, 754–59. As Erik Borgman rightly asserts, Schillebeeckx's theology is more related to the theology of liberation as it is presented in Gutiérrez's book. "Although Schillebeeckx tried to integrate other developments, this book, *Theology of Liberation* was for him the authoritative presentation of liberation theology . . . Gustavo Gutiérrez, whom he knew as a member of *Concilium's* board of directors, was his main conversation partner. This is probably at least partly due to the

theology, has a "universal significance."[95] Hence, as Erik Borgman states, Schillebeeckx was one of those "Catholic academic theologians in the First World who . . . tried to integrate the impulses of liberation theologies in their theological project."[96] In fact, in his book *Jesus*, Schillebeeckx acknowledges that his original intention is "to offer a summary view of the contemporary problem of 'redemption' and 'emancipation' or human self-liberation, partly with 'liberation theology' in mind."[97] Likewise, in the foreword of his book *Church*, Schillebeeckx says, "I want to offer what through my own reflection I have made my own as a liberating theology from and thanks to the great Christian tradition."[98]

Schillebeeckx certainly understands the method of liberation theology. He acknowledged that the method of liberation theology, in which "Praxis came first and theology was the second step," was also the model of his theology.[99] He recognizes the importance of experience in order to do liberation theology: "Before it is even possible to understand what Christians mean by liberation, it is necessary to have experienced some form of liberation."[100] Thus, we might ask if Schillebeeckx had some kind of praxis or experience with the reality of poverty in his own social context to develop his own version of liberation theology. It seems that Schillebeeckx had at least two experiential sources that gave him some personal knowledge of the reality of poverty. First, during his studies in Paris, Schillebeeckx was impressed by the theology of Marie-Dominique Chenu, who was part of the worker-priests movement. Although Schillebeeckx himself never got involved in such a movement, he was exposed under the mentorship of Chenu to the social struggles of men and women.[101] Second, Schillebeeckx assisted

---

fact that he had the feeling that he could easily relate to Gutiérrez's project because their theologies shared the same origin . . . It originates from the French theologian and Dominican Marie-Dominique Chenu . . . who was a master of both Schillebeeckx and Gutiérrez" (Borgman, "Theology as the Art of Liberation," 101). Martin Poulsom suggests that "the interaction between Schillebeeckx and liberation theology may well be a two-way interaction" (Poulsom, *The Dialectics of Creation*, 114). In other words, not only liberation theology had an impact on Schillebeecks's theology, but also the latter influenced theologically on the former. For an analysis of the mutual and critical correlation between Latin American liberation theology and Schillebeeckx's theology, see Borgman, "Theology as the Art of Liberation."

95. Schillebeeckx, *Church*, 54.
96. Borgman, "Theology as the Art of Liberation," 98.
97. Schillebeeckx, *Jesus*, 18.
98. Schillebeeckx, *Church*, xxiii. See Schillebeeckx, "Liberating Theology."
99. Schillebeeckx, *God is New*, 18.
100. Schillebeeckx, *Christ*, 740.
101. Schillebeeckx declares, Chenu "probably did more than anyone else to inspire

what were called "critical communities in Dutch Catholicism," which, according to Phillip Kennedy, were "somewhat akin to the basic ecclesiastical communities of Latin America."[102] Kathleen McManus observes, "the experience of the critical communities in which Schillebeeckx shared was an experience of suffering that would prove to be ongoing."[103] In any case, Schillebeeckx's theology shows through and through an honest and compassionate sensitivity to the suffering of people, which might indicate that he is theologically responding to "the griefs and the anxieties"[104] of those he met in different circumstances.

In the following sections I will present how critical negativity, especially the notion of negative experience of contrast, permeates Schillebeeckx's theology. This exploration will help us to systematize and expand the christological insights that we got from the experience of contrast in art, i.e., the understanding of the life, death, and resurrection of Jesus Christ as an event of contrast. This analysis will focus on the later theology of Schillebeeckx—that is, the writings from 1966 onwards—especially because the reality of suffering caused by unjust social conditions, as Rego observes, is a more prevalent theme in Schillebeeckx's later theological production than in his earlier work.[105]

Meaningfulness, Meaninglessness, and Suffering

Schillebeeckx sees an ambiguity in the world. On the one hand, he recognizes what is positive, good, and beautiful in the world. On the other hand, he detects what is negative, evil, and ugly. He often uses the term "meaningful" to describe the positive dimensions of reality, and the term "meaningless" to express the negative aspects. Something is meaningful that has a positive significance and a good purpose. Something is meaningless that has neither purpose nor positive significance. Thus, Schillebeeckx says, "in our world there is that constantly enigmatic mixture of good and evil, of meaning and meaninglessness." In fact, "This reality is full of contradictions." On the one hand, there is "the human experience of suffering and evil, of oppression

---

my theological thinking and he influenced not just by what he said, but by his whole personality" (Schillebeeckx, *God is New*, 15–16). See McManus, *Unbroken Communion*, 27; Kennedy, *Schillebeeckx*, 21–23.

102. Kennedy, *Schillebeeckx*, 27. See Schillebeeckx, *God is New*, 93–94.

103. McManus, *Unbroken Communion*, 18. Schillebeeckx declares: "I looked around and saw critical communities emerging in the Church. That was decisive for me . . . I wanted to go along with that movement" (Schillebeeckx, *God is New*, 82).

104. Vatican II, *Gaudium et Spes*, 1.

105. Rego, *Suffering and Salvation*, 10–11, 17, 38.

and unhappiness." On the other, "without doubt there is also much goodness and beauty, much to be enjoyed in this world . . . But all these fragments of goodness and meaning are constantly contradicted and crushed by evil and hatred, by suffering, whether blatant or dull, by the misuse of power and terror."[106] Therefore, "The real history of human beings occurs where sense and non-sense exist side by side, overlay each other and intermingle, where there is joy and suffering, laughter and tears . . . Human history is ambiguous, with flashes of light and clouds of impenetrable darkness."[107]

Schillebeeckx insists that we cannot resolve the ambiguity of history theoretically. He says, "We cannot rationalize the combination of meaning and meaninglessness—the very warp of history . . . —into a coherent theoretical project." Meaningfulness and meaninglessness "are interrelated in a tension which cannot be resolved theoretically."[108] There are at least three reasons why the tension between meaningfulness and meaninglessness cannot be resolved theoretically. Firstly, we cannot resolve such tension theoretically because any attempt to reconcile good and evil fails. Secondly, we cannot resolve such tension theoretically because such an attempt entails a justification of what is evil in the world. Schillebeeckx says, "on the basis of the insight that it has no justification for existence, [one can] refuse to give a theoretical answer to what is experienced as the darker reality of evil."[109] Finally, we cannot resolve such tension theoretically because such an attempt implies a sort of insensitivity towards the suffering of others. According to Schillebeeckx, "Theoretical talk about the ultimate, total meaning of history . . . would amount to a lack of sensitivity to world-historical and personal dramas."[110]

Schillebeeckx often looks at the negative aspects of reality from the perspective of suffering. We cannot say enough how central the reality of suffering is in Schillebeeckx's theology.[111] He states, "Of special importance, it seems to me, is the fact continually confronting us—that of . . . innocent suffering, in short, the story of human suffering."[112] Later I will refer to Schillebeeckx's distinction between meaningful and meaningless suffering, but in the meantime I want to focus on the negative side of suffering, that

---

106. Schillebeeckx, *Church*, 5.

107. Schillebeeckx, *Jesus*, 577–78.

108. Schillebeeckx, *Church*, 172.

109. Schillebeecks, *Christ*, 719.

110. Schillebeeckx, *Church*, 173.

111. Robert Schreiter claims, "Schillebeeckx's preoccupation with suffering" is one of his "most enduring contributions to theology for the twenty-first century" (Schreiter, "Schillebeeckx and Theology," 261–62).

112. Schillebeeckx, *Jesus*, 581.

is, on its meaninglessness. Schillebeeckx says, "there is an *excess* of suffering and evil in our history . . . There is too much *unmerited* and *senseless* suffering . . . , suffering in which men, without finding meaning for themselves, are simply made the crude victims of an evil cause which serves others . . . , unmerited suffering of so many of the nameless among us, in our immediate neighbourhood. Perhaps including our own suffering that we do not understand."[113] According to Schillebeeckx, in the same way that we cannot resolve the ambiguity of meaningfulness and meaninglessness in history theoretically, we cannot explain the existence of suffering and evil in history theoretically. For Schillebeeckx, "The so-called surplus of suffering, injustice and meaninglessness escapes the *logos* of theoretical reason."[114] Hence, suffering and evil are an "unfathomable, theoretically incomprehensible *mystery*."[115]

Theoretical reason cannot resolve the ambiguity of meaningfulness and meaninglessness in history, but human action is the right answer to such ambiguity. Theoretical reason cannot decide the meaning of history, yet practical reason can help to remove some meaninglessness from history. Schillebeeckx says, "the thematization of universal meaning can be accomplished meaningfully only with a practical-critical intention, i.e. in a perspective in which a bit of meaninglessness is done away with, step by step, through human action. The thematization or reflection must thus be supported by a praxis of gradual liberation which will prepare and free the way for total meaning. In other words, total meaning can only come about through historical experiences and commitment."[116] Theoretical reason cannot explain the existence of suffering and evil in history, and yet human action—the praxis of liberation—is the right answer to the reality of suffering and evil. Schillebeeckx claims, "The only meaningful reaction to this history of suffering is in fact to offer resistance . . . For one can refuse to allow evil the right to exist, on the basis of the insight that it has no

113. Schillebeeckx, *Christ*, 718.

114. Schillebeeckx, *Church*, 173.

115. Schillebeeckx, *Christ*, 718. Like Schillebeeckx, Rahner suggests that suffering is theoretically incomprehensible, and that the incomprehensibility of suffering is related to God's incomprehensibility. See Rahner, "Human Question of Meaning"; Rahner, "Why Does God Allow Us to Suffer?" Fritz says, "Rahner's connection of suffering's incomprehensibility with God's incomprehensibility is, in effect, a *reductio in mysterium* . . . This is not to say that Rahner calls suffering good or ultimately redemptive because it relates to God. Nor is it to say that Rahner posits primordial maliciousness in God, making God into a font of suffering. Nor, finally, is it to say that Rahner dismisses suffering . . . But it is to say that Rahner remains open to the goodness of God, even in the face of suffering" (Fritz, *Karl Rahner's Theological Aesthetics*, 201).

116. Schillebeeckx, *Church*, 173.

justification for existence, and therefore refuse to give a theoretical answer to what is experienced as the darker reality of evil . . . However, that is only consistent and coherent if this refusal is linked with a powerful involvement in resistance against all forms of evil. That means that *in practice*, too, people must refuse to allow evil the right to exist."[117] Therefore, "The only adequate response is a *praxis* of resistance to evil, not a theory about it."[118]

According to Schillebeeckx, the excess of suffering in human history is like an indelible stain that neither theoretical reason nor practical reason can wash away. "Because of their historical extent and their historical density, evil and suffering are the dark fleck in our history, a fleck which no one can remove by an explanation or interpretation which is able to give it an understandable place in a rational and meaningful whole."[119] In other words, "evil and suffering are a dark stain on our history which no one can remove or explain, which we cannot . . . erase with social critique and the resultant praxis (however necessary)."[120] Nevertheless, inasmuch as meaningless suffering is a stain in history that does not go away, it works as a memory that spurs human action. As Schillebeeckx says, "as memory, the meaningless residue of history which theoretical reason cannot grasp . . . , remains a power, a cognitive stimulus to practical reason . . . which seeks to remove the meaninglessness from history."[121] Therefore, "In theory, people may not be in a position to *explain* suffering and evil, but the *remembrance* of what has happened in very specific suffering in a particular historical context also belongs to the structure of human reason or critical rationality. The story of these specific remembrances therefore remains an inner stimulus for practical reason which seeks to be liberating and active."[122] Therefore, like Metz, Schillebeeckx maintains that the remembrance of unjust suffering in human history has a critical power.[123]

Schillebeeckx makes a distinction between meaningless and meaningful suffering. Meaningless suffering, as Rego says, "is the experience of sheer negativity."[124] According to Schillebeeckx, "We are concerned with our *suffering fellow man*, who suffers under exploitation and oppression or rejection

---

117. Schillebeeckx, *Christ*, 719.
118. Schillebeeckx, *Jesus*, 582.
119. Schillebeeckx, *Christ*, 718.
120. Schillebeeckx, *Jesus*, 582.
121. Schillebeeckx, *Church*, 174.
122. Schillebeeckx, *Christ*, 719.
123. According to Elizabeth Tillar, "Johann-Baptist Metz's overriding concern with remembered suffering reverberates in Schillebeeckx's theology" (Tillar, "Critical Remembrance and Eschatological Hope," 17).
124. Rego, *Suffering and Salvation*, 157.

not only from individual human beings but above all from socio-political, economic and bureaucratic systems, anonymous forces which are none the less real . . . He does not even suffer in any way *for* the kingdom of God or *for* a good cause. He suffers. And he suffers above all *from* something, not *for the sake* of a cause. Dumb suffering."[125] Men and women undergo meaningless suffering when they "are simply made the crude victims of an evil cause which serves others."[126] They are "totally passive victims."[127] Meaningless suffering is, for instance, the suffering caused by "violence, lust for power, coveting at the expense of others, enslavement and oppression; there is Auschwitz."[128]

However, Schillebeeckx asserts, "Not all suffering is meaningless."[129] He describes "meaningful" suffering as follows:

> it is suffering for a good, righteous or holy cause which is close to a man's heart . . . This is not suffering which man chooses or seeks for himself. What man does choose is the cause for which he gives himself wholly. That is vocation: obedience towards the good which summons us and which we think worth the trouble: man is better than the suffering which can bring this sacrifice with it. Thus suffering takes on significance as the *actual* implication of a call to, and a responsibility for, a true and good cause (fellow man, God). In *that* sense, this suffering is on the one hand not sought, and on the other freely accepted as an actual and possible consequence of a particular commitment. In this kind of suffering man is not concentrated on himself, nor on his own suffering, but on the cause which he takes up.[130]

Therefore, as Rego rightly asserts, meaningful suffering is still an experience of negativity. Yet, "in situations of suffering that can be rendered meaningful, the meaning comes 'from without,' from something good that stands apart from and transcends suffering. This is necessary if the suffering is to be justified as meaningful." Furthermore, "The important element in this experience of suffering is that the sufferer retains his/her personal autonomy. That is to say, the sufferer is the active and free agent in the experience and not an unfree and passive victim."[131]

125. Schillebeeckx, *Christ*, 640.
126. Ibid., 718.
127. Rego, *Suffering and Salvation*, 159.
128. Schillebeeckx, *Jesus*, 576.
129. Schillebeeckx, *Christ*, 717.
130. Ibid., 717–18.
131. Rego, *Suffering and Salvation*, 157.

Therefore, the difference between meaningful and meaningless suffering is that the former are "forms of suffering which enrich our humanity in a positive sense,"[132] whereas the latter are types of suffering which diminish and damage the *humanum*. Schillebeeckx often employs the suggestive term "*humanum*." Consistent with his understanding of critical negativity, he suggests that the *humanum* should "never be defined positively,"[133] because such positive definitions have the risk of "becoming megalomaniac in human terms."[134] In fact, "several modern theories claiming to protect the *humanum* . . . have in fact resulted in a degradation of humanity," for instance, Nazism.[135]

Although the positive content of the *humanum* cannot be formulated, "mankind clearly has some negative knowledge of it."[136] In other words, "The *humanun* that is sought only becomes a universally recognised value via a negative and indirect mediation, that is, via a resistance to the inhumane. All resistance to inhumane situations reveals, if only indirectly, an obscure consciousness of what must be confessed positively by human integrity; it manifests in a negative and indirect way the call of and to the *humanum*."[137] Therefore, by *via negativa*, we have a knowledge of the *humanum*, i.e., that which is "authentic humanity,"[138] "that which is worthy of human beings."[139] As Steven Rodenborn says, the term *humanum*, "intentionally unfamiliar," is "intended to function as a warning against positively conceptualizing in the present what human life should be, while simultaneously affirming that it is nonetheless possible to know what it should not be."[140] For Schillebeeckx, the *humanum* is a "call," something that "has to be realized here and now,"[141] and as such, McManus observes, the *humanum* refers to "humanity's positive potential," "the not-yet-seen fulfilment of all that it means to be human."[142] Thus, meaningful suffering contributes to the realization and the enhancement of the *humanum*, whereas meaningless suffering diminishes it.[143]

---

132. Schillebeeckx, *Christ*, 717.
133. Schillebeeckx, *Church*, 29.
134. Schillebeeckx, *Christ*, 788.
135. Schillebeeckx, *Understanding of Faith*, 82.
136. Schillebeeckx, *God*, 116.
137. Schillebeeckx, *Understanding of Faith*, 80.
138. Schillebeeckx, *Jesus*, 569.
139. Schillebeeckx, *Church*, 29.
140. Rodenborn, *Hope in Action*, 171 n. 3.
141. Schillebeeckx, *Jesus*, 569.
142. McManus, *Unbroken Communion*, 1.
143. Rego, *Suffering and Salvation*, 157 n. 45.

Negative Experience of Contrast

"Negative experience of contrast" is a central concept in Schillebeeckx's thought. As Kennedy says, a negative experience of contrast is a "double-edged experience." It "has both a negative and a positive face."[144] On the one hand, a negative experience of contrast has a negative aspect. It is an experience of negative dimensions of reality, i.e., an experience of what we called in the previous section the meaninglessness of history, or meaningless suffering. Schillebeeckx says, "What we experience as reality, what we also see and hear of this reality daily through television and other mass media, is evidently not 'in order'; there is something fundamentally wrong." Thus, for instance, the "human experience of suffering and evil, of oppression and unhappiness,"[145] is an experience of negative dimensions of reality.

However, a negative experience has a contrast, which is positive. This positive dimension includes several elements. First of all, the experience of negative aspects of reality can inflame our indignation. This indignation is a positive thing. As Schillebeeckx says, "suffering and evil can provoke indignation,"[146] and "a positive element in this fundamental experience of contrast, the second element in this basic experience, is this human indignation." In turn, this indignation involves a "no" and a "yes." The "no" is a "'no' to the world as it is." In other words, it is a "no" to what is wrong in the world. It is a "fundamental human 'no' to evil."[147] Therefore, the "holy wrath of indignation" is opposed to resignation,[148] since resignation is an acceptance of the world as it is, whereas indignation is a protest against the status quo. In fact, a negative experience can prompt a protest that says "this cannot go on."[149] For instance, "The contrast experiences of the two World Wars, the concentration camps, political torture, the color-bar, the developing countries, the hungry, the homeless, the underprivileged and the poor in countries where there is so much potential wealth, and so on—all these experiences make people suddenly say: 'This should not and must not go on.'"[150] However, indignation involves a "yes" too. According to Schillebeeckx, "This human inability to give in to the situation offers an illuminating perspective. It discloses an openness to another situation which has the

---

144. Kennedy, *Schillebeeckx*, 128.
145. Schillebeeckx, *Church*, 5.
146. Schillebeeckx, *Christ*, 718.
147. Schillebeeckx, *Church*, 5–6.
148. Ibid., 181.
149. Schillebeeckx, *God*, 95.
150. Ibid., 92.

right to our affirmative 'yes.' One can call it a consensus with 'the unknown,' the content of which cannot even be defined in a positive way: a better, other world, which in fact does not yet exist anywhere. Or, to put it in yet another way, the mere assumption of the possibility of improving our world: openness to the unknown and the better."[151] Therefore, "The fundamental human 'no' to evil," Schillebeeckx says, "discloses an unfulfilled and thus 'open yes' which is as intractable as the human 'no,' indeed even stronger, because the 'open yes' is the basis of that opposition and makes it possible."[152] Indeed, in a negative experience of contrast, the "no" of protest "is possible only on the basis of an implicit longing for happiness." It "presupposes a vague awareness of the possible positive significance of human integrity." It "implies an awareness of the positive call of the *humanum* and to the *humanum*."[153] In other words, hope is what makes human protest possible:

> the protest prompted by these negative experiences ("this cannot go on") is also the expression of the firm hope that things *can* be done differently, *must* improve and *will* get better through our commitment. The prophetic voice that rises from the contrast experience is therefore protest, hope-inspiring promise and historical initiative. To put it still more accurately: what makes the protest and the historical decision possible is the actual presence of this hope, for, without it, the negative experience would not prompt the contrast experience and the protest. Thus the negative experience itself shows the primacy of this hope for a better future.[154]

However, we can hope for a better future only if we have a vague idea of what this fulfilled *humanum* may be. The notion of a better world, this fulfilled *humanum*, can only be grasped negatively or indirectly, since any positive definition of the *humanum* has the danger of justifying the totalitarian actions of an individual or a group. We can indirectly or negatively have an idea of what this better future may be in two different ways. On the one hand, we can have a hint of what this better world may be in the fragmentary experiences of meaning in the present. As Schillebeeckx says, "human life includes particular experiences which are signs or glimpses of an ultimate total meaning of human life,"[155] experiences such as "friendship,

---

151. Schillebeeckx, *Church*, 6.

152. Ibid.

153. Schillebeeckx, *Christ*, 814; see Schillebeeckx, *Jesus*, 583.

154. Schillebeeckx, *God*, 95. For a study of the development of the concept of hope in Schillebeeckx's theology, see Rodenborn, *Hope in Action*, 69–198.

155. Schillebeeckx, *Understanding of Faith*, 84.

love, personal encounters and fidelity in marriage."¹⁵⁶ These "fragmentary but real experiences of meaning and happiness on both a smaller and a larger scale . . . constantly keep nurturing, establishing and sustaining the 'open yes.'"¹⁵⁷ Thus, the conception of an unthreatened, final, perfect world is to some degree formulated in a positive way in the partial experiences of meaning already undergone. On the other hand, a perfect world can be expressed negatively or indirectly through images and metaphors of a better world.¹⁵⁸ In this sense, Schillebeeckx claims, we need poets who can formulate such metaphors.¹⁵⁹ Indeed, as I said above, in their artworks, artists can present worlds, better worlds, as real possibilities.

Therefore, negative experiences of contrast can lead to action. "The absence of what ought to be is indirectly apprehended in the negative experience, and so one gets a glimpse of what has *to be done* here and now."¹⁶⁰ Furthermore, both indignation (provoked by the experiences of negativity) and hope (generated by the fragmentary experiences of what is positive) can energize liberating action. As Schillebeeckx says, "both meaning already experienced and the experience of refractory meaninglessness have an emotional force which can direct *actions*."¹⁶¹ Thus, "the critical *practical* force does not lie either in the positive or in the negative, but only in their dialectical tension, that is, *in* the contrast experience of suffering."¹⁶² Therefore, as McManus asserts, "Through the dynamic of negative contrast, suffering spurs human beings to the transformative praxis."¹⁶³

Thus, a negative experience of contrast has both a passive and an active dimension. A person who has a negative experience of contrast is both passive and active. On the one hand, the person is passive inasmuch as he or she undergoes the experience of negativity. The person who undergoes meaningless suffering is a passive victim. On the other hand, the praxis of protest and of resistance against meaningless suffering is an active and free reaction of the person who undergoes such a negative experience. To explain these two dimensions of negative experiences of contrast, Schillebeeckx employs the distinction between instrumental reason and aesthetic reason, which has appeared already in our study but in a different context. According to

---

156. Ibid., 85.
157. Schillebeeckx, *Church*, 6.
158. Ibid., 788; see Schillebeeckx, *Jesus*, 582.
159. Schillebeeckx, *Church*, 132 n. 12.
160. Schillebeeckx, *Jesus*, 583 (emphasis mine); see Schillebeeckx, *God*, 93.
161. Schillebeeckx, *Christ*, 788 (emphasis mine).
162. Ibid., 815 n. 77 (emphasis mine).
163. McManus, *Unbroken Communion*, 90.

Schillebeeckx, suffering has an epistemological force that cannot be reduced to "the purposive, emancipatory type of 'controlling knowledge' (that form of knowledge peculiar to science and technology)," or "to various forms of contemplative, aesthetic and playful, so-called 'purpose-free' knowledge."[164] In fact,

> the contrast experience of suffering (with its implicit ethical demand) is in a position to form an inner link between them, because only it displays characteristics of both forms of knowledge. For experiences of suffering come upon people in the form of a negative experience, quite different from the positive enjoyment of contemplative, playful and aesthetic experiences. On the other hand, under the aspect of the experience of *contrast* or critical negativity, the experience of suffering forms a bridge towards possible action [that] might remove both suffering and its causes. Because of this inner affinity, albeit in critical negativity, with both contemplative knowledge and with manipulative scientific knowledge, I would term this particularly "pathic" epistemological power of suffering both *practical* and critical.[165]

Here we can see that Schillebeeckx falls prey to what we have called aestheticism, that is, the exclusive association of aesthetics with the "contemplative, playful, useless and aimless 'let it be.'"[166] We have already discussed the shortcomings of such understanding. However, acknowledging that passive contemplation sometimes can be part of an aesthetic experience, we can accept Schillebeeckx's analogy between human passivity in an aesthetic experience and passivity in the experience of suffering.

Schillebeeckx did not develop a theological aesthetics.[167] However, as Robert Schreiter says, the concept of negative experience of contrast has "heuristic values."[168] In my judgment, it can be used to help us understand some artistic experiences. In fact, the negative experience of contrast is a promising concept for the development of a theological aesthetics that may work as "a corrective on the more inward-looking aesthetics found among some of the followers of [von] Balthasar."[169] In this study I am not applying,

---

164. Schillebeeckx, *Christ*, 813; see Schillebeeckx, *Jesus*, 582–83.

165. Schillebeeckx, *Christ*, 813–14; see Schillebeeckx, *Jesus*, 583.

166. Schillebeeckx, *Christ*, 801.

167. See Schillebeeckx, "Culture, Religion and Violence." In that article Schillebeeckx writes about culture and art from the perspective of language. Although it is a remarkable essay, we cannot conclude that Schillebeeckx developed a theological aesthetics just because he wrote one article about art and culture.

168. Schreiter, "Schillebeeckx and Theology," 261.

169. Ibid., 263.

but correlating Schillebeeckx's concept of negative experience of contrast with the notion of artistic experience of contrast. As I said above, an artistic experience of contrast not only shows the ugliness of reality, but also alludes to the beauty that is not there and should be there. In this way, the artistic experience of contrast is a "no" against the ugliness—of injustice, of violence, of poverty, etc.—in our world, and it is a "yes" to the beauty—of justice, of peace, of solidarity, etc.—that is not there in the world, but could and should exist in our world. Therefore, the artistic experience of contrast involves a protest and a hope that can energize the praxis of liberation. This experience of contrast in art is analogical to, correlative with—and an aesthetic expression of—the experience of suffering as a negative experience of contrast.

God, Salvation, and an Eschatological Proviso

The experience of meaningless suffering in our world provokes the question about God. The question can be formulated as follows: Is there any relationship between God and meaningless suffering? If there is such relationship, what is it? Here we are specifically talking about unjust suffering, that is, suffering caused by social injustice. Unjust suffering is meaningless, that is, it does not have any positive significance or purpose. Thus, the question about the relationship between God and unjust suffering is not easy to answer. As Schillebeeckx asserts, "suffering becomes a problem especially for the man who believes in God."[170] Therefore, as Rego says, suffering "poses a challenge to theology."[171] As we answer this question, though, we are not trying to justify God. As Schillebeeckx claims, "*We* cannot justify God." We cannot do so for two reasons. First, because "we are not God, and we think of God's omnipotence and goodness with petty human terms."[172] In fact, we cannot cover the infinite mystery of God with our limited human reason. Second, we cannot justify God because there is nothing to justify. In other words, God has not done anything wrong that needs our justification. Therefore, as we try to answer the question about the relationship between God and meaningless suffering, rather than trying to justify God, we are trying to express with "petty human terms" the reality of such relationship.

Consistent with his understanding of critical negativity, Schillebeeckx's answer to the question about the relationship between God and unjust suffering is both dialectical and practical. On the one hand, the answer is

170. Schillebeeckx, *Christ*, 664.
171. Rego, *Suffering and Salvation*, 5.
172. Schillebeeckx, *Christ*, 718.

dialectical, since the relationship between God and meaningless suffering is that of opposition. In other words, God opposes unjust suffering. The answer is practical, since the praxis of liberation from unjust suffering— i.e., the praxis of the kingdom of God as it is revealed in Jesus Christ—is the right answer to the reality of meaningless suffering. In the following paragraphs we will explore some aspects that are involved in this dialectical and practical response to the question about the relationship between God and unjust suffering.

"God is pure positivity."[173] This assertion means that the "God of Christians is 'not a God of the dead, but of the living' (Matthew 22:32). In other words, *this* concept of God assigns positivity simply and solely to God. 'God is love' (1 John 4:8,16); by nature he promotes the good and opposes all evil."[174] Like Gutiérrez, Schillebeckx claims that Christians worship "only a 'God of life,' not a God of life and death."[175] Thus, God wills the life of men and women, and not their death. God is the ground only of life, and not the ground of evil, suffering, and death.[176]

God is the principle of life. Is there any parallel principle of evil and death? For Christianity, the answer is "no," there is no first principle of evil. Christianity rejects dualism, i.e., "the existence of a twofold first and supreme principle, a principle of good and a principle of evil."[177] If God is not the ground of evil and death, and if there is no parallel first principle of evil and death, then what is the metaphysical origin of evil and death? The answer to this question is "we do not know." Schillebeeckx says, "Philosophy and theology alike are left speechless and confounded by the complexity of evil and [of] human suffering."[178] In fact, "The Christian message does not give an *explanation* of evil or [of] our history of suffering."[179] Resorting to Aquinas, Schillebeeckx very cautiously suggests that finitude might be the cause of evil and death. "As soon as there are creatures, there is the possibility (not the necessity) of a negative and original initiative of finitude, if I can put it that way."[180] However, this may be the only text in which Schillebeeckx tentatively make a hypothesis about the metaphysical origin of evil and death. In general, Schillebeeckx "does not delve into the metaphysics

---

173. Ibid., 720, 667.
174. Ibid., 776.
175. Schillebeeckx, *Church*, 32.
176. Schillebeeckx, *Christ*, 720.
177. Ibid., 665, 720.
178. Schillebeeckx, *Jesus*, 582.
179. Schillebeeckx, *Christ*, 721.
180. Ibid.

of evil,"[181] because for him, like for Rahner, suffering and evil "are not a *problem*, but an unfathomable, theoretically incomprehensible mystery."[182] However, we should specify that what remains a mystery is the *ultimate* origin of suffering and evil. "There are 'rational and comprehensible' aspects to suffering that are accessible to reason, and so to explanation and amelioration."[183] For instance, there are causes of evil and suffering "on a physical, psycho-somatic and social level" that are not a mystery, but a problem that can and should be resolved by means of human reflection and human praxis, although in a "partial and limited" way.[184] But even then, the ultimate origin of evil and death remains a mystery.

Therefore, as Rego remarks, Schillebeeckx "acknowledges the incomprehensible mystery of both, God and evil, without attempting to reconcile them." In fact, "any explanation of evil and suffering which compromises God's pure positivity, or makes God complicit in them, is unacceptable."[185] Thus, for instance, Schillebeeckx asks, "does someone perhaps want to give Buchenwald, Auschwitz or Vietnam (or whatever else) a specific structural place in the divine plan, which, as Christians believe, directs our history? No man, at any rate, who thinks it [is] important to be a man and to be treated as a man will do so."[186] As Rego says, Schillebeeckx "ultimately prefers to live with the mystery of God and suffering as irreconcilable. Therefore, innocent suffering can never be justified. Any attempt to do so is theological hubris."[187]

Furthermore, there is another reason why we should stop puzzling over the metaphysical origin of evil and death. For Schillebeeckx, the right answer to the reality of evil is not theoretical speculation about its origin, but the praxis of liberation from evil. As McManus asserts, Schillebeeckx "waves away such speculation as a waste of time when the concrete immediacy of suffering demands [practical] attention."[188]

To say that God wills the life of men and women means that God wills their salvation, i.e., salvation from evil, suffering, and death. God is the primary subject of the salvation of human beings. For Christians, the question about "the meaning and purpose of human life in nature and history, in a

---

181. Rego, *Suffering and Salvation*, 148–49.
182. Schillebeeckx, *Christ*, 718.
183. Rego, *Suffering and Salvation*, 167.
184. Schillebeeckx, *Christ*, 761.
185. Rego, *Suffering and Salvation*, 276.
186. Schillebeeckx, *Christ*, 718.
187. Rego, *Suffering and Salvation*, 334.
188. McManus, *Unbroken Communion*, 40.

context of meaning and meaninglessness, of suffering and moments of joy, has received a positive and unique answer surpassing all expectations: God himself is the guarantor that human life has a positive and significant meaning." God has decided the meaning and purpose of humankind, which is the wholeness and happiness of all humanity. In fact, "God's own honour lies in the happiness and salvation of mankind."[189] God's "glory lies in human happiness."[190] In this sense, Christianity understands "the cause of humankind as the cause of God."[191]

Like Rahner and liberation theologians, Schillebeeckx argues that the salvation of humankind comes from and is achieved primarily by God, who is transcendent, but from within the history of humanity. In other words, God saves humankind in history without losing his transcendence. Schillebeeckx observes, "Salvation lies in the line of the holy, good, beautiful, and enjoyable things that can be realized in our history, but in such a way that God remains free in a surprising gift which transcends all this."[192] Furthermore, God saves humankind without doing violence to human freedom. In other words, God saves humankind in and through the active freedom of men and women. Salvation is "a grace, but a grace which is effective in and through human action and not outside it, above it or behind it."[193]

What is this happiness and salvation of humankind? "What is to be a true and good, happy and free man . . . ? What is a livable humanity?"[194] According to Schillebeeckx,

> Conceptions of an unthreatened, final, perfect salvation applying to all are on the one hand to some degree formulated in a positive way because of partial experiences of meaning already undergone; on the other hand, however, within the real history of suffering within which we stand they can only be expressed negatively, in parables and visions: a world in which righteousness and love prevail, a world "without tears." However, our situation never allows us to define in positive terms what this will ultimately imply for human salvation, given the spiritual openness and the human "self-transcendence" still to be realized in history and, moreover, in view of the absolute freedom of God . . . Any positive definition runs the risk of either

189. Schillebeeckx, *Christ*, 627–28.
190. Ibid., 788.
191. See Schillebeeckx, *Jesus*, 239, 370, 569.
192. Schillebeeckx, *Christ*, 810–11.
193. Schillebeeckx, *Church*, 232.
194. Schillebeeckx, *Christ*, 725.

becoming megalomaniac in human terms or belittling God's possibilities.[195]

Therefore, Schillebeeckx does not give any "positivistic outline, or a pre-existing definition of 'human nature' in philosophical terms." Rather, he suggests some "anthropological constants," which form a kind of "system of co-ordinates of man and his salvation."[196] According to Schillebeeckx, "The height and breadth and depth of human salvation"[197] includes: (i) the "relationship with our human bodies, nature and the ecological environment," (ii) the relationship with other human beings, (iii) the "connection with social and institutional structures," (iv) the "conditioning of people and culture by time and space," (v) the "mutual relationship of theory and practice," (vi) the religious dimension of human beings, and (vii) an irreducible synthesis of the previous six aspects.[198]

> Thus *Christian salvation*, in the centuries-old biblical tradition called redemption, and meant as salvation from God for men, is concerned with the whole system of co-ordinates in which man can really be man. This salvation—the wholeness of man—cannot just be sought in one or other of these constants, say exclusively in "ecological appeals," in an exclusive "be nice to one another," in the exclusive overthrow of an economic system (whether Marxist or capitalist), or in exclusively mystical experiences: "Alleluia, he is risen!" On the other hand, the *synthesis* of all this is clearly an "already now" and a "not yet." The way in which human failure and human shortcomings are coped with must be termed one form of "liberation" (and perhaps its most important form). In that case that might then be the all-embracing "anthropological constant."[199]

Therefore, again like Gutiérrez who says that liberation is and should be integral, Schillebeeckx claims, "liberation or salvation, then, is the conquest of all human, personal and social alienation: it is the wholeness of man, human life and human history."[200] If salvation means "being whole," then it is threatened "to be less than wholeness when people seek all salvation in only

---

195. Ibid., 788. McManus asserts, for Schillebeeckx, "salvation can be articulated only in counterpoint to the reality of suffering" (McManus, "Suffering in the Theology of Edward Schillebeeckx," 477).

196. Schillebeeckx, *Christ*, 727–28.

197. Ibid., 725.

198. See ibid., 728–36.

199. Ibid., 737.

200. Schillebeeckx, *Jesus*, 585; see Schillebeeckx, *Christ*, 810.

one dimension of humanity—whether this is socio-political or personal." In fact, "it is impossible to reduce the causes of suffering and the saving and redemptive action directed towards them *either* to merely personal *or* to exclusively socio-political action. In that case the saving action would in fact be only half redemption and half liberation."[201]

The tension between the "already" and the "not yet" of salvation means that "we experience redemption and liberation only in finite fragments, in a history which *stands open* towards eschatological consummation."[202] In fact, "there are fragments of *eschatological joy* in our history."[203] For instance, Schillebeeckx says, "fragmentary salvation is realized where we encounter others in love."[204] Likewise, fragmentary salvation takes place whenever and wherever socio-political liberation occurs in history.[205] However, "human salvation is only salvation . . . when it is universal and complete. There cannot really be talk of salvation as long as there is still suffering, oppression and unhappiness."[206] Hence, Schillebeekcx claims that "man remains 'unquiet,' in the sense of 'dissatisfied,' so long as salvation is not realized universally and completely for each and every individual." However, "this 'discontent' which acts as a stimulus towards action . . . is part of the nature of Christian redemption."[207] In fact, the unquietness or the discontent that is provoked when we see that there is still injustice in the world can become "a spur to never give up realizing meaning in history and thus to challenge injustice and meaninglessness."[208]

Furthermore, the "not yet" of salvation is what we call the "eschatological proviso," which functions as critical negativity. The eschatological proviso is a "criticism of all presumptions to identify salvation exclusively in specific terms. Salvation cannot be identified exclusively with political

201. Schillebeeckx, *Christ*, 708.

202. Ibid., 815.

203. Ibid., 830. Schillebeeckx recognizes that the joy of the poor, here and now, is an anticipation of the kingdom of God. "The fact that, as I have repeatedly heard from Latin American liberation theologians, there is more laughing, dancing and celebration among the poor and oppressed is a clear indication, in keeping with Jesus' beatitude, that the kingdom of God now already belongs to the poor" (Schillebeeckx, *Church*, 112). For a theological and spiritual comment on the "Easter joy" of the poor, see Gutiérrez, *We Drink from Our Own Wells*, 114–21.

204. Schillebeeckx, *Christ*, 829.

205. For an analysis of both the identity and the difference between salvation and socio-political liberation according to Schillebeeckx's theology, see Simon, "Salvation and Liberation," 507–15.

206. Schillebeeckx, *Christ*, 719.

207. Ibid., 830.

208. Schillebeeckx, *Church*, 174.

liberation; exclusively with 'being nice to one another'; exclusively with ecological efforts; exclusively with identifying oneself either with micro-ethics or macro-ethics or mysticism, liturgy and prayer . . . , and so on."[209] Furthermore, the eschatological proviso rejects the identification of salvation with any human project of building a better society that has already been achieved in history, for Christian faith will "always keep this better future open to a constant transcendence of itself."[210]

The eschatological proviso rejects any understanding of salvation in purely human terms. In other words, the eschatological proviso reminds us, "mankind is not the subject of a 'universal providence.'"[211] Christian belief in salvation from God "is the downfall of any doctrine of salvation or soteriology understood in human terms, in the sense of an identity which is within our control and therefore can be manipulated."[212] Therefore, Christian faith "will always be critical of every form of individualism or of collective totalitarianism."[213] Christian faith is against "every image of man whose lines are strictly drawn or which presents itself as a positive and total definition."[214] In fact, "Christian faith resists any premature identification of the *humanum*. In its resistance . . . , Christianity remains critical and insists that it cannot accept any uniform positive definition of the *humanum*. The power to realise this *humanum* is reserved for God."[215] In other words, "Christian faith refuses to postulate a secular or universal subject of history . . . The Christian answer reminds man that such a universal subject of history . . . really exists, but cannot be given from history itself. Neither the human individual, nor the community nor any part of society, but only the living God is recognised in Christian faith . . . as the universal subject of history."[216]

However, according to Schillebeeckx, the eschatological proviso is not simply negative criticism. The "critical function of eschatological hope implies a criticism of all 'negative dialectics' whose critical negativity is sterile . . . and remains incapable of providing any positive contribution to the improvement of the condition of mankind as a whole."[217] If we were to take

---

209. Schillebeeckx, *Christ*, 776.
210. Schillebeeckx, *God*, 120.
211. Schillebeeckx, *Christ*, 776.
212. Ibid., 832.
213. Schillebeeckx, *God*, 120.
214. Ibid., 118.
215. Schillebeeckx, *Understanding of Faith*, 82.
216. Ibid., 81.
217. Schillebeeckx, *God*, 117.

only the negative critical function of the eschatological proviso, without the positive content of Christian faith, the eschatological proviso would rather cause damage to humankind, since it would not be able to give Christians any inspiration or any orientation in their choices.[218] Thus, "the eschatological vision of the future is the positive, 'utopian' and 'critical' norm for [our] particular concrete and changing situation."[219] The critical negativity of Christian faith would be "impossible and unintelligible without the justified trust that perfect meaningfulness . . . is not entirely beyond our reach." For Christian faith, it is possible for humankind to be in a state in which "meaningfulness and meaningless are no longer insanely interwoven and when fully realised meaning is actively experienced. This situation can be described as 'salvation,' being whole. It can also be called the *eschaton* or perfect fulfilment of meaning."[220] Therefore, "The message which Christianity brings to the secular world is this—humanity is possible!"[221] This message has "a positive power which continues to exert constant pressure in order to bring about a better world."[222] In this sense, Schillebeeckx says,

> Christian party politicians usually speak of a "*positive* Christian inspiration" with regard to the socio-economic and political ordering of temporal society. If what is meant by this is that the Christian faith exerts a positive pressure and insists that what is humanly impossible is indeed possible, then I can agree with it. If, on the other hand, it is to be understood in a different sense, then I am afraid that Christianity is thereby being narrowed down into a special kind of "ideology" . . . The gospel does not present us directly with any socio-economic or political plan of action.[223]

Therefore, for Christian faith, "humanity is possible through the resources of man himself, but that means through the resources of redeemed man with his 'new heart.'"[224] In other words, the fulfillment of the *humanum* is possible through the action of men and women who have faith and hope in the "God of promise," who "has bound himself to the realization of this also in Christ."[225]

---

218. Schillebeeckx, *Christ*, 774–75.
219. Schillebeeckx, *God*, 99.
220. Schillebeeckx, *Understanding of Faith*, 83.
221. Schillebeeckx, *God*, 117.
222. Ibid., 116.
223. Ibid., 119.
224. Ibid., 118–19.
225. Ibid., 116.

In fact, it is in Jesus Christ that God has revealed all the things that have been said in this section about God's self, salvation, and eschatology. It is in Jesus that God has revealed that God is a God of life, and not of death. As Schillebeecx says, the notion of God as pure positivity "appears from and in Jesus of Nazareth."[226] Jesus is the "pioneer in the fight for man's cause as God's cause."[227] In fact, the *humanum* has been "proclaimed and promised in Jesus Christ,"[228] that is, "the meaning or destiny of man, prepared for and intended from of old by God, has been disclosed and thus been made known . . . in the person, career and destiny of Jesus of Nazareth."[229] In other words, the fulfillment of the *humanum* has been anticipated in Jesus Christ. Therefore, eschatology is indeed "eschatological remembrance,"[230] since "for Christianity the foundation, norm and criterion of every future expectation is its relationship with the past, i.e. with Jesus of Nazareth and what has taken place in him."[231] As Rodenborn says, in Schillebeeckx's understanding of Christianity, "remembrance of the past and expectation for the future are essentially related,"[232] for "It is in Jesus Christ that Christians find the subversive memory capable of reenvisioning an alternative and better future."[233]

Jesus' Life, Death, and Resurrection

It is important to remember that here we are not planning to explain the whole Christology of Schillebeeckx. To do so is beyond the limits of our study, and it is unnecessary for our purposes. The goal of this section is to understand how the concept of contrast permeates Schillebeeckx's Christology, for it correlates, systematizes, and expands the christological insights that we got from the experience of contrast in art.

Like the liberation theologians, Schillebeeckx emphasizes the importance of the historical Jesus in order to understand Christian faith:

> the Christian faith entails not only the personal, living presence of the glorified Jesus, but also a link with his life on earth; for it is precisely that earthly life that was acknowledged and

---

226. Schillebeeckx, *Christ*, 776.
227. Ibid., 629.
228. Schillebeeckx, *Understanding of Faith*, 59.
229. Schillebeeckx, *Christ*, 628.
230. Ibid., 815.
231. Schillebeeckx, *God*, 114.
232. Rodenborn, *Hope in Action*, 151.
233. Ibid., 155.

empowered by God through the resurrection. For me, therefore, a Christianity or kerygma minus the historical Jesus of Nazareth is ultimately vacuous—not Christianity at all, in fact. If the very heart of the Christian faith consists in an affirmation of God's saving activity in history—decisively accomplished in the life history of Jesus of Nazareth—for the liberation of human beings . . . , then the personal history of this Jesus cannot be lost sight of.[234]

Remarkably like Sobrino, Schillebeeckx understands the concept "historical Jesus" differently from how some biblical scholars understand the term when they use a historical critical method. According to Schillebeeckx, by using critical scientific methods, biblical scholars gave to the Bible an objective value. In this way, scholars believed they could protect the Bible from subjective interpretation. However, this approach led to a break between the original unity between the text and the reader, between the Bible and the community of the church.[235] Therefore, Schillebeeckx says, "I hope, with my critical approach to the 'Jesus of history' to clear the way for a new interplay between the text and the reader of the Bible, so that the reader is stimulated by the text to become personally and socially emancipated and liberated."[236]

According to Schillebeeckx, again as for the liberation theologians, the kingdom of God is central in Jesus' life. The kingdom of God "is an *event* in which God begins to govern and act as king or Lord, hence an act in which God manifests his Godhead in the human world. Thus God's lordship or dominion is the divine power itself in its saving acts in our history, and *at the same time* the final, eschatological state that brings to an end the evil world, and initiates the new world in which God 'comes into his own.'"[237] Jesus proclaimed the kingdom of God through his life, his conduct, his words, his actions, that is, through his praxis. "Jesus makes a connection between the coming of God's kingdom and *metanoia*, that is, the actual praxis of the kingdom of God. The Lord's prayer suggests a fundamental connection between 'your kingdom come' and 'your will be done on earth': carrying out God's will in our earthly history has to do with the coming of his kingdom, always in the dialectics, so typical of Jesus, between present and future."[238] Therefore, Jesus leads his own life as an attestation of God's universal love for humankind. "Jesus' conduct of his own life presents not a theoretical but

---

234. Schillebeeckx, *Jesus*, 56.
235. Schillebeeckx, *God is New*, 20–21.
236. Ibid., 21.
237. Schillebeeckx, *Jesus*, 121.
238. Ibid., 132.

a practical, proleptic realization, an anticipation of the 'new earth' . . . Hence the sought after, totally other, better world—the kingdom of God . . . —is not vague and undefined: it acquired a historical likeness in the life and conduct of Jesus."[239] Therefore, "Jesus' praxis is nothing other than the praxis of God's kingdom."[240] His praxis includes, for instance, healing the sick, sharing the table with tax collectors and sinners, and friendship with social outcasts. Through his praxis, "Jesus brings God's message of his radical 'no' to the continuing history of human suffering . . . In Jesus' eschatological message we hear only God's radical 'no' to all forms of evil, all forms of poverty and hunger that lead to tears."[241] Therefore, in Jesus' proclamation of the kingdom of God, "the good news is for the poor . . . God and suffering are diametrically opposed; where God appears, evil and suffering have to yield. So there is no place for suffering and tears in the messianic kingdom, not even for death."[242]

Jesus' message, which implies a "connection between God's lordship and orthopraxis," is a call to his listeners to conduct their lives in Jesus' way, that is, in a way that unites "eschatological hope with a new praxis in this world."[243] Therefore, "Jesus' message of God's lordship and his kingdom is: God's universal love for mankind attested in and through Jesus' corresponding conduct, hence an appeal to us to believe in and hope for this coming salvation and kingdom of peace 'imparted by God,' and faithfully to manifest its coming in consistent praxis of that kingdom."[244]

Jesus' proclamation of the kingdom of God led him to have conflicts with those who had socio-political and religious power at that time, i.e., those who put him to death. Therefore, "The death of Jesus was no coincidence, but the intrinsic historical consequence of the radicalism of both his message and his life-style, which showed that all 'master-servant' relationships were incompatible with the life-style of the kingdom of God. The very radicalism of this proclamation provoked the fatal resistance of others." In fact, the "radical universality of a will of a salvation-for-all, without any exclusiveness, provoked the well-known and equally radical counter-reaction of 'this world.'"[245] The resistance of those who did not welcome

239. Ibid., 133.
240. Ibid., 192.
241. Ibid., 154–55.
242. Schillebeeckx, *Christ*, 686.
243. Schillebeeckx, *Jesus*, 132–33.
244. Ibid., 133.
245. Schillebeeckx, *Christ*, 791.

Jesus' message was not a necessary and obligatory reaction to his message, but a typical and very likely reaction of someone who sees his own power threatened.

Jesus "did not expect that his mission would inevitably lead to a violent death (even though that is the way in which it is in fact represented in the gospels)."[246] However, at the end of his life, Jesus recognized the "human, historical 'necessity'" of this "radical resistance to his message and his life-style. He assumed this human finitude, trusting in the non-finite God who has the last word." Jesus neither wanted his passion nor sought his own death.[247] Nonetheless, confronted with the possibility of a violent death, he came to terms with this probability.[248]

Therefore, "Jesus' death on the cross is the consequence of a life in radical service of justice and love, a consequence of his option for the poor and outcast, of a choice for his people suffering under exploitation and oppression. Within an evil world any commitment to justice and love is deadly dangerous."[249] In fact, "Suffering is the likely consequence . . . of any wholehearted efforts for a great cause: suffering through and for others, 'for the sake of the kingdom of God,' as scripture says."[250] Therefore, Schillebeeckx says,

> We may not isolate the death of Jesus from the context of his life, his message and his life's work; otherwise we are turning its redemptive significance into a myth, sometimes even into a sadistic and bloody myth. As soon as we fail to take account of Jesus' message and the life journey which led to his death, we obscure the Christian tenor of the saving significance of this death. The death of Jesus is the historical expression of the unconditional nature of his proclamation and life, in the face of which the significance of the fatal consequences for his own life completely paled into insignificance. Jesus' death was a suffering through and for others as the unconditional validity of a praxis of doing good and opposing evil and suffering.[251]

In other words, "We have to see the life and death of Jesus as one whole; we cannot consider the significance of his death by itself."[252] According to

---

246. Ibid., 824.
247. Ibid., 791.
248. Ibid., 824.
249. Schillebeeckx, *Church*, 124.
250. Schillebeeckx, *Christ*, 815.
251. Schillebeeckx, *Church*, 118–19.
252. Ibid., 119.

Schillebeeckx, "there is a continuity between the way of life of Jesus and his death." In his life, "Jesus identifies himself *par excellence* with outcast and rejected men and women, the unholy, so that he too himself finally becomes the one who is rejected and outcast. This identification is radical,"[253] especially in his death. Therefore, as Derek Simon observes, "Schillebeeckx brings to our attention a distinct dimension of the salvific meaning of the death of Jesus. God does not reject Jesus, but identifies with the Jesus rejected by a dominant minority of sociocultural and political-economic élites. This represents the extent of God's solidarity with all the marginalized and downtrodden ... Within the death of Jesus, God's solidarity with all the violated and vanquished is disclosed."[254]

If we consider Jesus' death in isolation, if we consider the cross in itself, without any reference to his life of solidarity with social outcasts, we can only say that the death of Jesus on the cross is sheer negativity. As Schillebeeckx says, "In Jesus' death, in and of itself, i.e. in terms of what human beings did to him, there is only negativity." In fact, in human history, "Thousands have been crucified, yet nevertheless their crucifixions have not been thought to have universal significance, nor have they been called atoning deaths. So the importance cannot lie in Jesus' death as such. Purely as the death of Jesus, this dying cannot have any redemptive or liberating force; on the contrary, death is the enemy of life."[255]

Nevertheless, Schillebeeckx, says, "*From beyond* the inherently negative nature of death, as it were, Jesus' death was given positive 'content,' carried as he was by his positive service to the cause of man as the cause of God."[256] In other words, if there is anything positive about Jesus' death, it does not come from death itself, since death is only negativity. The positive content of Jesus' death comes from outside—or "from beyond," using Schillebeeckx's words. The positive content of Jesus' death comes from his life of "service to the cause of man as the cause of God." In other words, the positive content comes from the "positivity which revealed itself in his actual life of solidarity with oppressed men and women on the basis of an absolute trust in God."[257]

Therefore, Schillebeeckx says, "Jesus could meaningfully endure what was meaningless—death—and even incorporate it into his offer of

---

253. Ibid., 123.
254. Simon, "Salvation and Liberation," 503.
255. Schillebeeckx, *Church*, 125.
256. Schillebeeckx, *Jesus*, 608 (emphasis mine).
257. Schillebeeckx, *Church*, 126.

salvation."²⁵⁸ To understand this assertion, we should recall Schillebeeckx's distinction between meaningful and meaningless suffering that we studied above. In fact, suffering *in itself* is meaningless. However, it is possible to say that suffering is meaningful if it is undergone for a good cause. As Rego says, this category of meaningful suffering "influences Schillebeeckx's Christology. It is the kind of suffering that Jesus endures in his career of proclaiming the kingdom of God."²⁵⁹ In fact, we can claim that Jesus' suffering is meaningful because it is undergone for a good cause, i.e., for the cause of humankind as the cause of God, for the kingdom of God, in solidarity with social outcasts. In fact, according to Schillebeeckx, the figure of the suffering servant in Deutero-Isaiah is an appropriate image of Jesus. However, Schillebeeckx interprets the suffering servant through 1 Peter to reach the conclusion that the suffering servant does not undergo suffering for the sake of suffering itself, but for the sake of others.²⁶⁰ Thus, the letter does not glorify suffering in itself, "but suffering *for the sake of* others and *at the hands of others*."²⁶¹

Hence, the saving significance of Jesus' suffering and death does not come from suffering and death themselves, but from the positivity of his life of solidarity with social outcasts. "Suffering is not redemptive in itself. But it is redemptive when it is suffering through and for others, for man's cause as the cause of [God]."²⁶² In other words, "the saving significance of Jesus . . . does not lie in the crucifixion taken in isolation." Rather, the saving significance of Jesus is in his life, which "finds its climax in the crucifixion."²⁶³ Nevertheless, even if we say that Jesus' death and suffering are meaningful and redemptive inasmuch as they are undergone for the sake of others, even then, Schillebeecks says, "that does not nullify or undo that meaningless death!"²⁶⁴ The negativity of Jesus' death "cannot be reasoned away."²⁶⁵

Schillebeeckx claims, God "did not put Jesus on the cross. Human beings did that."²⁶⁶ "It was not God but men and women who put Jesus to death."²⁶⁷ In fact, there is a "non-identity" between God and Jesus' death.

---

258. Schillebeeckx, *Jesus*, 608.
259. Rego, *Suffering and Salvation*, 157.
260. See Schillebeeckx, *Christ*, 213–18.
261. Ibid., 215.
262. Ibid., 629.
263. Schillebeeckx, *Church*, 123.
264. Schillebeeckx, *Jesus*, 608–9.
265. Ibid., 611.
266. Schillebeeckx, *Church*, 119.
267. Ibid., 125.

This reality of non-identity "removes [Jesus'] suffering from God's domain and leaves it in the worldly reality of the human condition and human freedom." Jesus' suffering and death are a "non-divine situation," since God does not will them.[268] In fact, "*Negativity* cannot have a cause or a motive in God. But in that case we cannot look for a divine *reason* for the death of Jesus either. Therefore, first of all, we have to say that we are not redeemed *thanks to* the death of Jesus but *despite* it."[269] In this "somewhat provocative statement," Rego observes, Schillebeeckx "sums up his position on the soteriological significance of Jesus' death," which includes three points. First, if death is negativity, then God saves us not thanks to the negativity of death, but in spite of it. Second, Jesus' death has indeed a saving significance, but it does not come from death itself, but from the positivity of his life. And third, God is not an accomplice in Jesus' death.[270] In this sense, Schillebeeckx says, "The messianic 'must suffer' of Jesus is not a 'divine' must. It is forced on God through Jesus by human beings."[271] As Simon says, "The dying and death of Jesus, according to Schillebeeckx, are in themselves neither salvific events nor intrinsically necessary as an act of obedience to a divine demand for sacrificial compensation. The death of Jesus is not the result of God's wish or imperative, not the result of Jesus' obedience to a sadistic parent, nor a moral teaching on suffering as an end in itself, or even a means to glory."[272] In fact, this understanding of God in a dialectical or opposed relationship with the negativity of the cross is a corrective to the theologies of the cross of Sobrino and von Balthasar, who suggest that Jesus' death on the cross was God's will.

Not only Jesus' death, but also his resurrection should always be seen in connection with his life. As Schillebeeckx's says, "Just as the death of Jesus cannot be detached from his life, so his resurrection cannot be detached from his life and death. To extrapolate the death and resurrection of Jesus so that they become the nucleus of the Christian message is ultimately to twist the prophetic content of the whole ministry of Jesus."[273] This connection between the life and the resurrection of Jesus is in two directions. On the one hand, the life of Jesus is an anticipation of the resurrection. As Schillebeeckx says, Jesus' "'going around Palestine doing good' was itself already the beginning of the kingdom of God, of a kingdom in which death and injustice

---

268. Schillebeeckx, *Jesus*, 611.
269. Schillebeeckx, *Christ*, 722.
270. Rego, *Suffering and Salvation*, 295–96.
271. Schillebeeckx, *Church*, 127.
272. Simon, "Salvation and Liberation," 503.
273. Schillebeeckx, *Church*, 128.

no longer have a place. [Therefore] In Jesus' praxis of the kingdom of God his resurrection is already anticipated."²⁷⁴ As Simon says, for Schillebeeckx,

> Jesus' lifepraxis and fidelity even into death, communicating God's solidarity with human beings as a solidarity intent upon justice and reconciliation, are a partial, advance realization of the Resurrection as God's sovereign power over evil and suffering. In other words, the Resurrection event is not only the definitive manifestation beyond history of the actual reversal of the history of suffering. The Resurrection is already historically enacted in the praxis and message of Jesus . . . The Resurrection is provisionally and proleptically communicated, even embodied, by the historical praxis and message of Jesus as the eschatological beginning of this reversal of suffering.²⁷⁵

On the other hand, the resurrection is a divine affirmation of the positivity of Jesus' life. As Schillebeeckx asserts, "the resurrection of Jesus is God's yes to the person and the life of Jesus."²⁷⁶ In fact, "In the resurrection from the dead, God's eschatological action with reference to Jesus the crucified one becomes God's own verdict on Jesus, and only in this way does God's evaluation of Jesus and his message, life and death also become clear to believers."²⁷⁷ God's verdict or evaluation is that Jesus' way of life has "permanent validity *in and of itself* . . . In this sense the resurrection of Jesus does not provide ratification by correction of what has gone before, of what was still lacking from the earthly life of Jesus."²⁷⁸ In fact, "In the resurrection God authenticates the person, message and whole way of life of Jesus. He puts his seal on it."²⁷⁹ Hence, by raising Jesus from the dead, "God identified with him, who in his lifetime had identified with God's cause, his coming reign; Jesus Christ himself was the reign of God. So Jesus, who proclaimed not himself but the reign and lordship of God, as it were and without suspecting it, was proclaiming 'himself': the proclaimer *is* the proclaimed one."²⁸⁰

Furthermore, the resurrection is not only a divine affirmation of the positivity of Jesus' life; it is also a divine negation of the negativity of Jesus' death. As Schillebeeckx claims, in the resurrection, God "speaks out against

---

274. Ibid., 127. According to Schillebeeckx, "Without effective anticipations of the resurrection in the earthly life of Jesus, Easter is an ideology" (ibid., 126).

275. Simon, "Salvation and Liberation," 506.

276. Schillebeeckx, *Christ*, 795.

277. Schillebeeckx, *Church*, 127.

278. Schillebeeckx, *Christ*, 792.

279. Schillebeeckx, *Church*, 128.

280. Schillebeeckx, *Jesus*, 503.

what men and women did to Jesus."²⁸¹ In other words, "the resurrection is God's corrective to the negative of death." In fact, "In Jesus, God overcame the negativity of this and any death."²⁸² Schillebeeckx writes,

> the resurrection of Jesus is also a corrective, a victory over the negativity of suffering and even death. From the point of view of the Christian Bible, for anyone who thinks historically it is not a question of "divine permission" for evil and unmerited suffering . . . , but of God's *victory* over this particular initiative of the finite. Only in the overcoming of it can we say that the negative aspects in our history have an indirect role in God's plan of salvation: *God is the Lord of history.* That is why Mark 8:31 could say intuitively, "The Son of Man *must* suffer many things." We shall never be able to give a reason (any more than Mark could) for the significance for salvation history of this improper expression "the divine must." On the one hand it contains the insight that man is redeemed by Jesus *despite* the death of Jesus, seen as negativity . . . On the other hand, this "despite" is so transcended by God, not because he permits it in condescension but because through the resurrection of Jesus from the dead he *conquers* suffering and evil and *undoes* them, that the expression "despite the death" in fact does not quite say enough. However, the terms in which we could fill this unfathomable "does not say enough" in a positive way, with finite, meaningful categories, escape us.²⁸³

It is in this sense that we can understand Schillbeeckx's expression, "It was not God but men and women who put Jesus to death; at the same time, however, this execution is the material prepared for God's supreme self-revelation by human beings, as emerges from New Testament belief in the resurrection of Jesus."²⁸⁴ In other words, God does not will Jesus' death. However, this unjust execution is a sort of "material" made by human beings, in which the revelation of God's glory is revealed, not so much by allowing Jesus' death, but by overcoming it in the resurrection.²⁸⁵

281. Schillebeeckx, *Church*, 128.
282. Schillebeeckx, *Christ*, 795.
283. Ibid., 722–23.
284. Schillebeeckx, *Church*, 125.
285. Schillebeeckx has some reservations about the idea of a God who "permits" or "allows" suffering and evil. As Robin Ryan says, Schillebeeckx "thinks that talk about God's permitting evil and suffering can be misleading." For instance, "Schillebeeckx finds permission language problematic when it is applied to particular instances of human suffering, e.g., God's 'allowing' this woman to contract breast cancer . . . Such God-talk can easily evoke the idea of God as a neutral bystander to the suffering of human

Therefore, we can see both the critical negativity and the notion of contrast in Schillebeeck's understanding of Jesus' life, death, and resurrection. For Schillebeeckx, Jesus' death *in itself* is an experience of negativity. Jesus' death can be considered as something positive if it is understood as a death for a good cause, i.e., for the cause of humankind as the cause of God, for the kingdom of God, in solidarity with social outcasts. However, this positive content of Jesus' death does not come from death itself, but from outside his death, i.e., from his life. Thus, even if we see the positive meaning of Jesus' suffering, the negativity of his suffering and death remains, since there is no possible reconciliation between the negativity of death and the positivity of God. In fact, the negativity of Jesus' death is in contrast with the positivity of Jesus' life and resurrection. "He went about doing good" (Acts 10:38) is one of the best descriptions of the positivity of Jesus' life. As proclamation of the kingdom of God, Jesus' life was an anticipation of the resurrection. In fact, the resurrection is both God's affirmation of the positivity of Jesus' life, and God's critical negation of the negativity of Jesus' death. Therefore, Jesus' life and resurrection stand in contrast or in opposition to the negativity of Jesus' death.

Christian Life

The God that is revealed in Jesus Christ is a God of life, and not of death. Therefore, "God does not want mankind to suffer."[286] According to Schillebeeckx, "The insight that God does not want men to suffer but wills to *overcome* suffering where it occurs in our history . . . , throws us back on *our own history* . . . The New Testament says with bold realism: 'Be imitators of God' (Eph 5:1)."[287] In other words, to be a Christian involves imitating God in the praxis of overcoming suffering.

To be a Christian means to imitate Jesus in his praxis of solidarity with social outcasts, and, as it happened to Jesus, the proclamation of the kingdom can provoke the resistance and the rejection of people who feel threatened by such a message. As Schillebeeckx says, "What applies to Jesus in the New Testament applies to all Christians: to follow Jesus to the point of

---

beings, one who simply stands back and watches people suffer. For Schillebeeckx, we should never speak of God actively willing or causing evil and suffering, nor should we speak of God permitting or allowing it. We should simply say that God is busy about the work of overcoming evil and suffering" (Ryan, "Holding on to the Hand of God," 122–23).

286. Schillebeeckx, *Christ*, 717.

287. Ibid., 723.

suffering through and for others."[288] Thus, suffering and death for the kingdom of God are a possibility, a likely consequence of imitating Jesus' way of life. As Schillebeeckx says, "what happened to Jesus can still happen to many people: murder of the innocent."[289] However, it is necessary to remember that Christianity does not advocate any kind of "dolorism."[290] Death and suffering do not have positive significance *in themselves*.

The suffering and death of Jesus—and of any follower of Jesus—have a saving significance if they are understood and undergone for a good cause, i.e., for the cause of humankind as the cause of God, for the kingdom of God, in solidarity with social outcasts. "The New Testament does not praise suffering but only suffering in and with resistance against injustice and suffering. It praises suffering 'for the kingdom of God' or 'for the sake of the gospel' (Mark 8:35; 10:29), 'for the sake of righteousness' (1 Peter 3:14) . . . , 'for the good' (1 Peter 3:17) . . . , in solidarity with one's brothers (Heb 2:17f)."[291] Therefore, "The redemptive and ultimately truly liberating significance of suffering lies for the New Testament precisely in the suffering which man has to take upon himself in his responsible concern to overcome suffering."[292] Therefore, as Rego asserts, "For Schillebeeckx, suffering *per se* is not salvific. Not all experiences of suffering are redemptive . . . The salvific meaning of suffering lies in the intention of the sufferer, namely, the reason for which suffering is endured. Suffering is salvific to the extent that it is undergone in love, for the good of others—after the manner of Jesus, who is salvation from God. Jesus' experience of and engagement with suffering is the norm and criterion for assessing the salvific significance of suffering."[293]

As we said above, the suffering servant is an appropriate image of Jesus. Thus, for Schillebeeckx, 1 Peter presents the suffering servant of God—the suffering Jesus Christ—as the model of all Christians. However, it is important to remember that the suffering servant does not undergo suffering for the sake of suffering itself, but for the sake of others. Therefore, "it is the calling of Christians to be prepared to accept this innocent suffering for others."[294]

Furthermore, consistent with his understanding of critical negativity, the remembrance of Jesus' death has for Schillebeeckx a critical force. It has

288. Ibid., 687.
289. Schillebeeckx, *Jesus*, 629.
290. Schillebeeckx, *Christ*, 668.
291. Ibid., 629.
292. Ibid., 687.
293. Rego, *Suffering and Salvation*, 335.
294. Schillebeeckx, *Christ*, 215.

a rebellious character. As Elizabeth Tillar says, "*Anamnesis*, or the remembrance of Christ's passion and the history of suffering humanity, is defined by Schillebeeckx in terms of its prophetic and critical function."[295] For Schillebeeckx, indeed, the remembrance of the negativity of Jesus' death—and of any unjust death—can provoke the indignation and the protest that says, "unjust death should never happen." Hence, the *memoria passionis Christi* can be a source of Christian praxis that opposes injustice and meaningless suffering in the world.[296] As Robin Ryan says, for Schillebeeckx, Christians are called to be "people of memory and action." The memory of human suffering—the memory of the ongoing passion of humanity—and the memory of the story of Jesus' life, death, and resurrection, can be a source of liberating praxis as long as memory "leads believers to thoughtful, reflective action in seeking to alleviate human suffering and to fight against the causes of suffering . . . In the face of evil and suffering, then, Christians are those who remember and who act."[297]

Therefore, Schillebeeckx is against what he calls "*lijdensmystiek*"[298]—a mystique or "mysticism of suffering."[299] With this term, Schillebeeckx seems to suggest spiritualities, practices, theologies, and understandings of Christian faith that give a "mystical and positive significance" to suffering.[300] For such a kind of mysticism, suffering is not considered as suffering for a good cause. Rather, suffering is positive *in itself*. Furthermore, for this type of mysticism, suffering is understood as something willed by God. According to Schillebeeckx, the image of Jesus especially in the Middle Ages as "the one who bears the suffering of mankind"[301] became central in the spiritual practices of Christians; "this opened a way to concentration on one's *own* suffering, detached from suffering *for a cause*; in this way a cult of suffering could arise, detached from the critical and productive force of suffering. The suffering and death of Jesus were at the same time detached from the historical circumstances which brought him suffering and death. 'Suffering in itself,' no longer suffering through and for others, took on a mystical and positive significance."[302] In tandem with this experience of Jesus as "the one who bears our sufferings," theologians started to "systematize" suffering.

---

295. Tillar, "Critical Remembrance and Eschatological Hope," 15.
296. Schillebeeckx, *Christ*, 816
297. Ryan, "Holding on to the Hand of God," 123–24.
298. Schillebeeckx, *Gerechtigheid en Liefde*, 203, 642, 669.
299. Schillebeeckx, *Christ*, 215, 692, 721.
300. Ibid., 691.
301. Ibid., 690.
302. Ibid.

> From the moment when the death of Jesus took on independent significance, detached from the historical events which made it a suffering through and for others because of his critical preaching, people also began to theologize this death. The death of Jesus became a necessary ingredient in the reconciliation of sinful man with God, who was defending his divine honour. God laid the sins of the world on the innocent Jesus; he had to do penance for the crimes of others for which they could not do penance completely themselves. Thus suffering and death become "a divine necessity" . . . Suffering as suffering (in whatever way) takes on a positive significance: God's honour, as theologians imagined this honour, is avenged through suffering and blood. True, this is not the exact significance which Anselm gave to his theory of atonement, but that was the way in which in fact it lived on in many spiritual books.[303]

The problem with this mysticism of suffering is that it "both weakens and 'tames' the critical force of the crucifixion of Jesus," it "perpetuates the 'existing order' in church and society."[304] In other words, those "theological speculations which neglect the circumstances of Jesus' death and consider the death in and of itself" have a "critical barrenness."[305] As Rego says,

> [Schillebeeckx's] concern is that, in the Christian tradition, an uncritical appeal to the cross and death of Jesus has been used to legitimise unjust and oppressive suffering. In this perspective, whatever the nature and source of one's suffering, a pious appeal is often made to stoical suffering with patience and with due submission, to make reparation to the divine majesty for one's sins and those of the world. In this way the cross has frequently been employed as an ideological tool, both by the perpetrators of suffering and also by those who seek a facile reconciliation between suffering and God.[306]

Thus, according to Schillebeeckx, the idea that God himself casts Jesus out as a sacrifice for our sins "puts us on a false trail." The claim that "God himself required the death of Jesus as compensation for what *we* make of our history" is blasphemous and not authentically Christian, since this "sadistic mysticism of suffering is certainly alien to the most authentic tendencies

---

303. Ibid., 691–92.
304. Ibid.
305. Ibid., 790.
306. Rego, *Suffering and Salvation*, 272–73.

of the great Christian tradition."[307] Therefore, suffering and death, in Jesus' case and in any case, should never be *mysticized*. In the original Dutch version, Schillebeeckx says: "*Lijden en dood blijven dan absurd en mogen niet, ook niet in Jezus' geval, gemystificeerd worden.*"[308] This text has been translated in English as follows: "In that case suffering and death remain absurd, and even in Jesus' case may not be mystified."[309] In my judgment, "mystified" is a mistranslation of "*gemystificeerd.*" In English, the verb "mystify" means making something obscure or mysterious.[310] Schillebeeckx is not talking about making suffering and death obscure or mysterious. Rather, he is referring to *lijdensmystiek*—the mysticism of suffering. What Schillebeeckx is saying, then, is that suffering and death should not be mysticized. Therefore, Schillebeeckx is not criticizing the "mystification" of suffering, as Rego claims.[311] Rather, Schillebeeckx is criticizing the "mysticization" of suffering.[312]

The resurrection also has a critical force in Christian life. As Schillebeeckx says, "The source of hope for a life after death is not a flight from the present; the source of any glance towards this future is life *today*." On the one hand, the resurrection affects Christian life here and now, since "what is done in the present is what will be confirmed by God on the other side of death because of its intrinsic goodness, or cannot be confirmed by him because of its inhumanity."[313] On the other hand, the resurrection of Jesus is the ground of hope. This expectation of the future motivates and orients the lives of Christians. Belief in the resurrection demands that Christians live in accordance with their hope. If what they hope is the fullness of life of all, then their way of life should enhance the lives of all. In fact, "Christian belief in the resurrection . . . will have to be 'proved' again and again, here and now, from [a] corresponding behaviour on the part of Christians, from their activities in this world. Without such consistency, what Christians assert is

---

307. Schillebeeckx, *Christ*, 721.

308. Schillebeeckx, *Mensen als verhaal van God*, 147.

309. Schillebeeckx, *Church*, 127.

310. Another meaning of the verb "mystify" is "to confuse or to bewilder someone," but such a meaning does not apply to Schillebeeckx's text.

311. Rego, *Suffering and Salvation*, 7, 131, 273, 336.

312. To be sure, Schillebeeckx is not criticizing Christian mysticism, but the mysticization of suffering. In fact, Schillebeeckx has a great appreciation for a type of mysticism that includes political action. "Our mystical relationship with the one whom we, following Jesus' example, call 'our Father' ought to inspire us to do justice. Mysticism and solidarity with the poor form a single whole! Mysticism on its own, without any socio-political consequences, can come to nothing" (Schillebeeckx, *God is New*, 118). See Schillebeeckx, *On Christian Faith*, 65–75.

313. Schillebeeckx, *Christ*, 796.

in fact incredible; furthermore, it has no power of attraction and above all gives no hope to the world."[314]

CORRELATING SCHILLEBEECKX'S THEOLOGY AND AESTHETICS

In the previous section we studied some aspects of Schillebeeckx's theology. We paid attention especially to the notions of critical negativity and of contrast in his theology and Christology. With such an exploration, we tried to systematize and expand the theological and christological insights that we found in the experience of contrast in art. As a summary of this chapter, then, I will explain now how the main points of Schillebeeckx's theology correlate with aesthetics.

According to Schillebeckx, the reality of our world is ambiguous. The positive dimensions of reality—such as friendship, love, and justice—are meaningful. The negative aspects of reality—for instance, poverty, social marginalization, and violence—are meaningless. The ambiguity of meaningfulness and meaninglessness in history cannot be resolved or reconciled theoretically. We cannot explain theoretically the existence of suffering and evil in history. However, action—i.e., the praxis of liberation from meaninglessness—is the right answer to the ambiguity in history. In view of the reality of unjust suffering and evil, the right answer is the praxis of resistance to evil. In correlation with aesthetics, we should say then that in the world we find both the beauty of love and justice, and the ugliness of hate and injustice. Beauty and ugliness cannot be reconciled theoretically. However, the right answer to what is horrific in history is the praxis of resistance to what is evil.

Schillebeeckx makes the distinction between meaningful and meaningless suffering. On the one hand, meaningless suffering is the kind of suffering that people undergo as victims of injustice. That kind of suffering does not have any positive purpose. On the other hand, meaningful suffering is the sort of suffering that men and women undergo for a good cause. The meaning of such kind of suffering is not intrinsic, it comes from outside. While meaningful suffering enhances the *humanum*, meaningless suffering diminishes it. If we correlate this distinction with aesthetics, we should say that meaningless suffering is awful, horrendous. Meaningful suffering is beautiful, life-enhancing, attractive. However, the beauty of meaningful suffering does not come from suffering itself, but from outside. The beauty

---

314. Ibid., 797.

of meaningful suffering is not in the suffering itself, but in the good cause of enhancing the *humanum*.

Meaningless and unjust suffering can be a negative experience of contrast. Unjust suffering is an experience of negativity. However, it has a contrast, which is positive. The experience of unjust suffering can incite indignation, protest, and liberating action, which are both a "no" to the injustice in the world, and a "yes" to a better world that is possible. This hope for a better future is what makes protest possible. Art can be a mediation of a negative experience of contrast, since art can show the ugliness of reality. As such, art can incite indignation, protest, and liberating praxis. Art can express a "no" of protest against the ugliness—of injustice, of violence, of poverty—in our world, and it can express a "yes" to the beauty—of justice, of peace, of solidarity—that is not there in the world, but could be there and should be there. In fact, art can present the reality of a better world, which can generate a yearning for such a world, a yearning that can be a source of liberating action.

According to Schillebeeckx, God is pure positivity. God is a God of life, and not a God of death. Therefore, God wills the fullness of life of human beings. In other words, God wants to save human beings from suffering, evil and death. In terms of a theological aesthetics of liberation, we can say that God is pure beauty. God's liberating action and his preferential option for the social outcast are beautiful. There is no trace of ugliness in God. God is not the ground of what is horrific in the world, for instance, injustice, violence, and the meaningless suffering of the poor.

The saving action of God through men and women takes place now in history, and will reach its fulfillment in the eschatological future. Eschatology has a negative critical function in Christian faith. It reminds us that salvation should not be identified exclusively with any human project of building a better society, and that the primary subject of salvation is God. However, the eschatological proviso is not simply critical negativity. It has a positive dimension inasmuch as the eschatological vision of a perfect and beautiful world is a source of hope that can energize liberating praxis. Precisely, art can present the vision of a better world as a possibility. At the same time, the experience of beauty in art can be an anticipation of the joy that belongs to the kingdom of God.

The eschatological future, the fulfillment of the *humanum*, has been promised and anticipated by God in Jesus Christ. In fact, God has revealed in Jesus Christ what God wills for all human beings, that is, salvation for all. The central message that Jesus communicated to the people, namely, the kingdom of God, consists precisely in the good news that God is actively present now in history, saving people from suffering, evil, and death.

Therefore, the kingdom of God is especially good news for the poor. Jesus communicated the kingdom of God with his life. In fact, the beauty of Jesus' life consists precisely in his praxis of the kingdom of God, which includes healing those who suffer and sharing his table with sinners. In other words, the beauty of Jesus' life consists in his love for those whom society considers ugly and disgusting, that is, the poor. By being in solidarity with social outcasts, Jesus shows the beauty of God's love for the poor.

However, Jesus provoked the resistance of those who saw in his message a threat to their own power. They were those who put Jesus to death. Jesus neither wanted his passion nor sought his own death. However, he came to terms with this possibility. The death of Jesus should not be isolated from his life. Jesus' death in itself is pure negativity, and as such, it is not intrinsically redemptive. If Jesus' death has a positive and saving significance, it comes from outside, that is, from his life. In other words, Jesus' death has a positive significance only if it is considered as death for a good cause, that is, for the cause of humankind as the cause of God, for the kingdom of God, in solidarity with social outcasts. However, even if Jesus died on the cross for a good cause, the negativity of Jesus' unjust death remains. Therefore, Jesus' death on the cross is not beautiful in itself, as von Balthasar suggests. If there is anything positive or beautiful about Jesus' death, it does not come from death itself, since unjust death is only horror and negativity. The beautiful dimension of Jesus' death comes from his life, that is, it comes from his faithful service to the cause of the liberation of humankind as the cause of God. However, even if it is possible to find this dimension of beauty in Jesus' death, the ugliness and horror of his unjust death are still there.

The continuity between the life and death of Jesus can be found also in his solidarity and identification with the poor. As McCormick says, the gospels depict Jesus befriending and breaking bread with social outcasts. "But what is even more striking is that the gospels portray Jesus himself as an alien and outcast."[315] In fact, "Jesus' radical table fellowship put him in the company of all manner of outcasts and aliens. But this practice of breaking bread with sinners and strangers also rendered Jesus an unclean outcast in the eyes of many of his contemporaries." However, his solidarity and identification with social outcasts reach their climax in his passion and death. As McCormick says, "Jesus is revealed as the ultimate outcast in his passion, death, and resurrection. In his arrest, torture, mock trial, and execution Jesus is mistreated, abandoned, ridiculed, abused, and murdered; he is torn from the safety of civil society and cast into a dark wasteland

---

315. McCormick, *God's Beauty*, 102.

where he may be abused with every injustice and cruelty."[316] As I said above, social outcasts are those considered by society to be ugly and disgusting. Consequently, Jesus' solidarity with the poor makes him ugly in the eyes of a world that despises social outcasts. Thus, in his crucifixion, "Like all the other strangers who have been degraded and dehumanized until we can no longer recognize their humanity, Jesus has been rendered ugly."[317]

Jesus' identification with the poor manifests God's solidarity with all social outcasts. However, Viladesau suggests, "God is not merely in 'solidarity' with human suffering, but is also genuinely identified with it."[318] In this sense, "the God revealed in the cross of Christ may be unattractive . . . because of the divine *identification* with the subhuman, the suffering, the poor, the ugly."[319] In other words, God associates God's self with the poor. God recognizes and regards God's self as sharing the same characteristics as those of social outcasts. God does not identify God's self with the ugliness of injustice, but with those who are considered ugly by an unjust society. A God who identifies God's self with the cause of the poor is certainly disgusting for many in society.

God did not put Jesus to death, as Sobrino and von Balthasar suggest. The beauty or the glory of God does not shine in the event of Jesus' death itself. That would be a "mysticization," glorification, and beautification of unjust suffering and death. As Viladesau claims, "theology cannot fall into the delusion of a mysticism of evil."[320] Rather, the beauty or the glory of God is shown in the resurrection of Jesus Christ, which is both a divine negation of the negativity of Jesus' death, and a divine affirmation of the positivity of Jesus' life. In other words, the resurrection of Jesus Christ is both a divine negation of the ugliness of Jesus' unjust death on the cross, and a divine affirmation of the beauty of Jesus' life of solidarity with the poor. As Viladesau says,

> The cross is not beautiful or good in itself: it is beautiful only insofar as it represents Christ's ultimate faithfulness and self-gift to God, even to the point of death, and insofar as this act is given eternal validity by God's overcoming of death itself. That is, the cross only has beauty as the expression of an act of love; and love is "beautiful," theologically speaking, precisely because it is finally not defeated, but victorious . . .

316. Ibid., 108.
317. Ibid., 109.
318. Viladesau, *Theological Aesthetics*, 196.
319. Ibid., 194.
320. Ibid., 196.

> The cross is not a beautiful thing; it is the symbol of a beautiful act—on Jesus' part, as self-giving, and (inseparably) on the part of the Father, in raising Jesus from death.[321]

It is true that the cross is beautiful only as long as it represents Jesus' faithfulness and self-gift to God. However, in the theological aesthetics of liberation that we are developing here, we always remember and point out that the liberation of humankind, especially the liberation of the poor, is the cause of God. Therefore, we should rather say that the cross is beautiful insofar as it represents Christ's faithfulness and self-gift to the cause of human liberation as the cause of God. Likewise, it is also true that the cross is the symbol of a beautiful act. But what is this beautiful act? Somewhere else in the same book, Viladesau writes: "although the other may not be beautiful, generous self-giving love for the needy other is nevertheless perceived by the eyes of faith as a (morally, spiritually) beautiful act . . . It is in this sense that we may speak of the 'beauty' of the cross."[322] Thus, we should always specify that the cross is the symbol of the beautiful act of loving those whom society considers ugly. It is the beauty of loving the poor that is affirmed by God in the resurrection of Jesus Christ. Hence, the glory of God does not shine in the cross itself. Rather, the beauty of God shines in the victory over unjust suffering and death, that is, in the liberation of social outcasts.

In his article, "The Beauty of the Cross," Viladesau suggests that there are "two complementary but different theological perspectives on the cross that are found already in the New Testament." On the one hand, in John's gospel and in the theology of Paul, "the cross is seen above all as the expression of the salvific will of God." On the other hand, in the Letter to the Hebrews and in the speeches of Peter in the Acts of the Apostles, we find a theology that "is probably a more primitive theology of the cross," which emphasizes that "the cross has a negative character . . . Here the cross is indeed part of God's plan of salvation; yet there is a contrast. Jesus' death on the cross is the work of sinful humanity, opposing God's will; but God nevertheless triumphs, by raising Jesus. The cross is the evil work of humanity; the resurrection is God's triumphant response of victory over evil. The whole is the realization of God's 'plan'; but its elements are different in their relation to God."[323]

According to Viladesau, these two theologies are "contrasting but not contradictories," that is, they are "different perspectives of the same reality." He explains: "The cross and the suffering are evil . . . ; they are not to be

---

321. Ibid., 197.
322. Ibid., 207.
323. Viladesau, "Beauty of the Cross," 135–36.

glorified in themselves; they are not God's will. Yet they fit into God's plan of salvation: God saves not by miraculously taking evil out of the world, or by sparing his beloved son from it, but by using it. God makes good come from evil, life from death. In this sense, we may see God as the author of the event of the cross."[324] I agree with Viladesau to some extent. Indeed, these two theologies can be complementary as long as we see the cross in connection with his life. We can consider the cross as God's will if we see it as the culmination of Jesus' faithfulness to the cause of the poor as the cause of God. However, instead of saying that God saves by using evil, it would be better to say that God saves by overcoming evil. Indeed, Viladesau recognizes, "That God brings good out of evil does not mean that evil has become good; if God brings beauty even out of suffering, it does not mean that suffering is beautiful. As Augustine says, Jesus was beautiful, even in the bearing of the cross. This does not mean the cross was beautiful in itself . . . the tension remains. Hence the 'contrast theology' of the early church remains valid and necessary, even once we have adopted the Johannine perspective on God's glory."[325] In other words, the "contrast theology" is a necessary corrective to the Johannine approach to the cross. Although Viladesau himself does not make the following correlation, the Johannine theology of the cross is the model of von Balthasar's theology, while the other theology corresponds to Schillebeeckx's. Hence, Schillebeeckx's "theology of contrast" is a necessary correction to von Balthasar's theology of the cross.

For Christian life, seeing the beauty of Jesus' praxis of the kingdom can inspire his followers to imitate him in his praxis. Likewise, the vision of the ugliness of Jesus' unjust death and of any unjust death can provoke indignation and protest. It can nourish the beautiful act of working for the liberation of the poor. Furthermore, Jesus' identification with social outcasts is a source of Christian solidarity with those whom society considers ugly. Viladesau suggests, "God's presence in the poor and suffering cannot be taken to mean that these conditions are 'godly,' but that they contain within themselves an inextinguishable possibility of transcending the present evil in the direction of goodness. This means that God's presence is experienced by the suffering as hope, and by those who encounter the suffering as the imperative to be engaged in the reversal of their suffering condition."[326] In fact, loving a God who identifies God's self with the poor necessarily entails the demand of loving those who are social outcasts. Viladesau writes: "The glorifying of God demands from us above all the spiritual beauty of agapic

---

324. Ibid., 136.

325. Ibid., 142.

326. Viladesau, *Theological Aesthetics*, 197.

love."[327] Nevertheless, for a theological aesthetics of liberation, agapic love includes the struggle for social justice. Thus, both the beauty of God and the glorifying of God shine in the liberation of social outcasts.

---

327. Ibid., 213.

Conclusion

This work has explored a possible correlation between liberation theology and theological aesthetics. The result of this correlation can be called *a theological aesthetics of liberation*. This work does not pretend to be the only way, but one way of establishing such a correlation. The assumption of this study is that the articulation of such a correlation between liberation theology and theological aesthetics will be beneficial for both disciplines in their attempt to understand God in his relationship with human beings, especially with those who have been excluded from society. On the one hand, liberation theology should pay attention to art as long as aesthetics is an important dimension of the liberation of social outcasts. On the other hand, theological aesthetics should heed the plight of the poor if it means to be relevant in a world marked by social injustice.

According to Gustavo Gutiérrez, liberation theology is a reflection on praxis in the light of the gospel. Therefore, liberation theology is an understanding of God in his relationship with humanity based on a specific event, namely, the liberation of social outcasts. Wherever there is liberation in history, it is possible to formulate a theology of liberation. Gutiérrez's definition of liberation theology expresses its methodology. That is to say, the experience of liberation is a prior stage before we develop theology as an intellectual reflection. Thus, liberation theology agrees with the transcendental method of Karl Rahner, in which the transcendental experience of the subject is the starting point of theological reflection. However, for liberation theology, the transcendental experience of theological reflection is concretely the praxis or the experience of liberation of the poor.

Applying the same method, the starting point of this theological aesthetics is the praxis or the experience of liberation of social outcasts in and through art. This supposition implies that some experiences of art can be liberating. To understand the liberating power of art, we reject a purist notion of aesthetics—what we have called "aestheticism"—which comprehends aesthetics as an isolated realm. In a purist understanding of aesthetics, art is only for art's sake, art is useless or non-instrumental, and art is only for contemplation. Contrary to a purist notion of aesthetics, here we understand aesthetics as a distinctive field, but in relationship with other dimensions of reality, such as politics and religion. Disagreeing with Roberto Goizueta, who understands aesthetic praxis only as an end itself, here we suggest that aesthetic praxis can also have goals that are external to the artistic action itself. For example, when we sing a song as a lullaby, or when we paint a mural as a memorial, putting a baby to sleep or remembering a tragic event are goals that are external to the action of singing or painting. Therefore, aesthetic delight is not the only purpose of art. Art as action or praxis can have other goals, such as the liberation of those who are social outcasts.

Art is liberating in at least three ways. Firstly, some works of art have the power to liberate when they present what is evil and ugly in our reality. In this way, art can function as a protest against the horrors that have occurred in our human history and still occur today. Likewise, some works of art can present a world that is good and beautiful as a real possibility. In this way, art can elicit hope in a better future. Therefore, as an instrument of protest and hope, art can collaborate in the process of liberation of social outcasts. Secondly, art is liberating when it is an experience of creative freedom for the artist. Finally, art is liberating in so far as it has the power to transform the whole being of its recipients. By transforming human beings, art has the power to transform society. However, art can only transform people when they are open to participate in the experience of art.

Based on this experience of liberation in and through art, we suggest two theological points. The first point is that the Spirit of God works in the experience of liberation through art. The second is that the life, death, and resurrection of Jesus Christ can be interpreted as an event of contrast. The first point is a theological reading of the phenomenon of art. The second is an aesthetic interpretation of the event of Christ. These two points should be read in a hermeneutical circle, since it is the Spirit of God who inspires artists to create works of art that express and mediate aesthetically the experience of contrast, and it is thanks to the experience of contrast in art that we can interpret analogically the life, death, and resurrection of Jesus Christ as an event of contrast.

The first theological assertion claims that the Spirit of God works in the experience of liberation through art. According to Rahner, art is an expression and mediation of transcendental experience. Art is a mediation of a God who wants to communicate God's self to human beings. In other words, art is another mediation of God's saving action in the lives of men and women. In this sense, we can say that the experience of liberation in and though art is a mediation of God's saving action in the history of human beings. It is the Spirit of God who inspires some artists to create works of art that show what is evil and ugly in our world, and it is the Spirit who inspires the creation of works that artistically present alternatives to the world that we currently have. God's grace is actively present both in the experience of creative freedom of the artist, and in the experience of transformation of those who freely and actively participate in the experience of art as recipients. Theologically speaking, it is not art that saves; rather it is God who liberates through art. It is not the artist who builds or brings the kingdom of God through his or her works of art—as Jon Sobrino would suggest; rather, it is God who reigns in and through the creative freedom of the artist and through the free participation of the recipient in the experience of art.

The second theological assertion states that the life, death, and resurrection of Jesus Christ can be interpreted as an event of contrast. We make this assertion based on the experience of contrast in art. As we said above, some works of art have the power to show what is evil and ugly in our reality. By contrast, those works recall the beauty that is not there, but could and should be there in the world. In other words, by showing what is evil and ugly in our reality, some artworks express a "no" of indignation to what is evil and ugly in the world, and by contrast, they entail a "yes" to what is beautiful, which is not there, but could be there. "Beautiful" is an unfitting word to describe those works of art that show what is dreadful in our world. "Grotesque," "disturbing," and "shocking" are aesthetic concepts that describe better those works that present the horrors of humanity. These concepts that express negative dimensions of reality should not be integrated or subsumed under the concept of beauty, for they express precisely the opposite of the beautiful. Certainly there are artworks that express beauty. However, some of those works are also experiences of contrast, in so far as they provoke a sense of longing for a beauty that is not there in our world, but could and should be there.

Relying on the experience of contrast in art, we interpret analogically the life, death, and resurrection of Jesus Christ as an event of contrast. We support this interpretation with the theology of Edward Schillebeeckx, which is a necessary corrective to the Christologies of Jon Sobrino and Hans Urs von Balthasar. Here we suggest that Jesus' death on the cross has two aspects that should always be distinguished and held in tension. On the one hand, the cross has a passive-negative dimension. The cross is something that is done to Jesus. It has a negative dimension because it is the unjust suffering and violent murder of a just man. In this sense, the cross is ugly. On the other hand, the cross has an active-positive dimension. Jesus freely accepts to undergo the suffering of the cross as the culmination of a life of solidarity with the poor. The cross indicates Jesus' faithfulness to the cause of the poor as the cause of God. As such, the cross has a positive aspect, which does not come from the cross itself, but from Jesus' life. In this sense, the cross refers to the beauty of Jesus's life of solidarity with all social outcasts. The cross in itself is ugly, but by contrast, it refers to the beauty of Jesus' life. God does not will Jesus' death on the cross, as von Balthasar and Sobrino suggest; what God wants is that Jesus remains faithful to the mission of announcing the kingdom of God. Indeed, the resurrection manifests both God's negation of the negativity of the cross, and God's affirmation of the positive aspect of Jesus' life. Therefore, God's beauty does not shine in the cross itself, as von Balthasar claims. Rather, God's glory radiates in Jesus' life of solidarity, which is vindicated by God in the resurrection.

Consequently, we should recognize that suffering in itself does not have any positive value for the life of a Christian. Suffering has a positive meaning if it is undergone for a good cause, such as the cause of liberation. Indeed, God's beauty does not shine when his people suffer from material poverty and from social exclusion. Rather, God's glory shines in the liberation of all who are social outcasts.

Bibliography

Adams, James Luther, and Wilson Yates, eds. *The Grotesque in Art and Literature: Theological Reflections*. Grand Rapids: Eerdmans, 1997.
Aquinas, Thomas. *Summa Theologiae*. Translated by Fathers of the English Dominican Province. New York: Benziger, 1947.
Arya, Rina. *Francis Bacon: Painting in a Godless World*. Farnham: Lund Humphries, 2012.
Austin, Michael. *Explorations in Art, Theology and Imagination*. London: Equinox, 2005.
Balthasar, Hans Urs von. "Current Trends in Catholic Theology and the Responsibility of the Christian." *Communio* (1978) 77–85.
———. *The Glory of the Lord: A Theological Aesthetics*. Vol. 1, *Seeing the Form*. Edited by Joseph Fessio and John Riches. Translated by Erasmo Leiva-Merikakis. San Francisco: Ignatius, 2009.
———. "Liberation Theology in the Light of Salvation History." In *Liberation Theology in Latin America*, edited by James V. Schall, 131–46. San Francisco: Ignatius, 1982.
———. *The Moment of Christian Witness*. Translated by Richard Beckley. San Francisco: Ignatius, 1994.
———. *Mysterium Paschale: The Mystery of Easter*. Translated by Aidan Nichols. San Francisco: Ignatius, 2000.
———. *Theo-Drama: Theological Dramatic Theory*. Vol. 1, *Prolegomena*. Translated by Graham Harrison. San Francisco: Ignatius, 1988.
———. *Theo-Drama: Theological Dramatic Theory*. Vol. 4, *The Action*. Translated by Graham Harrison. San Francisco: Ignatius, 1994.
———. *The von Balthasar Reader*. Edited by Medard Kehl and Werner Löser. Edinburgh: T. & T. Clark, 1982.
Bauerschmidt, Frederick Christian. "Theo-Drama and Political Theology." *Communio* 25 (1998) 532–52.
Begbie, Jeremy S. *Voicing Creation's Praise: Towards a Theology of the Arts*. Edinburgh: T. & T. Clark, 1991.
Boeve, Lieven. "Experience according to Edward Schillebeeckx: The Driving Force of Faith and Theology." In *Divinising Experience: Essays in the History of Religious Experience from Origen to Ricœur*, edited by Lieven Boeve and Laurence P. Hemming, 199–225. Leuven: Peeters, 2004.

Bibliography

Boff, Clodovis. "Methodology of the Theology of Liberation." In *Systematic Theology: Perspectives from Liberation Theology*, edited by Jon Sobrino and Ignacio Ellacuría, 1–21. Maryknoll, NY: Orbis, 1996.

Boff, Leonardo. *Church: Charism and Power: Liberation Theology and the Institutional Church*. Translated by John W. Diercksmeier. New York: Crossroad, 1992.

———. *Ecclesiogenesis: The Base Communities Reinvent the Church*. Translated by Robert R. Barr. Maryknoll, NY: Orbis, 1986.

———. *Jesus Christ Liberator: A Critical Christology of Our Time*. Translated by Patrick Hughes. London: SPCK, 1983.

———. *Liberating Grace*. Translated by John Drury. Maryknoll, NY: Orbis, 1979.

Borgman, Erik. "Theology as the Art of Liberation: Edward Schillebeeckx's Response to the Theologies of the EATWOT." *Exchange* 32 (2003) 98–108.

Brown, Frank Burch. *Good Taste, Bad Taste, and Christian Taste: Aesthetics in Religious Life*. New York: Oxford University Press, 2000.

———. "Is Good Art Good for Religion?" In *Theological Aesthetics after von Balthasar*, edited by Oleg V. Bychkov and James Fodor, 153–68. Aldershot: Ashgate, 2008.

———. *Religious Aesthetics: A Theological Study of Making and Meaning*. Princeton: Princeton University Press, 1989.

Casaldáliga, Pedro, and José María Vigil. *The Spirituality of Liberation*. Translated by Paul Burns and Francis McDonagh. Tunbridge Wells: Burns & Oates, 1994.

Comblin, José. *Called for Freedom: The Changing Context of Liberation Theology*. Translated by Phillip Berryman. Maryknoll, NY: Orbis, 1998.

———. "Grace." In *Systematic Theology: Perspectives from Liberation Theology*, edited by Jon Sobrino and Ignacio Ellacuría, 205–15. Maryknoll, NY: Orbis, 1996.

———. "The Holy Spirit." In *Systematic Theology: Perspectives from Liberation Theology*, edited by Jon Sobrino and Ignacio Ellacuría, 146–64. Maryknoll, NY: Orbis, 1996.

———. *The Holy Spirit and Liberation*. Translated by Paul Burns. Maryknoll, NY: Orbis, 1989.

———. *People of God*. Edited and translated by Phillip Berryman. Maryknoll, NY: Orbis, 2004.

Crammer, Corinne. "One Sex or Two? Balthasar's Theology of the Sexes." In *The Cambridge Companion to Hans Urs von Balthasar*, edited by Edward T. Oakes and David Moss, 93–112. Cambridge: Cambridge University Press, 2004.

Dalzell, Thomas G. *The Dramatic Encounter of Divine and Human Freedom in the Theology of Hans Urs von Balthasar*. Bern: Peter Lang, 1997.

———. "Lack of Social Drama in Balthasar's Theological Dramatics." *Theological Studies* 60 (1999) 457–75.

Dawson, Andrew. "The Origins and Character of the Base Ecclesial Community: A Brazilian Perspective." In *The Cambridge Companion to Liberation Theology*, edited by Christopher Rowland, 109–28. Cambridge: Cambridge University Press, 1999.

Dillenberger, John. *A Theology of Artistic Sensibilities: The Visual Arts and the Church*. London: SCM, 1987.

Dych, William V. "Theology and Imagination." *Thought* 57 (1982) 116–27.

Eggemeier, Matthew T. "A Mysticism of Open Eyes: Compassion for a Suffering World and the Askesis of Contemplative Prayer." *Spiritus* 12 (2012) 43–62.

Faricy, Robert. "Art as a Charism in the Church." *Thought* 57 (1982) 94–99.

Farley, Edward. *Faith and Beauty: A Theological Aesthetic*. Aldershot: Ashgate, 2001.

Francis. *Evangelii Gaudium.* http://w2.vatican.va/content/francesco/en/apost_exhortations/documents/papa-francesco_esortazione-ap_20131124_evangelii-gaudium.html.

Fritz, Peter Joseph. *Karl Rahner's Theological Aesthetics.* Washington, DC: The Catholic University of America Press, 2014.

García-Rivera, Alejandro. *The Community of the Beautiful: A Theological Aesthetics.* Collegeville, MN: Liturgical, 1999.

―――. "On a New List of Aesthetic Categories." In *Theological Aesthetics after von Balthasar*, edited by Oleg V. Bychkov and James Fodor, 169–83. Aldershot: Ashgate, 2008.

―――. *A Wounded Innocence: Sketches for a Theology of Art.* Collegeville, MN: Liturgical, 2003.

Goizueta, Roberto S. *Caminemos con Jesús: Toward a Hispanic/Latino Theology of Accompaniment.* Maryknoll, NY: Orbis, 1995.

―――. *Christ Our Companion: Towards a Theological Aesthetics of Liberation.* Maryknoll, NY: Orbis, 2009.

―――. "Theo-Drama as Liberative Praxis." *CrossCurrents* 63 (2013) 62–76.

Green, Garrett. *Imagining God: Theology and the Religious Imagination.* Grand Rapids: Eerdmans, 1998.

Gruchy, John W. de. *Christianity, Art and Transformation: Theological Aesthetics in the Struggle for Justice.* Cambridge: Cambridge University Press, 2001.

Gutiérrez, Gustavo. *The Density of the Present: Selected Writings.* Maryknoll, NY: Orbis, 1999.

―――. *The God of Life.* Translated by Matthew J. O'Connell. London: SCM, 1991.

―――. *On Job: God-Talk and the Suffering of the Innocent.* Translated by Matthew J. O'Connell. Maryknoll, NY: Orbis, 1987.

―――. "The Task and Content of Liberation Theology." In *The Cambridge Companion to Liberation Theology*, edited by Christopher Rowland, 19–38. Cambridge: Cambridge University Press, 1999.

―――. *Teología de la Liberación: Perspectivas.* Salamanca: Sígueme, 1990.

―――. *A Theology of Liberation: History, Politics, and Salvation.* Edited and translated by Caridad Inda and John Eagleson. Maryknoll, NY: Orbis, 2007.

―――. *We Drink from Our Own Wells: The Spiritual Journey of a People.* Translated by Matthew J. O'Connell. Maryknoll, NY: Orbis, 2008.

Harries, Richard. *Art and the Beauty of God: A Christian Understanding.* London: Mowbray, 2000.

Harrington, Daniel J. *Jesus: A Historical Portrait.* Cincinnati: St. Anthony Messenger, 2007.

―――. "What Got Jesus Killed? Sobrino's Historical-Theological Reading of Scripture." In *Hope and Solidarity: Jon Sobrino's Challenge to Christian Theology*, edited by Stephen Pope, 79–89. Maryknoll, NY: Orbis, 2008.

―――. *Why Do We Suffer? A Scriptural Approach to the Human Condition.* Franklin, WI: Sheed and Ward, 2000.

Hogan, Linda. "Rahner and the Theologies of Liberation." In *Karl Rahner: Theologian for the Twenty-first Century*, edited by Pádraic Conway and Fáinche Ryan, 163–70. Bern: Peter Lang, 2010.

Jaén, Néstor. *Hacia una Espiritualidad de la Liberación.* Santander: Sal Terrae, 1987.

John XXIII. *Humanae Salutis.* https://w2.vatican.va/content/john-xxiii/es/apost_constitutions/1961/documents/hf_j-xxiii_apc_19611225_humanae-salutis.html.

Johnson, Elizabeth A. *She Who Is: The Mystery of God in Feminist Theological Discourse.* New York: Crossroad, 2007.

Kennedy, Philip. *Schillebeeckx.* London: Geoffrey Chapman, 1983.

Kilby, Karen. *Balthasar: A (Very) Critical Introduction.* Grand Rapids: Eerdmans, 2012.

———. "Balthasar and Karl Rahner." In *The Cambridge Companion to Hans Urs von Balthasar,* edited by Edward T. Oakes and David Moss, 256–68. Cambridge: Cambridge University Press, 2004.

Kundera, Milan. *The Unbearable Lightness of Being.* Translated by Michael Henry Heim. London: Faber and Faber, 1985.

Lamb, Matthew L. "David Tracy." In *A Handbook of Christian Theologians,* edited by Dean G. Peerman and Martin E. Marty, 677–90. Cambridge: Lutterworth, 1984.

Lassalle-Klein, Robert. "Jesus of Galilee and the Crucified People: The Contextual Christology of Jon Sobrino and Ignacio Ellacuría." *Theological Studies* 70 (2009) 347–76.

Leeuw, Gerardus van der. *Sacred and Profane Beauty: The Holy in Art.* Translated by David E. Green. London: Weidenfel and Nicolson, 1963.

Little, Brent. "Anthropology and Art in the Theology of Karl Rahner." *Heythrop Journal* 52 (2011) 939–51.

Marmion, Declan. "Rahner and His Critics: Revisiting the Dialogue." *Irish Theological Quarterly* 68 (2003) 195–212.

Martinez, Gaspar. *Confronting the Mystery of God: Political, Liberation, and Public Theologies.* New York: Continuum, 2001.

McCormick, Patrick T. *God's Beauty: A Call to Justice.* Collegeville, MN: Liturgical, 2012.

McDade, John. "Catholic Theology in the Post Conciliar Period." In *Modern Catholicism: Vatican II and After,* edited by Adrian Hastings, 422–43. London: SPCK, 1991.

McGovern, Arthur F. *Liberation Theology and Its Critics: Toward an Assessment.* Maryknoll, NY: Orbis, 1989.

McManus, Kathleen. "Suffering in the Theology of Edward Schillebeeckx." *Theological Studies* 60 (1999) 476–91.

———. *Unbroken Communion: The Place and Meaning of Suffering in the Theology of Edward Schillebeeckx.* Lanham, MD: Rowman & Littlefield, 2003.

Metz, Johann Baptist. *Faith in History and Society: Toward a Practical Fundamental Theology.* Edited and translated by J. Matthew Ashley. New York: Crossroad, 2007.

———. *A Passion for God: The Mystical-Political Dimension of Christianity.* Edited and translated by J. Matthew Ashley. New York: Paulist, 1998.

———. *Theology of the World.* Translated by William Glen-Doepel. London: Burns & Oates, 1969.

Mieth, Dietmar. "What is Experience?" In *Revelation and Experience,* edited by Edward Schillebeeckx and Bas van Iersel, 40–53. New York: Seabury, 1979.

Mongrain, Kevin. *The Systematic Thought of Hans Urs von Balthasar: An Irenaean Retrieval.* New York: Crossroad, 2002.

O'Collins, Gerald. "Theology and Experience." *Irish Theological Quarterly* 44 (1977) 279–90.

O'Donovan, Leo J. "A Journey into Time: The Legacy of Karl Rahner's Last Years." *Theological Studies* 46 (1985) 621–46.

---. "Orthopraxis and Theological Method in Karl Rahner." *Proceedings of the Catholic Theological Society of America* 35 (1980) 47–65.

O'Hanlon, Gerard. "The Jesuits and Modern Theology: Rahner, von Balthasar and Liberation Theology." *Irish Theological Quarterly* 58 (1992) 25–45.

---. "The Legacy of Hans Urs von Balthasar." *Doctrine and Life* 41 (1991) 401–7.

---. "May Christians Hope for a Better World?" *Irish Theological Quarterly* 54 (1988) 175–89.

---. "Theological Dramatics." In *The Beauty of Christ: An Introduction to the Theology of Hans Urs von Balthasar*, edited by Bede McGregor and Thomas Norris, 92–111. Edinburgh: T. & T. Clark, 1994.

Pattison, George. *Art, Modernity and Faith: Restoring the Image*. London: SCM, 1998.

---. "Is the Time Right for a Theological Aesthetics?" In *Theological Aesthetics after von Balthasar*, edited by Oleg V. Bychkov and James Fodor, 107–14. Aldershot: Ashgate, 2008.

Piar, Carlos. *Jesus and Liberation: A Critical Analysis of the Christology of Latin American Liberation Theology*. New York: P. Lang, 1994.

Pilario, Daniel Franklin. *Back to the Rough Grounds of Praxis*. Leuven: Leuven University Press, 2005.

Pitstick, Alyssa Lyra. *Light in Darkness: Hans Urs von Balthasar and the Catholic Doctrine of Christ's Descent into Hell*. Grand Rapids: Eerdmans, 2007.

Poulsom, Martin G. *The Dialectics of Creation: Creation and the Creator in Edward Schillebeeckx and David Burrell*. London: T. & T. Clark, 2014.

Rahner, Karl. "Art against the Horizon of Theology and Piety." In *Theological Investigations*, translated by Joseph Donceel and Hugh M. Riley, 12:162–68. London: Darton, Longman and Todd, 1992.

---. *Faith in a Wintry Season: Conversations and Interviews with Karl Rahner in the Last Years of His Life*. Edited by Paul Imhof and Hubert Biallowons. Translated by Harvey D. Egan. New York: Crossroad, 1990.

---. *Foundations of Christian Faith: An Introduction to the Idea of Christianity*. Translated by William V. Dych. New York: Crossroad, 2005.

---. "The Human Question of Meaning in the Face of the Absolute Mystery of God." In *Theological Investigations*, translated by Edward Quinn, 18:89–104. London: Darton, Longman and Todd, 1984.

---. *Karl Rahner in Dialogue: Conversations and Interviews 1965–1982*. Edited by Paul Imhof and Hubert Biallowons. Translated by Harvey D. Egan. New York: Crossroad, 1986.

---. "On the Theology of Books." In *Mission and Grace*, translated by Cecily Hastings, 3:98–126. London: Sheed and Ward, 1966.

---. "Priest and Poet." In *Theological Investigations*, translated by Karl-H. Kruger and Boniface Kruger, 3:294–317. London: Darton, Longman & Todd, 1967.

---. "Reflections on the Unity of the Love of Neighbour and the Love of God." In *Theological Investigations*, translated by Karl-H. Kruger and Boniface Kruger, 6:231–49. London: Darton, Longman & Todd, 1969.

---. "The Theology of the Religious Meaning of Images." In *Theological Investigations*, translated by Joseph Donceel and Hugh M. Riley, 13:149–61. London: Darton, Longman and Todd, 1992.

---. "Why Does God Allow Us to Suffer?" In *Theological Investigations*, translated by Edward Quinn, 19:194–208. London: Darton, Longman and Todd, 1984.

Rego, Aloysius. *Suffering and Salvation: The Salvific Meaning of Suffering in the Later Theology of Edward Schillebeeckx*. Louvain: Peeters, 2006.

Richard, Pablo. *Fuerza Etica y Espiritual de la Teología de la Liberación en el Contexto Actual de la Globalización*. La Habana: Caminos, 2004.

———. "Liberation Theology: A Difficult but Possible Future." In *The Future of Liberation Theology: Essays in Honor of Gustavo Gutiérrez*, edited by Marc H. Ellis and Otto Maduro, 502–10. Maryknoll, NY: Orbis, 1989.

Ritt, Paul E. "The Lordship of Jesus Christ: Balthasar and Sobrino." *Theological Studies* 49 (1988) 709–29.

Rodenborn, Steven M. *Hope in Action: Subversive Eschatology in the Theology of Edward Schillebeeckx and Johann Baptist Metz*. Minneapolis: Fortress, 2014.

Rowland, Christopher. "Introduction: The Theology of Liberation." In *The Cambridge Companion to Liberation Theology*, edited by Christopher Rowland, 1–16. Cambridge: Cambridge University Press, 1999.

Ryan, Robin. "Holding on to the Hand of God: Edward Schillebeeckx on the Mystery of Suffering." *New Blackfriars* 89 (January 2008) 114–25.

Schillebeeckx, Edward. *Christ: The Christian Experience in the Modern World*. Translated by John Bowden. The Collected Works of Edward Schillebeeckx 7. London: Bloomsbury, 2014.

———. *Church: The Human Story of God*. Translated by John Bowden. The Collected Works of Edward Schillebeeckx 10. London: Bloomsbury, 2014.

———. "Culture, Religion and Violence." In *Essays: Ongoing Theological Quest*, translated by Edward Fitzgerald and Peter Tomlinson, 163–82. London: Bloomsbury, 2014.

———. *God: The Future of Man*. Translated by N. D. Smith. The Collected Works of Edward Schillebeeckx 3 London: Bloomsbury, 2014.

———. *Interim Report on the Books Jesus and Christ*. Translated by John Bowden. The Collected Works of Edward Schillebeeckx 8. London: Bloomsbury, 2014.

———. *Gerechtigheid en Liefde: Genade en Bevrijding*. Bloemendaal: Nelissen, 1977.

———. *God is New Each Moment: Edward Schillebeeckx in Conversation with Huub Oosterhuis and Piet Hoogeveen*. Translated by David Smith. Edinburgh: T. & T. Clark, 1983.

———. *Jesus: An Experiment in Christology*. Translated by Hubert Hoskins and Marcelle Manley. The Collected Works of Edward Schillebeeckx 6. London: Bloomsbury, 2014.

———. "Liberating Theology: Reflection on J. B. Metz's Political Theology." In *Essays: Ongoing Theological Quest*, translated by Edward Fitzgerald and Peter Tomlinson, 69–84. London: Bloomsbury, 2014.

———. *Mensen als verhaal van God*. Baarn: Nelissen, 1989.

———. *On Christian Faith: The Spiritual, Ethical and Political Dimensions*. Translated by John Bowden. New York: Crossroad, 1987.

———. *The Understanding of Faith*. Translated by N. D. Smith. The Collected Works of Edward Schillebeeckx 5. London: Bloomsbury, 2014.

Schreiter, Robert J. "Schillebeeckx and Theology in the Twenty-First Century." In *Edward Schillebeeckx and Contemporary Theology*, edited by Lieven Boeve et al., 252–64. London: T. & T. Clark, 2010.

Schüssler Fiorenza, Francis. "Method in Theology." In *The Cambridge Companion to Karl Rahner*, edited by Declan Marmion and Mary E. Hines, 65–82. Cambridge: Cambridge University Press, 2005.

Segundo, Juan Luis. *Liberation of Theology*. Translated by John Drury. Dublin: Gill and Macmillan, 1977.

Sherry, Patrick. *Images of Redemption: Art, Literature and Salvation*. London: T. & T. Clark, 2003.

———. *Spirit and Beauty: An Introduction to Theological Aesthetics*. London: SCM, 2002.

Simon, Derek J. "Salvation and Liberation in the Practical-Critical Soteriology of Schillebeeckx." *Theological Studies* 63 (2002) 494–520.

Sobrino, Jon. "Central Position of the Reign of God in Liberation Theology." In *Systematic Theology: Perspectives from Liberation Theology*, edited by Jon Sobrino and Ignacio Ellacuría, 38–74. Maryknoll, NY: Orbis, 1996.

———. *Christ the Liberator: A View from the Victims*. Translated by Paul Burns. Maryknoll, NY: Orbis, 2001.

———. *Jesus the Liberator: A Historical-Theological Reading of Jesus of Nazareth*. Translated by Paul Burns and Francis McDonagh. Tunbridge Wells: Burns & Oates, 1994.

———. "Karl Rahner and Liberation Theology." *The Way* 43 (October 2004) 53–66.

———. *The Principle of Mercy: Taking the Crucified People from the Cross*. Maryknoll, NY: Orbis, 1994.

———. *Spirituality of Liberation: Toward Political Holiness*. Translated by Robert R. Barr. Maryknoll, NY: Orbis, 1988.

Stålsett, Sturla. *The crucified and the Crucified: A Study in the Liberation Christology of Jon Sobrino*. Bern: Peter Lang, 2003.

Steiner, George. *Real Presences: Is There Anything in What We Say?* London: Faber and Faber, 1989.

Stoker, Wessel. "Beauty as a Theological Concept: A Critical Examination of the Aesthetics of Hans Urs von Balthasar and Gerardus van der Leeuw." In *At the Crossroads of Art and Religion: Imagination, Commitment, Transcendence*, edited by Hetty Zock, 153–71. Leuven: Peeters, 2008.

Thiessen, Gesa Elsbeth. "Karl Rahner: Toward a Theological Aesthetics." In *The Cambridge Companion to Karl Rahner*, edited by Declan Marmion and Mary E. Hines, 225–34. Cambridge: Cambridge University Press, 2005.

———. *Theology and Modern Irish Art*. Dublin: Columba, 1999.

Tillar, Elizabeth. "Critical Remembrance and Eschatological Hope in Edward Schillebeeckx's Theology of Suffering for Others." *Heythrop Journal* 44 (2003) 15–42.

Tillich, Paul. *On Art and Architecture*. Edited by John Dillenberger and Jane Dillenberger. New York: Crossroad, 1987.

Tracy, David. *The Analogical Imagination: Christian Theology and the Culture of Pluralism*. New York: Crossroad, 1981.

———. *Blessed Rage for Order: The New Pluralism in Theology*. Chicago: The University of Chicago Press, 1996.

Vatican II. *Gaudium et Spes*. http://www.vatican.va/archive/hist_councils/ii_vatican_council/documents/vat-ii_const_19651207_gaudium-et-spes_en.html.

Viladesau, Richard. "The Beauty of the Cross." In *Theological Aesthetics after von Balthasar*, edited by Oleg V. Bychkov and James Fodor, 135–51. Aldershot: Ashgate, 2008.

———. *Theological Aesthetics: God in Imagination, Beauty and Art*. New York: Oxford University Press, 1999.

Voiss, James. "Rahner, von Balthasar and the Question of Theological Aesthetics: Preliminary Considerations." In *Finding God in All Things: Celebrating Bernard Lonergan, John Courtney Murray, and Karl Rahner*, edited by Mark Bosco and David J. Stagaman, 167–81. New York: Fordham University Press, 2007.

Vorgrimler, Herbert. *Understanding Karl Rahner: An Introduction to His Life and Thought*. Translated by John Bowden. London: SCM, 1986.

Williams, Rowan. "Balthasar and Rahner." In *The Analogy of Beauty*, edited by John Riches, 11–34. Edinburgh: T. & T. Clark, 1986.

Wolterstorff, Nicholas. *Art in Action: Toward a Christian Aesthetic*. Grand Rapids: Eerdmans, 1980.

———. *Art Rethought: The Social Practices of Art*. Oxford: Oxford University Press, 2015.

———. "Beyond Beauty and the Aesthetic in the Engagement of Religion and Art." In *Theological Aesthetics after von Balthasar*, edited by Oleg V. Bychkov and James Fodor, 119–33. Aldershot: Ashgate, 2008.

Yates, Wilson. "Francis Bacon: The Iconography of Crucifixion, Grotesque Imagery, and Religious Meaning." In *The Grotesque in Art and Literature: Theological Reflections*, edited by James Luther Adams and Wilson Yates, 143–191. Grand Rapids: Eerdmans, 1997.

www.ingramcontent.com/pod-product-compliance
Lightning Source LLC
Chambersburg PA
CBHW051054230426
43667CB00013B/2297